The Future of British Foreign Policy

The Future of British Foreign Policy

Security and Diplomacy in a World after Brexit

Christopher Hill

polity

First published in 2019 by Polity Press

Polity Press
65 Bridge Street
Cambridge CB2 1UR, UK

Polity Press
101 Station Landing
Suite 300
Medford, MA 02155, USA

ISBN-13: 978-1-5095-2461-7 (hardback)
ISBN-13: 978-1-5095-2462-4 (paperback)

A catalogue record for this book is available from the British Library.

Typeset in 11 on 13 pt Sabon
by Toppan Best-set Premedia Limited

The publisher has used its best endeavours to ensure that the URLs for external websites referred to in this book are correct and active at the time of going to press. However, the publisher has no responsibility for the websites and can make no guarantee that a site will remain live or that the content is or will remain appropriate.

Every effort has been made to trace all copyright holders, but if any have been overlooked the publisher will be pleased to include any necessary credits in any subsequent reprint or edition.

For further information on Polity, visit our website: politybooks.com

Contents

Preface and Acknowledgements   vi
Abbreviations   xi

1   Brexit and UK Foreign Policy   1

2   Falling Back on Europe   24

3   Does Britain Need European Foreign Policy?   51

4   Britain's à La Carte Menu   74

5   Regional or Global?   99

6   A Tale of Two Special Relationships –
    Paris and Washington   128

7   Nothing Good Out of Europe?   155

Further Reading   179
References for Further Reading   182
Notes   185
Index   213

Preface and Acknowledgements

Writing a book about a moving target is always a high-risk strategy, let alone in conditions of speeded-up politics like the present. It is quite possible that by the time the present volume is published there will have been further sea-changes in Britain's relationship with the European Union as the result of the volatile interactions between the Article 50 negotiations and domestic politics. But how can I not write about such an important subject as my country's decision to leave the most significant cooperative endeavour yet created by sovereign states in favour of an unknown voyage on the open seas of international politics? This is especially the case given that the flood of writing which Brexit has engendered is in large part concerned with the issues – vital as they are – of economics, sovereignty, migration and the Irish border? Foreign policy has been relatively neglected, even though the professionals in government, and those outside who follow these things, know that the decision to leave the EU represents a foreign policy shift of the first magnitude, both in the general sense of our 'place in the world' and technically, in terms of the policy-making process. These issues too need serious discussion.

I have been writing about British foreign policy for all my professional life, which has coincided almost exactly with the United Kingdom's membership of the EC/EU. For much of the time I have also focused on Europe's attempts to coordinate national foreign policies so as to 'speak with one voice' in relations with third parties. I have always been sceptical of the view that a European superpower could and should be created but at the same time have recognized that Britain's ability to influence events alone is increasingly limited. This is the starting-point of the analysis in this short book, which seeks to be even-handed in assessing the dilemmas facing British foreign policy as a result of the referendum vote in 2016, but at the same time argues that – in or out of the EU – we are first and foremost a European power. What happens in Europe and its neighbourhood is both a major concern for the UK and the theatre in which our foreign policy is most likely to be effective.

In order to limit the vulnerability of the book to new events I have chosen an historical and thematic approach. This places UK foreign policy in the context of Britain's gradual, often reluctant, move towards the project of European integration, showing that foreign policy was the only area in which it was 'present at the creation', and which (not coincidentally) turned out to cause fewest clashes with other Member States. The book analyses in Chapter 3 the nature of the system of cooperation in classical diplomacy known first as European Political Cooperation and then as the Common Foreign and Security Policy, showing that it allowed Britain to enjoy both influence and independence. The discussion then opens up to focus on the wider concept of 'external relations', which includes such things as monetary diplomacy, enlargement policy, security in the broadest sense and migration. Here the UK has been able to pursue, with relative success, what I term an à la carte approach, opting in to some common systems and opting out of others.

Moving back towards a macro perspective, that of how Britain operates on the international scene more generally,

Chapter 5 takes on the dilemma of regionalism versus glo-
balism – is it possible or desirable to be a global power,
inside or outside the EU, or is a regional destiny more
practicable, even inevitable? That issue in turn leads in
Chapter 6 to an assessment of Britain's principal bilateral
relationships, with France and with the United States. France
is a close analogue country for the UK and will face similar
foreign policy issues in the future even as an EU member.
As for the United States, it has had the paradoxical impact
on Britain of both encouraging its EU membership and on
occasions drawing it into global geopolitics in ways which
have created tensions on the European front. The book
ends with a consideration of whether a country which
enjoyed opt-outs as a Member State finds itself in the position, now that it is facing life outside the Union, of seeking
opt-ins to foreign and security policy cooperation, and
whether that is a feasible or desirable outcome. Is Britain
therefore indelibly 'European' from a geopolitical point of
view? What are the interests that British governments, and
the British people, seek to pursue through foreign policy?

In completing this project, many debts have been accu-
mulated. I am first of all most grateful to Louise Knight,
my editor at Polity, for her invitation to write the book
and for her encouragement throughout. Her colleague
Nekane Tanaka Galdos has also been both patient and
professional in providing the support that every author
needs. On the academic front I was fortunate in the immediate aftermath of my retirement from Cambridge University
in being offered the post of the Wilson E. Schmidt Distin-
guished Chair of International Relations at the School of
Advanced International Studies (SAIS), Johns Hopkins
University, Bologna. In the Fall semester of 2017 I ran a
European Research Seminar on the subject of this book
with some excellent master's students, who contributed a
great deal to my thinking by their sharp insights, enthusiasm
and external perspectives on UK foreign policy. So my
gratitude goes to: Vassilis Coutifaris, Francesco Diegoli,
Malte Helligsøe, Caroline Mayr, Ginevra Poli, Juan Manuel

Reyes, Umberto Speranza, Xiuqun Sun, Veerle Verhey and Lucie Webster. Also at SAIS, my colleagues Bart Drakulich, Erik Jones and Filippo Taddei have provided many stimulating ideas and discussion. Mark Gilbert took the time to read the historical part of the text and to make invaluable comments. I am also most grateful to SAIS Director Professor Michael Plummer for his welcome and assistance, and to Paolo Forlani, Gail Martin, Bernadette O'Toole and Barbara Wiza for indispensable and friendly administrative support.

Cambridge University's Department of Politics and International Studies (POLIS) is my other academic home. There my colleagues Chris Bickerton, Geoffrey Edwards, Mette Eilstrup-Sangiovanni, Brendan Simms, Julie Smith and Helen Thompson represent a formidable concentration of expertise in British and European politics on which I have been fortunate enough to draw. As a Fellow of Sidney Sussex College I also benefit from regular contact with James Mayall, whose judgement on international politics is always to be trusted. The College environment also means I can lean on the expertise of colleagues from other disciplines such as Kenneth Armstrong, professor of European Law and Eugenio Biagini, Professor of Modern and Contemporary History. I am grateful to the Master of Sidney Sussex, Richard Penty, for permission to spend the autumn at SAIS, and to Robbie Duschinsky, Mette Eilstrup-Sangiovanni, Bernhard Fulda, James Mayall and Rupert Stasch for kindly having covered for my supervising and interviewing duties during that term.

Lastly, I must thank a range of colleagues who have advised me on particular aspects of this work, encouraged me in various ways to proceed, or simply challenged my views. They might not always realize how helpful they have been, but I have not forgotten. So I acknowledge with sincere thanks my debts to: David Allen, Massimo Ambrosetti, Fraser Cameron, Charles Clarke, Marta Dassù, Renaud Dehousse, Helen Drake, Spyros Economides, Georgios Evangelopoulos, Andrew Geddes, Catherine Gegout, Charles

x   Preface and Acknowledgements

Grant, Michel Kenny, Alan Knight, Christian Lequesne, Benjamin Martill, Maria Grazia Melchionni, Anand Menon, Anthony Milton, Tariq Modood, Robin Niblett, Tim Oliver, Alice Pannier, Mario and Annalisa Poli, Karen Smith, Michael Smith, Rick Stanwood, Eva Stolte, Nathalie Tocci, Uta Staiger, Richard Whitman and Jan Zielonka.

I am also indebted to various organizations for their invitations to speak during recent years on subjects related to the theme of this book, notably St Antony's College, Oxford, the London School of Economics (both its European Institute and its Diplomacy Commission), the University of Cologne, the Franco-British Council, the Greek Public Policy Forum in Chania, Crete, the Hay Literary Festival, the Istituto Affari Internazionali, Rome, the Libera Università Internazionale degli Studi Sociali, Guido Carli (LUISS), Rome, and the SAIS Alumni Association, Washington DC.

My fondest thanks, however, as always, go to my wife Maria McKay, who shows true devotion in reading everything I write and in putting up with the private agonizings of the author. We met as History students at Oxford at a time when Britain's attempt to join the EEC finally looked like succeeding. Our grown-up off-spring, Alice and Dominic, are fully European in their outlook. We only hope that the open Europe we benefited from will survive for them and for future generations.

Christopher Hill
12 June 2018

Abbreviations

ACP	African, Caribbean and Pacific group of countries
ASEAN	Association of Southeast Asian Nations
BBC	British Broadcasting Corporation
BRICS	Brazil, Russia, India, China, South Africa
CANZUK	Canada, Australia, New Zealand, United Kingdom
CAP	Common Agricultural Policy
CFSP	Common Foreign and Security Policy
CSDP	Common Security and Defence Policy
CSSF	Conflict, Security and Stability Fund
COREU	CORrespondance EUropéenne
DEXIT	Department for Exiting the EU
DFID	Department for International Development
EAW	European Arrest Warrant
EC	European Community/Communities
ECOWAS	Economic Community of West African States

ECSC	European Coal and Steel and Community
EDC	European Defence Community
EDF	European Development Fund
EEA	European Economic Area
EEAS	European External Action Service
EEC	European Economic Community
EFP	European Foreign Policy
EFTA	European Free Trade Association
EMU	European Monetary Union
ERM	Exchange Rate Mechanism
EU	European Union
EU-27	European Union of 27 Member States (i.e. without the UK)
EURATOM	European Atomic Energy Community
FCO	Foreign and Commonwealth Office
G7	Group of Seven (Canada, France, Germany, Italy, Japan, UK, USA)
G20	Argentina, Australia, Brazil, Canada, China, France, Germany, India, Indonesia, Italy, Japan, Mexico, Russia, Saudi Arabia, South Africa, South Korea, Turkey, UK, USA, plus the EU)
GA	General Assembly of the UN
GCHQ	Government Communications Headquarters
GDP	Gross Domestic Product
GKN	Guest, Keen & Nettlefolds engineering company
GNI	Gross National Income
HMG	Her Majesty's Government
IAEA	International Atomic Energy Agency
IGC	Intergovernmental Conference
IGO	Intergovernmental Organization
JCPOA	Joint Comprehensive Plan of Action (Iran nuclear deal)
MEP	Member of the European Parliament

MERCOSUR	Common Market of the Southern Cone
MOD	Ministry of Defence
NAFTA	North American Free Trade Agreement
NATO	North Atlantic Treaty Organization
NGO	Nongovernmental Organization
NPT	Non-Proliferation Treaty
NSC	National Security Council
ODA	Official Development Assistance
OECD	Organization for Economic Cooperation and Development
OPEC	Organization of Petroleum Exporting Countries
OSCE	Organization for Security and Cooperation in Europe
ONS	Office for National Statistics
PESCO	Permanent Structured Cooperation on Security and Defence
PSC	Political and Security Committee
SACEUR	Supreme Allied Commander Europe
SEM	Single European Market
SIS	Schengen Information System
UDI	Unilateral Declaration of Independence
UKIP	United Kingdom Independence Party
UNSC	United Nations Security Council
WEU	Western European Union

1

Brexit and UK Foreign Policy

All kinds of metaphors can be used to describe Britain's relationship with European integration since the start of the process in 1950 – we have missed the bus, dragged our feet and tried to slow down the Franco–German locomotive driving the project forward. Finally, in 2016, the British people voted clearly, if by a small majority, to get off the train altogether. In our various moods, and by means of governments from both major parties, we had persistently and with some success attempted to put a brake on integration over 43 years of membership. But whether because Britain itself had changed, with hardening views towards Europe, or because the European Union (EU) itself had run into ever more serious problems, this strategy was deemed insufficient. Britain would have to leave, to renegotiate fundamentally its relationship with its closest neighbours, and thus to seek both a new identity and a new role in world politics.

In this book I focus on the foreign policy dimension of the decision to leave, looking first backward, then at the uncertainties that face the country in the process of departing from the EU, and finally at the likely longer term consequences of such a seismic event. This is at once a large

task and a limited one. Large, because foreign policy has
come to encompass a wide range of issues, many bridging
the external and internal divide. Limited, because it is neither
possible nor desirable in a short book to cover every aspect
of the United Kingdom's (UK's) relationship with the EU
and of the agonizing negotiations over its departure. The
negotiations focus mostly on finance, on the Irish border,
on the rights of citizenship and on a post-Brexit trading
deal. All of these have foreign policy aspects and implications that will occupy much of the energy of the Foreign
and Commonwealth Office, but they are highly technical
and space-consuming questions. How they are settled will
certainly shape Britain's future role in the world but, until
then, our thinking about foreign policy is better focused
on the broader questions of orientation, identity, security
and power.

   This is, in part, a work of futurology. As it seeks to
identify the likely effects of Brexit on Britain's foreign policy
it is subject to the vicissitudes of events. Brexit might mean
'Brexit', as Prime Minister Theresa May initially asserted
but, as there are no precedents for a sovereign state seceding from the EU we cannot – by definition – know what
that entails in detail. Britain faces a moving target and a
'journey to an unknown destination', to adapt Andrew
Shonfield's famous characterization of the European
Community.[1]

   The journey might entail a complete break with the Single
European Market and the 'four freedoms' of movement
for people, goods, services and finance, or it might involve
any number of intermediate positions between that and
EU membership, especially given the need for a transition
period. After the divisions and deadlock evident in the
result of the general election of 8 June 2017, called by Mrs
May to give her a free hand in the negotiations, it might
even mean no Brexit at all, or (after a brief intermission)
a Brit-turn.

   Yet, despite these uncertainties and the fast-moving nature
of events it should still be possible to analyse systematically

the parameters of the problem, meaning the country's historical relationship with Europe, the 'givens' of its geographical and power position, the domestic drivers and constraints of policy, and the attitudes of third states towards what is increasingly a dis-United Kingdom. The distance provided by an academic perspective should provide some buffer against the intrusion of polemics in what is the longest-running issue of contention in British politics.

If the UK is undergoing the most momentous transition in its relations with the outside world since EEC entry in 1973, and arguably since the Second World War, then, once that is over, the scope and targets of its foreign policy will by definition have changed. Pressed against the windows of the Europa Building in Brussels as Council meetings proceed inside without them, British diplomats will have to get used to treating the EU and its Member States as objects of 'foreign' policy – whereas for decades now the Foreign and Commonwealth Office (FCO) and its embassies around Europe have been used to a multilateral, semi-internalized system of diplomacy in which they have often made the running. They will also be excluded from the European External Action Service (EEAS), which seeks to produce common positions both in Brussels and in the capitals of non-EU states, and in principle from decision-making in relation to the various missions sent abroad by the Common Security and Defence Policy (CSDP).

More generally, the Brexit decision means that the common tendency of the British to refer to 'Europe' as something 'over there' will take on a distinctly practical meaning. The UK population will no longer be part of a common endeavour and will depend for travel and economic activity on particular arrangements, which may well be subject to periodic change. It might be that France and Belgium will no longer operate UK passport controls in Paris, Brussels and the Channel ports, leading to longer queues at home. Unless the UK joins the European Free Trade Area (EFTA) and the European Economic Area (EEA), or negotiates some unusually favourable conditions, Britons will no longer be able to identify themselves as European citizens, let alone have access to the rights that status bestows in terms of access to healthcare, education, residence and driving licences. In short, Europe and the EU will move from being a central part of our political, legal and institutional life into our external environment, to become a foreign policy problem. This is, of course, precisely how the 'leave' campaigners have viewed them, rejecting the narrative of amity and partnership created over nearly half a century.

The basic questions driving this inquiry, therefore, are: what will Britain's position in the world be after Brexit is achieved, and what choices exist for the country in that new environment? Are there alternative multilateral fora in which shelter may be found? Which bilateral relationships will be crucial, and how much continuity will there be in that respect? What will be the balance between new freedoms and new vulnerabilities? Will the government need to devote more, less or the same amount of resource to foreign and security policy? These questions have received much less attention than those of sovereignty, regulation, migration and freedom of movement in the referendum campaign and that of the 2017 general election, but they are just as important in the long term.[2] The European Union is the most developed form of multilateralism in which the UK has participated, and its absence will be felt in diplomacy and security as much as in economics. In response, Conservatives tend to argue that a new 'global Britain' will emerge, the Liberal Democrats foresee only isolation and weakness and the Labour Party has avoided concrete predictions, while stressing its commitment to internationalism, and to an 'ethical' foreign policy.

Given that the political debate has been so inadequate on the foreign policy side, it falls to academics to make up the deficit. Some foundations have already been made. The book-length analysis by Michael Emerson and colleagues of the issues facing voters in the 2016 referendum contained a sharp treatment of the foreign and security policy dimension.[3] The overview of UK foreign policy by Jamie Gaskarth raises some of the key strategic issues, although it was written three years before the Brexit vote.[4] Brendan Simms' invigorating historical treatise is indispensable for anyone seeking to understand the past, present and perhaps the future trajectories of the country's role.[5] Julie Smith focuses on party politics, which is integral to our understanding of why Europe has been such a source of suspicion for many, internationally as much as domestically.[6] Inevitably there is also much coverage by journalists, commentators and experts, which is in the nature of things ephemeral. But some represents a significant contribution to the debate, as in the discussions of the possible impact of Brexit on European security, and in Kenneth Armstrong's breaking down of the issues chronologically and conceptually.[7] The essays in the collection edited by Benjamin Martill and Uta Steiger address the various levels of interconnection between Britain's future and that of the EU, Brexit or no Brexit.[8]

The world after Brexit

The British, like everyone else but a touch more so, tend to exaggerate their own importance in the eyes of the rest of the world. Most people would be surprised at how little attention the US media pay to events in the UK (apart from the doings of the royal family) and indeed to Europe more generally.[9] Even inside the EU, Brexit has come to be regarded as a nuisance to be got out of the way as quickly as possible, and as by no means the most serious of the problems facing the Member States. In the wider world it is being followed with interest and some degree of concern by those who have major trade and foreign policy dealings with Britain and/or the EU, but it is rare for anyone to have the feeling that a great deal hangs on the outcome, as New Zealand did over Britain's original entry to the EC in 1973. No one is eagerly expecting great gains from relations with a 'liberated' UK.

The divisions inside the country have been so severe as to produce a collective solipsism, which inevitably increases the chances of neglecting or misperceiving events in the external world. While the UK is preoccupied with internal debate and with the transaction costs of the complex leave negotiations, other states inside and outside Europe are able to focus on more substantive economic and political issues. All states turn inwards from time to time, as Turkey did after the attempted coup of 2017, but there are few examples of a stable democracy undergoing major upheaval internally and externally of its own volition.

It is to be doubted that many of those voting to leave in 2016 were concerned about the possible diplomatic losses entailed in a Brexit. The informed minority would have expected Britain's place in NATO and its good bilateral relations with some of its European partners to have continued – the historic maritime ties to Portugal, the geographical and military closeness to Belgium and the Netherlands, the shared sense of a peripheral status with Norway. And these might indeed survive, for what they are worth. But the two critical relationships – those with France and Germany – are far less certain, as we shall see in more detail later in this book. One of the reasons for Britain's semi-detached posture within the EU has long been its inability to work as well with either Paris or Berlin as those two do with each other. Whether this is a cause or an effect of British distancing is difficult to ascertain – probably both. What is certain is that leaving the EU will not make it easier for London to develop those important bilateral ties, while it will definitely rule out any possibility of a European leadership triumvirate. As for the EU itself, while it is possible in time that the UK will be able to square the circle of its wish to have both independence and effective cooperation, the conflictual nature of the exit negotiations is likely to reverberate for some time.

The British need to realize that they have become a considerable source of irritation to those remaining in the EU, who resent the political energy absorbed by the referendum and its fallout, the damage done to the stability, budget and profile of the organization, and the sheer distraction from other pressing problems. Among these are the troubles of the eurozone, the migration crisis, relations with Russia and the USA, and a highly unstable neighbourhood. In this context Brexit looks like a relatively minor shock, but an immensely time-consuming one. Even before 19 June 2017, when the formal negotations began, European Council members had made it clear that there was much other business to be conducted. Just running the EU on a daily basis is a complex and burdensome task, quite apart from the need to consider strategy, to manage existing crises and to avert future ones. They are all familiar with the warnings of past leaders like Harold Macmillan and James Callaghan that it is the unforeseen or apparently minor event that can end by blowing policy off course.[10] European leaders themselves are all too aware, given the Russian invasion of the Crimea in 2014 and the dramatic exodus of Syrian refugees in September 2015, that 'life is what happens to you when you are busy making other plans'.[11] The officials of the FCO, DEXIT (Department for Exiting the European Union) and the Department of Trade, therefore, will be operating on the assumption that the hopes of their political masters for a rapid and clear process of disengagement are likely to be disappointed, as other priorities start to push the British question away from the centre of EU concerns.

Inside and outside reframed

However tiresome they are, the problems over negotiating an exit from the EU must eventually come to an end, and even the elements of ill-will generated on both sides will fade. Yet British foreign policy will then have to grapple with some rather more fundamental consequences and dilemmas, all of them crossing the conventional divide between internal and external policies and thus creating confusion over how and where they should be handled. They can be divided into four categories: (i) the scope of foreign policy, given that issues previously intra-EU now need a new definition;

(ii) decision-making, or the changing responsibilities of the great departments of state; (iii) society, meaning how citizens might relate to the outside world once they have lost the extra protective shelter (and constraint) of the European Union; and (iv) identity, which here refers to the collective need for a new self-understanding, incorporating not only Britain's new outsider status but also its centuries of shared history with continental neighbours.

To begin with the scope of foreign policy: we have already seen that in principle the EU and its Member States will move from the current grey area, where they are half familiar, half-alien to each other, into the realm of foreign policy proper. The UK will also miss the economics and politics of scale associated with participation in the collective exercise, through regular meetings of foreign ministers (formal and informal) and of heads of government, and through access to shared reporting from missions in third countries, most recently via the European External Action Service (EEAS). If joining the European Community in 1973 was partly designed to find a new role, Britain having lost its empire, then leaving it will resurrect that dilemma by casting the country adrift from its major multilateral framework of action. Winston Churchill talked in 1946 of Britain's unique position at the intersection of three circles – Atlantic, imperial and European. Of these only the Atlantic and the Commonwealth will remain post-Brexit, and even the nostalgics rarely argue that either represents a solid platform for British foreign policy in the twenty-first century.[12] Isolationism, in the sense of keeping external commitments to the minimum and always giving obvious domestic needs the priority, is a theoretical possibility but unlikely ever to be seriously considered in a country of Britain's history and cosmopolitan character. This leaves as the only option, at least in terms of looking for a distinctive 'role', that of 'global Britain', espoused by the pro-Brexit camp, and picked up by the May government in its struggle to find a way forward. It is a conception that appeals to various constituencies, but is difficult to define in structural terms. What, indeed, would *not* be included in such an approach?

Yet the close institutional networks of a regional organization might not be as necessary to conduct a successful foreign policy as the enthusiasts for the EU have come to believe. Given Britain's inevitable continued profile as a leading Western state, it could benefit from an increased flexibility within its general orientation. For example, practical cooperation will probably continue on the ground with other European states in third countries, particularly where conditions are testing, while the UK will doubtless regularly align itself with them in the many international organizations, especially under the UN umbrella, where they all participate. In that sense nothing much might change, since every Member State has always had the capacity to defect from any common position in the strictly intergovernmental system of the Common Foreign and Security Policy (CFSP), which Britain has never felt constrained by. On the one hand Britain cannot, any more than other rich states, escape its image in the world as a capitalist liberal democracy. It has a long history, which has earned both respect and anger, depending on who is talking. These mixed memories, of power and responsibility but also empire and oppression, can fade only over the course of generations. They define Britons' self-images as well as those held by outsiders. On the other hand, even within the EU Britain has retained full sovereignty over its foreign and defence policies. Indeed, its sovereignty (meaning the ultimate ability to make one's own decisions) has only been qualified with respect to trade, agriculture, fisheries and the Single Market – admittedly things that 52 per cent of those voting in the 2016 referendum saw as critical impediments to their democratic rights.

Given this historical matrix Britain has a limited but real margin of diplomatic manoeuvre, which has been evident throughout its membership of the EU, and arguably might be enlarged after its departure. If it can avoid the sycophantic clichés of the 'special relationship' it should still be able

to benefit from a pattern of cooperation with the United
States that has now lasted nearly eighty years, even if much
depends on the variable of US foreign policy, itself in part
a function of the personality of the president. On this side
of the Atlantic the Europeans may well be tired with the
difficulties Britain has caused them but they will not treat
it as a pariah, especially in matters of geopolitics. Casting
the net more widely, even if new strategic partnerships are
unlikely, London should still be able to work closely with
familiar partners like Australia, Canada, India, Nigeria and
South Africa according to the issue of the moment. Commonwealth membership does not guarantee interests in
common, but it does facilitate cooperation once that has
been identified as desirable.

This potentially positive scenario is overshadowed,
however, by the conundrum of how far Britain should
attempt to keep the states of the European region in the
innermost circle of its foreign policy. Are the 49 years of
diplomatic cooperation a mere wasting asset, or can they
be used to maintain privileged partnerships? The answer
varies according to the bilateral relationship in question –
given the various rounds of EU enlargement some states
have been partners for longer than others, just as historical
closeness has varied. But it seems unlikely that any British
government would wilfully throw away the painful gains
achieved since 1945 in building closer relations with the
Federal Republic of Germany, or in managing the always
brittle entente with France. Italy, Poland and Spain have
also become countries with whom good working relations
are necessary. In fact there are few European capitals in
which British diplomacy could afford to be inactive even
outside the EU.

Decision-making on foreign policy will present future
governments at Westminster with some interesting choices
– even assuming that by then Scotland will not be en route
to independence. The FCO has had to surrender its monop-
oly on dealings with the outside world over the last half
century as advances in communications have enabled other

government departments to make direct contacts with their equivalents abroad. This role will not be coming back. But membership of the EC/EU opened new doors for the FCO, given the key role of foreign ministers first in European Political Cooperation (EPC) and then in European law through the role of foreign ministers in the General Affairs Council. British diplomats soon earned a high reputation for professional competence in Brussels, backed by the weight that their state carried. Thus the FCO carved out a new function for itself as the coordinator of the diverse strands of UK external relations. The European system was its primary focus but, given the acceptance after 1968 that a truly world role had been consigned to the past, and the growing degree of coordination between European embassies in third countries, this meant that it continued to hold a strategic position in Whitehall. The Cabinet Office, in conjunction with the Prime Minister's office and the prominence there of special (political) advisers (SpAds), has naturally come to see itself as the primary coordinating body, but limitations of space and staff mean that it still relies heavily on the FCO for external policy. After all, no one else specializes in 'the international'.

This has not prevented the inhabitants of King Charles's Street from regularly being denigrated, in the press, in parliament, and even by a few of its own, as being unfit for modern purpose and as having lost their high standing in the Cabinet room.[13] Once Britain has left the EU, this view will have to be faced. Despite being denuded of much of its daily rationale, the FCO will have no choice but to present itself as the only ministry capable not just of coordinating policies across the board, but also of helping the National Security Council (NSC) to provide strategic direction – unless it loses its nerve and surrenders external policy to Number 10 and to its bureaucratic rivals. The Prime Minister, like most of her recent predecessors, will seek to determine the *grandes lignes* of British diplomacy, leaving Cabinet colleagues to fight over implementation and resources – in the shadow of the Treasury's administrative primacy. The Foreign Office will be only one player, with the Ministry of Defence also a potential source of policy initiatives towards the outside world, given its direct links to the military inside various important states, notably the USA. Another system in parallel is inhabited by the intelligence services, even if they, like the defence diplomats, need the FCO's network of embassies as the elephant perch from which to observe other states and societies.

These are the traditional turf rivals over foreign policy, whose position will not change markedly after Brexit given that the EU has never made serious inroads into national defence and intelligence activity. But others will be advantaged, at least in the narrow departmental sense, by the change. The National Security Council, for example, established in 2010, consists not only of the PM, Chancellor of the Exchequer, Foreign Secretary and Defence Secretary but also the Home Secretary, Attorney General, and the Secretaries of State for International Development, and Business, Energy and Industrial Strategy, with others attending on an issue-related basis. Leaving the EU will remove an important set of pressures to present a coherent face in external policy, a process in which the FCO played a central part. It thus opens the door for other departments to behave more independently.

The Department of International Development, for example, is already a significant rival given the large budget at its disposal and the increasing tendency to see development as a critical means of pre-empting radicalization, conflict and migratory pressures. It has been a major player in EU development policy, setting norms and contributing (in 2014) 14.7 per cent of the total European Development Fund (EDF), which was the third largest share behind Germany and France.[14] This money, amounting to more than 10 per cent of the UK's overall Official Development Assistance (ODA), will come back into the budget of the Department for International Development (DfID) as a virtually untouchable instrument of policy, given that

Parliament has legislated to commit the UK to spending at least 0.7 per cent of GDP on aid.

Although development specialists complain about conditionality and the diversion of money to help refugees settle in the UK, such politicization gives DfID the right to a say in the setting of external policy goals. Other ministries too will look for seats at the table when major international issues are discussed. In the case of the Department of Trade, limited to export promotion by the existence of the EU's Common Commercial Policy, the referendum vote has already given it a strategic responsibility for securing deals with the states or regions that might prove key markets or sources of raw materials for the UK economy. The Department of the Environment, Food and Rural Affairs will also have a high global profile assuming that government policy continues to take climate change seriously. Food security and the many health issues associated with it must require complex discussions with other states, with the UN's Food and Agriculture Organization – and with the EU, given the influence its Common Agricultural Policy has on world food trade. Such matters have long involved direct relations between specialists, which is why so many home civil servants have been seconded to the UK's permanent representations in Brussels and Geneva, and to embassies like Washington or Tokyo. But they have worked under the supervision of the FCO and its diplomats, a process made easier by the existence of the EU and the way it operates. What is more, while home civil servants may feel at their ease in comfortable Western capitals, being posted to Abuja, Beijing, Moscow, New Delhi or many others is a different story. The Foreign Office will have to fight its corner in the post-Brexit administrative free for all, but Whitehall's loss of the domesticated environment of the EU will arguably place a premium on specialist diplomatic knowledge of the diversity present in the international system.

The first issue to be raised once the prospect of negotiations over Brexit had become real was the fate of the people whose status would change. Inside the UK the position of the three million or so citizens of other EU countries living here was suddenly thrown into doubt just as the Britons living in France, Spain, Italy and elsewhere on the continent were alarmed at the prospect of losing residence rights and access to welfare – particularly as over 20 per cent of the expatriates are pensioners.[15] Many expected humanitarian gestures on both sides of the negotiating table to settle the matter. Indeed, the Joint Report issued in December 2017 at the end of the preliminary Brexit negotiations did commit to allowing EU citizens resident in the UK, and UK citizens resident elsewhere in the EU, at the time of withdrawal, to stay. But important uncertainties remained, with legal wrangles certain for years to come, regardless of the final UK–EU deal. Much hinges on the bigger issue of Britain's access to the Single Market, with its commitment to the free movement of peoples, and on the practical consequences of labour market needs in Britain and on the continent.

Another dimension of this problem for UK citizens is their ease and safety of travel. Unless the UK accepts the need to be part of the EEA, with all the qualifications of a Brexit that entails, the British are unlikely to be able to use the 'EU citizens' line at airports. At present this facility means that despite being outside the Schengen zone they suffer minimal inconvenience. The return to a national (blue) passport after relinquishing the maroon EU format will please some but it will also pick out British citizens more easily in any context with the potential for hostility to the old imperial power. They will be identified more with their own country's foreign policy (and that of the United States, with which it often aligns) rather than being able to shelter under the cover of Europe. In the most extreme circumstances, of being taken hostage, or as visitors in a conflict zone, this could even prove fatal.[16]

Less dramatically, the increasing tendency for EU Member States to cooperate in helping each other's citizens in third states, which could lead to common consular services in future, might not be available to UK citizens, although the tendency of developed democracies to show solidarity in emergencies would probably over-ride that theoretical disadvantage. Visas are another matter. As the UK has never entered the Schengen system of open borders it has also not used the common visa scheme that Schengen operates, and which led to 13.9 million visas being granted in 2016 (out of 15.2 million applied for) allowing their holders to travel freely within most of the EU for a limited period.[17] The UK has preferred to take on the extra work of issuing its own visas, forcing foreign visitors who then want to travel on to, say, France to go to the trouble of obtaining another document. It makes sense to have Europe-wide agreement on which nationalities should and should not have visa-free access, so Britain is likely to continue to shadow such EU decisions as the 2017 removal of the visa requirement for Ukrainians. It might prove diplomatically awkward if London has a different line from the majority, but that is the price of autonomy.

At the same time London has sought access, for security and law enforcement reasons, to the Schengen Information System, which collates data on the movements of third country nationals, including vehicle registrations. It will certainly wish to continue to have this privilege, which helps law enforcement and border controls. In the interests of counter-terrorist strategy the EU is not likely to make difficulties. Furthermore EU Visa Facilitation Agreements with third countries are linked to Readmission Agreements about the return of irregular migrants to their home countries – e.g. with Hong Kong in 2004 and Albania in 2006. Britain has a strong interest in working closely with these arrangements, if not actually being party to them. It also works with Denmark, France and the Netherlands to operate a visa-free scheme for the ex-dependencies on the OCT list (Overseas Countries and Territories), which could now be called into question. As for the individuals seeking visas or residency, life will become more complicated and family reunions more difficult. All things considered, therefore,

Brexit is likely to add to the procedural labyrinth for both ordinary people and national bureaucracies, at a time when the complexities of migration (and asylum) policy are crying out for rationalization and harmonization.

British foreign policy, like the citizens it works for, will face an identity dilemma after Brexit. This will not present itself immediately, in the way that new barriers to trade or the free movement of people will have a visible impact. But over a period of time the issue of how Britain sees itself in relation to the rest of the world will have to be addressed – after half a century in which it has seemed settled – through a series of practical, incremental, steps. Across a range of issues decisions will have to be made on whether to go it alone, to seek alignment with erstwhile EU partners or to act in conjunction with more distant states, notably the US. In every case, apart from defence – where NATO will remain the default setting – the balance of costs and benefits will have to be assessed individually, as compared to the current procedure of working through the CFSP unless there is a positive reason to break ranks.

In the early 1960s it was evident, even without Dean Acheson's caustic reminder, that Britain was desperate to identify a new role for itself.[18] The period after the first application to join the European Economic Community (EEC) in 1961 was marked by uncertainty about this new destiny but that ended with the referendum which confirmed membership in 1975. Thereafter, despite the lack of enthusiasm in sections of both major political parties, it became accepted that Britain needed to work with its European neighbours – to compensate for its 'descent from power' and to offset the risks of full dependence on the US, itself in a state of uncertainty post-Vietnam.[19] It was only in the period since the election in 2005 of David Cameron to leadership of the Conservative Party, and the associated rise of UKIP, that a serious debate arose about the possibility of actually leaving the EU, and thus of finding a new niche in international affairs, political and economic.[20]

The difficulty with the 2016 decision that then followed was that there was no obvious next step, no line of least resistance, as there had been after the Suez crisis of 1956. In the 1960s the new European project promised so much: a large market, a stimulus to change, and a means of developing the 'continental commitment' without serious sacrifices of sovereignty, given that General de Gaulle was in the process of knocking back the supranational ambitions of the Commission. There were moral and political difficulties about abandoning the close trade ties with Commonwealth countries like New Zealand, but given the US support for British entry it increasingly seemed like an historically irresistible move to make. Now, however, despite the liberation from a legal straitjacket in which a majority of British voters seems to have been chafing, there is no alternative safe haven, regional or institutional, to head for.

It may be that this kind of metaphorical thinking, of havens, niches, roles, circles and the rest, associated with the search for a single dominant identity, is simply irrelevant to actual needs. Most people do not have great problems in accepting that they are not only British but also English, Northern Irish, Scottish or Welsh, while members of ethnocultural minorities may further define themselves in terms of the country of their, or their parents', origins.[21] Thus it should not in principle be a problem to extend the process to include the idea of being also European, 'Western' or citizens of the world, whatever formal alliances or legal commitments Britain may have entered into. Since people are now more at ease with multiple cultural identities they will understand the need for their state to vary its orientations according to the issue at stake. Even in times of sharp disagreement France and Britain have displayed great solidarity when either has come under terrorist attack, indicating that the tie between neighbours cannot be discounted, and that the nature of the issue is crucial. This country, whether via its government or a vocal public opinion, might equally present itself as Atlanticist in relation to Russia, European over the Iran nuclear deal, as a concerned player in the southern hemisphere (given responsibilities in the Antarctic and the Falkland Islands), and as a leader on functional issues like climate change.

Argument and structure

This book is not written as an open-ended enquiry, whereby the final destination comes into view only in the course of the journey. Nor is it the product of a lengthy research project whose findings need to be summarized. It is instead a brief and concentrated analysis that aims to show where British foreign policy stands at this critical point of juncture in its modern history, looking both back and forward. This must involve some contestable value-judgements about the nature of the choices at stake, just as the moving-target nature of the issue is bound to show up the foolishness of making predictions. Still, it should be possible to identify the trends and parameters that British foreign policy-makers will have to take into account, regardless of their preferences.

The aim is to treat the subject dispassionately – but not uncritically. To that end a straightforward argument under-pins everything that follows in the book: namely, the view that whatever legal relationship the UK arrives at once the tortuous process of negotiating an exit from the EU is concluded, it is not going to be able to detach itself politically from the fate of that organization, and even less from the region that we call Europe. It is Britain's historical, geographical and cultural destiny to be entangled with the affairs of the continent. As a result, the fundamental issue is less that of membership or otherwise of the European Union than it is the nature and the terms of the relation-ships that have to be formed with the states of the region and with the organizations they have generated.

After the scene-setting of this introductory chapter the book proceeds to an historical account of the key steps and missteps in British diplomacy towards the European project. The aim here is to explain how over 65 years a combination of ambivalence, divisions and no little hypocrisy has brought the country to reverse what had been thought to be a once and for all strategic decision, not just about the economy but about Britain's place in the world. This decision was made during a period of angst about identity and foreign policy, not unlike the current ferment, after having stood complacently on the sidelines during the original construction of the EEC in the 1950s. Chapter 3 then proceeds to analyse the relationship between Britain's independent national foreign policy and the processes of diplomatic coordination that have taken place in the EC/EU since 1970 – often at British instigation. The focus here is mainly on the contemporary situation but inevitably it harks back to key formative episodes – from Maastricht through the Iraq War to Europe's financial crisis – when the Member States have sometimes come together and sometimes splintered, with Britain and France usually the leading players in one way or other. A question of particular importance here is the extent to which these two states have become 'Europeanized' in their foreign policies, meaning that as middle powers they have come to rely on their regional grouping in order to have effective, influential, foreign policies. On such a logic even leaving the EU does not mean that Europeanization automatically ceases, for no British government will find attractive the binary choice between harnessing itself unequally to the US, and pursuing unilateralism. Whoever is in power will have to find a way of associating itself with the EU's Common Foreign and Security Policy (CFSP), albeit from a weakened position on the sidelines.

The fourth chapter will deal with Britain's historic preference for an à la carte approach to the European policy menu – that is, to adopt some areas willingly, even enthusiastically, but to resist others to the point of opting out altogether. Defence, for example, has always been seen in Britain as strictly in NATO's domain. On the other hand 'security', which lies between defence and foreign policy, has increasingly been the terrain of the EU and its Member States. Because it relates to trans-border activity rather than conventional territorial defence it is one of those areas in which even after Brexit Britain will have little choice but to engage with its European neighbours. Cooperation with myriad agencies on police, judicial and counter-terrorism work is bound to continue in some form or other, if with higher transaction costs. This has been effectively recognized by the British government during the first year of the post-referendum negotiations. More difficult in terms of opting in or out have been the trade and financial services sectors, where zero-sum games are perceived by both Britain and the EU to be at stake. Yet tensions may be mitigated by the fact that the health of the eurozone economy and the level of the euro are matters of vital interest to a country whose commercial life will remain oriented to the continent for a long time, whatever efforts are made to diversify.

The single issue of external policy that most embodies British ambivalence towards the EU, is enlargement. London has persistently supported the policy of enlarging the EU, partly for geopolitical reasons and partly as a tactic to dilute the influence of the federalists among the original Six. In many respects the policy and the tactic have succeeded, but they have also backfired, with Russia in a state of alienation and the extension of the Single Market to eastern Europe leading to the increased immigration that has so destabilized the UK's domestic politics. How and why British governments took this line, and whether it could have been handled better, are still controversial questions, although increasingly a matter for the historians. Yet crucial problems remain for decision: is there anything to be salvaged from the current mess, in terms of the sensible management of migration, not just into Britain but at the EU's southern and eastern borders? How are the strategic issues, such as the stability of eastern Europe and the credibility of European foreign policies to be managed? It can hardly be doubted that the issue of the EU's membership, growing or reducing, will remain of vital importance to the UK even after a departure from the Union. If others were to follow the British lead in departing that would transform the nature of the European international order. Conversely, were the remaining Balkan states, to say nothing of Turkey or the Ukraine, to be given the green light for accession that would dramatically change the parameters of the UK's own external strategy.

The complexities of choice and of prioritizing lead naturally into Chapter 5, where the book addresses the question that plagues the CFSP and will remain a real dilemma for Britain on its own: are Europeans destined, in a post-colonial world of emerging powers, to limit themselves to a regional power role, or should they still aspire to global political influence? If the world is to become, as so often mooted, multipolar, it is hardly realistic for Britain to expect to constitute a pole by itself. Even the EU as a whole has struggled to live up to that expectation. Thus we need to ask about the specificities of the UK's vital interests, where they lie geographically, how the country might be able to promote them, and in conjunction with whom. If 'global Britain' is to be more than a campaigning slogan what will it entail in terms of partnerships, priorities and resources? The pursuit of new 'strategic partnerships' is one intriguing possibility but the meaning and feasibility of the policy needs critical analysis, as does the notion of the 'Anglosphere', often mooted in certain quarters. A more obvious framework for foreign policy is the Commonwealth, but there are obvious doubts as to its homogeneity, effectiveness and sympathy for Britain. Yet if the question-marks over these various options lead Britain to conclude that its influence is still primarily to be exerted in the Euro-Atlantic region, then how far can that approach be pursued independently of cooperation with the EU? Can NATO be employed not just as a defence framework but also for diplomacy? Does Britain's role in the UN Security Council imply closer coordination with France, as the other European power with weight in that forum?

This last question is central to Chapter 6. Assuming that the UNSC remains critical to the UK's foreign policy, and to its self-image in international relations, then it is logical to give specific attention to the two bilateral relationships upon which Britain has relied since 1945, and which seem likely to continue: with France, and with the USA. The three states together make up the Western contingent on the UNSC. France has been a key ally (for better or worse) in two world wars, at Suez, in the Balkans and most lately during the action against Libya of 2011. Furthermore the St Malo meeting of 1998 and the Lancaster House Treaties of 2010 remain the two most significant developments in Europe's attempts at building an architecture of security cooperation independent of the US. The two countries are also Europe's only two nuclear powers, and its only permanent members of the UN Security Council, while they share a similar imperial history. They may not always see eye to eye but they are destined to be closely engaged. As for the United States, acres of print have been spent on the 'special relationship', which now – political rhetoric notwithstanding – only looks special in very limited respects. Yet after Brexit Britain will be both more dependent on support from Washington and more vulnerable to the vicissitudes of US foreign policy. The relationship is complicated by the fact that France has grown closer to the US since its return to the NATO command structure. The triangular diplomacy between London, Paris and Washington will pose significant challenges for all parties, with Britain having little choice but to accept that its relationships with the other two Western members of the UNSC foreign policy will be critical for the foreseeable future – as indeed will be that with Germany, the most powerful state in the EU and one whose foreign policy will face new demands in the absence of the UK.

There is more than enough material in the issues surveyed above to fill a much longer book than this one. Ultimately the aim is to provide an assessment of where the UK stands in the world after the Brexit referendum, of how much change is inevitable, or even possible, and of the extent to which continuing links between society at home and events in continental Europe will shape our identity, economy and external influence. For whatever the legal relationship between Britain and the EU, at every other level the connections are bound to remain of profound concern to both sides. Margaret Thatcher popularized the glib view that 'nothing good [comes] out of Europe', but whatever political position or value-judgement we adopt one thing is clear: as an off-shore island the United Kingdom has never been able to ignore what happens on the continental land-mass next door. After Brexit, therefore, the key questions must be: will the UK continue to be European despite itself? Might it even remain to some extent under the EU roof?

2

Falling Back on Europe

The question of whether Britain is 'a European country' is both banal and unanswerable. In one sense the country is all too clearly European. Until the 1950s its demography was almost exclusively the product of waves of migration from the continent over many thousands of years. Culturally its art and music has been persistently influenced by continental achievements from the Norman cathedrals through Palladio and Handel to Monet, Holst and Le Corbusier. Its monarchy has been at various times francophone, Dutch-speaking and Germanic. Politically it has been shaped by the Reformation, and by reactions against the French revolution and Soviet communism.

On the other hand, Britain also has important characteristics that set it apart.[1] It was the source and for a long time the centre of a global Anglophone network that took much from the Westminster system of government, with its customary law and a gradualist approach to political change – in contrast to a continent accustomed to Roman law and sharper struggles over ideas and ideology.[2] Britain's location and maritime tradition kept it turned outwards towards the Atlantic, the Caribbean and the southern oceans for longer than the other seaboard powers of Portugal,

Spain, the Netherlands and France, which also had to look towards their landward defences. The British could mostly avoid having to maintain a standing army, with all the associated costs and implications for executive power.[3] In the second half of the twentieth century the country also became, earlier and to a greater degree than other EU members, multicultural with large Caribbean and south Asian minorities. In contrast to the French preference for assimilation, Britain celebrated its new cosmopolitanism, which was the other side of the coin from its lukewarm attitude towards European integration.[4]

The general argument about Britain's Europeanness is thus irresolvable. The country has been influenced by many of the same forces that have shaped its neighbours, but is also distinctive and is thus seen by them as part of an alien 'Anglo-Saxon' world, which includes the United States, Australia, New Zealand and (apart from Quebec) Canada – no matter that the Angles and Saxons were largely Germanic, and that other countries using the Westminster model, such as India or South Africa, can hardly be so described. In any case, this debate is beside the point when placed in a geopolitical context. Not only has Britain been subject to continual pressure from the continent, through invasion, the threat of invasion, and dynastic successions, but its governments have taken a keen interest in the nature of the European political order. As a modern English state emerged in the sixteenth century, and its relative power grew, pro-active interventions in the balance of power became more frequent – from Elizabeth I's campaign in the Spanish Netherlands to Marlborough's victories in the war of the Spanish Succession. By the time of Napoleon's defeat in 1815 Britain had become Europe's leading power, assuming its role of balancer against any potential hegemon but resisting the temptation of any permanent military presence on the continent. At this level, then, relating to co-existence and survival, Britain's fate has always been tied in with that of the landmass from which it is separated by only a narrow waterway. Indeed, as Brendan Simms has pointed out, its politicians have always 'had a very clear sense of the link between the Continental and the colonial or maritime spheres'.[5] This was because Britain's global role depended on a European order that did not put it at risk.

Paradoxically it was in the middle and later nineteenth century, when Britain's primacy was unchallenged, that its foreign policy seemed most detached from Europe. The confidence bestowed by industrial progress led to a watching brief while the growth of nationalism undermined the Austrian and Russian empires. At the same time France was struggling to cope with the consequences of revolution and defeat. The heroes of Blenheim and Waterloo were coming to be linked with both the Whig story of a free island people reaching back to Alfred through Magna Carta and the new dramas of empire, in Mysore, Khartoum and Natal. Yet the unification of Germany through war between 1860 and 1871 sounded alarm bells that in due course led British diplomacy once again to fear the threat of an emerging continental hegemon, and eventually to make common cause with France against Berlin – which seemed ready to use its growing economic strength and fortress position in central Europe as a base from which to challenge the Royal Navy and to engage in imperial competition. From around 1890, when new alliances began to form among the powers, and certainly from 1904 when the Entente Cordiale was formed, the European balance of power was once again the Foreign Office's major preoccupation.[6] In one form or other this continued to be the case over the century that followed.

Britain fought two 'world wars' between 1914 and 1945, but the first was primarily a European contest, and the second ultimately destroyed its position as a leading global power. Between those two conflicts, as after 1815, it had to take responsibility for making the post-war settlement work, while still being reluctant to make a practical reality of Baldwin's observation in 1934 that 'when you think of the defence of England you no longer think of the chalk cliffs of Dover; you think of the Rhine'.[7] In fact the United

Kingdom was torn between policies of deterrence and of internationalism, as it was between making a full commitment to European security and watching on events. It fell fatally between two stools, allowing the League of Nations to founder while failing to deter Germany through rearmament and alliances.[8] Its vital interest in the political order of Europe was only recognized far too late, first feebly at Munich in September 1938, and then symbolically with the issue of formal guarantees to Poland, Greece and Romania six months later. When war then came Britain was in no position to use its forces in France to carry the fight to Hitler.

Absent at the creation

Europe was devastated at the end of the Second World War, when all the powers agreed that Germany must be divided and disarmed, and a new more permanent security system be devised. This turned out to take the form of the bipolarity created by the mutually hostile armed camps of NATO and the Warsaw Pact. So far as Britain was concerned it was clear that there could be no more shilly-shallying about the continental commitment. If the priority was to pull the USA into defending Europe against the Soviet Union, then the price was that Britain became one of the four occupying powers in a divided Germany, heading the European contribution to the Atlantic alliance. In this respect while Europe remained a central concern, it was more an object of foreign policy than a source of identity – or perceived destiny.

It was at this point, soon after the war, that the project of European integration got going. The story of how the UK remained aloof from the first phases, of the European Coal and Steel Community (ECSC), the European Defence Community (EDC) idea and finally the EEC itself, is well known.[9] Given that it was not 'present at the creation', as it had been with NATO, this was to make it difficult, once accession had finally been sought and achieved, to shape the evolution of an organization whose founding principles, enshrined in the Treaty of Rome, could not be gainsaid. Some of the underlying reasons why the bus had been missed in the 1950s are relevant to contemporary British foreign policy even if the context has changed dramatically from those early Cold War years.

For one thing, there was a consensus in political opinion that Britain was a country apart – as a victor nation, and one that had stood heroically alone against Hitler, it was not about to work on equal terms with a group of defeated and failed states seeking to rebuild by transcending national sovereignty.[10] For the UK the principle of untrammelled sovereignty was still sacred, for its own sake but also because of its symbolic attachment to the conjoined images of island defence and parliamentary democracy. In any case, since sovereignty is vested in 'the Crown in Parliament' and in an unwritten constitution it was not exactly negotiable. Thus although the new continental military commitment was now unquestioned, and Britain continued to attempt to shape the regional order diplomatically, it still did so from the margins, consistent with the off-shore balancer tradition. Lastly, this was the first of many occasions on which Britain under-estimated France and Germany, separately and together. Understandable at first given the weakness of both states in the early 1950s, by the 1960s it was an indication of myopia in Westminster, and it continues to be so. The assumption that London could either divide and rule the Paris-Berlin couple, or join it in a triumvirate, was regularly proved wrong. France and Germany consistently overcame their own differences, while making it clear that any change in the EU's shape or direction depended on their joint agreement. At this early stage of European integration, however, Britain did not appreciate how quickly the two war-time enemies would recover, get on close terms, and make a great success of the Common Market. The combined effect of France's *trente glorieuses* and Germany's *wirtschaftswunder* was to leave the United Kingdom chasing the game.

The struggle to join

The years between the first recognition that Britain needed to join the EEC and the endorsement of its membership in a referendum vote, that is from 1961 to 1975, were a difficult time for the country internationally. Still recovering from the setback of the Suez crisis in 1956, when Washington had forced the Franco–British forces to withdraw from Egypt, the UK also had to manage the final disintegration of its empire and cope with the consequences of Sterling being seriously over-valued.[11] What is more, its declared wish to join the EEC was rebuffed twice by General de Gaulle – paradoxically given that his intergovernmentalist view of organization would have found strong support from across the Channel, while it was the smaller, more supranationalist, Member States who favoured bringing Britain in.[12]

On top of these humiliations the Labour government of the 1960s, which was not in itself anti-American, had to face the fact that the 'special relationship' with the United States could not be relied upon. This had been brought home first over Suez 1956 and then when the Kennedy administration cancelled the Skybolt missile without regard to the fact that it had been promised to the UK. The subsequent compensatory agreement to provide access to the Polaris system on generous terms had more than a touch of condescension about it.[13] But it was the brutal prosecution of the Vietnam War during the second half of the 1960s which made it clear that US global policy was out of line with British interests and capabilities. The Wilson government successfully kept its distance under strong American pressure to join the war but Lyndon Johnson's White House fobbed off its attempts to broker peace in harness with Soviet premier Kosygin.[14] This episode tended to confirm the growing sense of the cross-party political class that, however important NATO was for defence, the UK could not afford to be identified too closely with US grand strategy.

It was, in any case, increasingly apparent that global activism was no longer an option for Britain. Under the weight of its newly independent members the Commonwealth was in no mood to accept leadership from Britain, which was on the defensive over its ambivalent relations with racist regimes in South Africa and Southern Rhodesia. What is more the weakness of the economy, leading to the devaluation of Sterling in November 1967 and the decision soon afterwards to withdraw forces from East of Suez, forced the recognition on London that the end of empire had negative consequences for the bigger question of Britain's world role – a connection that seems obvious now but up to then had been elided for two decades. The logical corollary, that foreign policy cooperation with the Europeans provided the only other feasible option, was soon understood – and given practical expression with the setting up in 1969 of European Political Cooperation. This was the one EC institution in which Britain was able to participate from the outset, thanks to de Gaulle's resignation and German pressure to allow the three new candidate countries to join in before actual accession.[15]

Officials and politicians

These developments followed on from the crisis of confidence in British foreign policy, which had begun after the Suez debacle and had continued with the avalanche of African decolonization that followed. Given that 'the real significance of the empire for Britain was that it cushioned her fall in the world', the end of empire meant coming to terms with a tough new reality.[16] The Foreign Office was in the eye of the storm, and its reconstitution as the Foreign and Commonwealth Office (FCO) in 1965 did nothing to change that. It was an obvious scapegoat given its popular image (even then outdated) as a refuge for foppish aristocrats and/or appeasers. Despite the fact that diplomats tended to be ahead of general opinion in seeing the opportunities represented by the EEC, it did not protect them against demands for modernization. It is revealing that these focused on the need for training in economics, given that the Common Market was seen primarily as an economic venture at this time. Opinion across the board was shifting away from the old customs, as indicated by the start of the Anglo-French Concorde project in 1962, and by Prime Minister Wilson's call in 1963 for a new Britain 'to be forged in the white heat of this [scientific] revolution'.[17] At the same time generational change was sweeping through popular culture, making the experiments like EEC seem like the way of the future.

As a result the Plowden Report of 1964 on the civil service called for more specialized training for diplomats, to be followed by the Duncan Report of 1969, commissioned by the government 'to report urgently on the means of obtaining the best value for money from our overseas representation'.[18] The Report argued that as a 'major power of [only] the second order' Britain would have to prioritize, primarily within the Euro-Atlantic 'area of concentration'.[19] It also criticized the FCO's lack of expertise in planning and economics – it had been excluded from the decision on the devaluation of the Pound in 1967. The Report had been produced by three men whose background indicated the business orientation intended: Sir Val Duncan, the Chairman of Rio Tinto-Zinc, the economist Andrew Shonfield, and the diplomat Sir Frank Roberts. They set the tone for the retrenchment in British foreign policy to come, with cuts in postings matching those in global military deployments, and the hopes for an economic revitalization through access to the growing European market. By 1977 the Berrill Report was criticizing British diplomacy for still aspiring to a Rolls Royce performance in the age of the Mini, while two years later Sir Nicholas Henderson's dramatic valedictory letter as Ambassador in Paris argued that economic performance was the key to foreign policy. He called for Britain to stop underestimating Franco–German leadership and to make a proper success of EC membership: 'there is no doubt that our general stance in the Community has made us look an uncooperative member, with inevitable results'.[20]

At the political level attitudes in the Conservative Party had gradually swung round to approve of the new European orientation, partly because it coincided with a wish to seem more modern and democratic after 20 post-war years under an ailing Winston Churchill and then the patrician figures of Anthony Eden, Harold Macmillan and Sir Alec Douglas-Home. It was no coincidence that in 1965 they elected Edward Heath, who was both from humble origins and a strong supporter of joining the Common Market. With Harold Wilson as Labour Prime Minister Britain seemed finally to have joined the meritocratic age and at the same time to have shuffled off its imperial hangover (even if Wilson did say in 1965, to please India, that 'our frontiers are on the Himalayas').[21] Nonetheless the Labour Party at first proved to be the more reluctant Europeans, notwithstanding Wilson's application to join the EEC in 1967 and the restarting of negotiations in 1969. It was Heath who signed the Treaty of Accession in 1973, only for his government to be brought down by a miners' strike. The Labour government that succeeded him had to be circumspect on the EEC, which many on its left wing saw as designed to weaken the nation-state's right to pursue socialism. This suspicion was not enough, however, to counter the modernizing *zeitgeist*. Wilson saw a referendum (never used previously in British politics) as a way of achieving legitimacy for this major foreign policy and constitutional change. The device worked triumphantly, with the British people voting by 2 to 1 to accept membership, on a turnout of 64 per cent.[22] The business community, with strong influence inside the Conservative Party, was desperate to take advantage of the opportunities that the European Community (EC), as it was by then being termed, presented for a fragile UK economy. The press, too, was strongly supportive.[23]

Conflicting and confusing conceptions

Part of the difficulty that Britain had, and has, with the European project arises from competing views of what it amounts to at any given time, and more importantly where it is going – the famous question of a *telos*. Given that no one can know whether the EU will ever become an equivalent to the United States, whether it will collapse or whether it will simply continue on its *sui generis* way, stagnating at times, with bursts of change at others, it is not easy to weigh those views against each other. Yet there is no doubt that some predictions and fears have been wilder than others, just as some hopes and expectations have been driven more by faith than understanding. Furthermore the diversity of perceptions in these crucial years of adaptation to the EC itself caused confusion and conflict inside the UK, in particular because it occurred within the two big political parties as much as between them.

The specific difficulties of British foreign policy arising from the European connection will be discussed in the central part of this book. But there are some more general attitudinal issues that were evident from the earliest days and which cannot be reduced to simple ideological dichotomies. They are important because they have continued to swirl around the domestic debates, to obstruct consensus and to bewilder outsiders.

The first is the sheer unfamiliarity, even ignorance, seen on all sides of the debate in the UK. This was inevitable in the first half of the 1950s, when the ideas for the ECSC and EDC were new-fangled. As late as actual accession in 1973 it was difficult to acquire true expertise in EEC policy-making, from which by definition British officials were excluded. Parliament and public opinion, while regularly attuned to foreign affairs, were preoccupied with the life and death issues of the Korean War, Suez, decolonization, Vietnam and the debate about nuclear disarmament. When Europe did figure it was through such Cold War dramas as the Hungarian uprising or the crises over Berlin. But there was also a lack of understanding of how Monnet, Schuman and the rest saw their new project. As François Duchêne, who worked closely with Monnet, observed, 'where Churchill and Macmillan meant to take the lead on Europe and the Commonwealth, Monnet saw Britain very much as one among equals'.[24] Yet the legacy of perceived betrayals at Dunkirk and Mers-el-Kebir impeded intimacy with France, while Germany and Italy were still seen as problems to be resolved rather than potential partners.

This was part of the under-estimation of the new project mentioned earlier. But it is also consistent with a common pathology of decision-makers, namely the tendency to live in their own worlds and to be insufficiently sensitive to the perceptions of others.[25] This makes adaptation to external constraints, and to change, difficult. In the circumstances of the 1950s where Britain was finally seeing some of the fruits of victory, with a welfare state at home and nuclear weapons seeming to guarantee the status of great power abroad, a degree of solipsism was even more natural. The national awkwardness with foreign languages, and the distance created not just by the Channel but by the fact that Britain had not suffered the trauma of foreign occupation, exacerbated this sense of apartness.

In practical terms the problem was that few on any part of the political spectrum had come to a settled view on the type and extent of international cooperation that might be desirable. As ideas about interdependence, let alone globalization, were still embryonic, the importance of multilateralism for an ex-great power like Britain was not yet understood. True, the NATO alliance gradually became institutionalized, but this was seen in traditional terms, as a defensive bulwark against the threat of world communism and as a way of guaranteeing a US military presence. The United Nations was accepted, especially by the Labour Party, as the expression of internationalist values, but since Britain was unshakeably installed as a veto power on its Security Council there was no danger of being subject to any supranational decisions. In general it was assumed, as indeed it still often is, that international cooperation could be opted in and out of, so that it need not become a thickening web of permanent commitments.

The left remained attached to sovereignty so as to defend the gains of the reforming post-war Labour government. It saw no need to risk losing control of mines and furnaces by joining the ECSC. For its part the right clung to the idea of Britain at the head of a great empire, and when imperial decline could no longer be denied it fell back on the metaphor of the three circles, and the country's apparent indispensability to them all. What both shared was a slowness to recognize the loss of great power status and an inability to translate abstract beliefs about roles into detailed thinking about how the national position might actually be strengthened through joint ventures – what Alan Milward was later to call, in relation to the EEC Six 'the European rescue of the nation-state'.[26] Perhaps the efforts put in to getting the United States to commit to Europe through the Marshall Plan and NATO had exhausted British creativity. It is interesting to note that the Messina conference, which launched what was to become the EEC, took place only a week after the 1955 British general election. Prime minister Anthony Eden was fully preoccupied with other matters.[27] But the real problem was that his government (and party) had a completely different conception of European cooperation from that emerging among the Six, and did not yet grasp the import of what was happening across the Channel.

Even when it came to the momentous accession decision later on, there was much ambiguity over what kind of entity the UK would be joining. There was some sleight of hand in playing down the political aims of the federalists in Brussels, Rome and Berlin – indeed after de Gaulle's slapping down of the Commission in the 1960s no one could be sure what kind of progress would feasible – but there was also self-deception and cognitive dissonance. While Prime Minister Heath was clear that European integration was in itself a good thing, as were the Liberals, most other supporters were prepared to sign up for a limited degree of supranationalism on the assumption that once in the EC Britain would be able to brake the train from the front. Alternatively it was unthinkable that such derogations of sovereignty as were involved would call into question Britain's existence as a proudly independent country. That this latter belief was hardly compatible with the fact that the UK had had to go cap in hand to the members of the EC, and would henceforth have to submit to the primacy of European law, was not often acknowledged.

The holding of a given view at any one time was no guarantee that it would be sustained. Over the first few decades of Britain's engagement with the EC the official views of both main parties shifted from hostility to grudging acceptance. Within them, individuals were even more volatile. Labour heavyweights Tony Benn and Denis Healey each oscillated between support and scepticism in the 1970s.[28] On the Tory side Margaret Thatcher had happily campaigned for accession in 1975, only to become steadily more hostile to the EC once serving as Prime Minister. For his part the Chancellor of the Exchequer Nigel Lawson prevailed upon her in 1989 to agree to join the European Exchange Rate Mechanism (ERM), only to emerge as a leading Eurosceptic in the years that followed. Even Edward Heath, the most *communautaire* of prime ministers, had changed his view quite abruptly: 'I believed until recently that we could carry on fairly well outside the EC'.[29] Some of this inconsistency was the result of a learning process, which went both ways: familiarity breeding either acceptance or disillusion. But the oscillations were to continue with some unfortunate consequences in the following decades – most dramatically in the case of Margaret Thatcher's change from midwife of the Single Market to the enemy of the Commission tasked with implementing it.

Another form of the uncertainty that bedevilled British thinking was over the nature of the EC itself. Was it strong and getting stronger, which might make it a threat to a Britain that remained outside, or might it be a new platform on which British power in the world could be revived? Or was it simply a shelter for states in rehabilitation, fatally divided between the federalists and the believers in '*Europe des patries*'? There could be no definitive answer to this question, given that the Community was all too obviously a work in progress – and that its enthusiasts had great, if unrealistic, plans for it. That helps to explain why Roy Jenkins took the view in 1983 that 'public debate on the topic of Britain and the EEC is in this country all too frequently obscured by doubtfully informed and polarized comment'.[30] But there was more to it than that. Observation of the Community was rarely cool and dispassionate. Rather, it was inflected by strong feelings about what kind of future it represented for a Britain in crisis.

Particularly for those in the Labour movement, the EC had strong ideological connotations, producing in these pre-accession years the fear among many on the left that it would prove to be a graveyard for workers' rights. Despite Labour's internationalist tradition, sovereignty was seen as the precondition of socialism, not an obstacle to it. Commonwealth ties trumped Europe, especially with vulnerable ex-colonies needing help, and war-time friends expecting loyalty. Conservatives shared these last concerns, while also holding suspicions about continental social democracy. Still, given how the European issue cut across party lines, debate was often fudged. The leading Tory William Whitelaw recalled that his party 'had been in no position to think about Europe in any detail before 1970, as any attempt to do so only opened divisions in the party'.[31] Thus, European integration is the one issue that has defied the traditional cohesiveness of British political parties. Neither the Conservative nor the Labour Party has ever been able to achieve a settled position on Europe, let alone one in harmony with continental colleagues.

The capacity for initiative

Over the years the original Six of the EC have had various partners that have intermittently caused headaches – Japan, Turkey, the United States, and within the system Austria,

Greece, and now Hungary and Poland. But Britain has been the most persistent source of difficulties. It is not that the UK has broken the rules. Its governments have been among the most scrupulous in implementing European law while its civil servants are respected for the major contributions they have made to the smooth running of the Brussels institutions. The problem has been that Britain has broken the political consensus, having so often been at odds with majority opinion on how the Community should develop, and on the future of the nation-state. It is piquant that now, just as the UK's view on the latter is starting to find some supporters, especially among the newer members of the 28, it has decided to disrupt the whole enterprise by isolating itself once again.

British governments of different stripes have been well aware of the need to be constructive, not least because until recently they have assumed that membership was permanent and that if the EC/EU were to be beneficial to the UK then it would be essential to engage with the major issues and the major players. The main area in which this was true was classical foreign policy – EPC as it was until 1993, and the CFSP thereafter. It is easy to see why. On the one hand Britain has been one of the two weightiest member-states in terms of international politics, and on the other it was present at the creation of foreign policy cooperation, which had not been part of the Treaty of Rome. The Six had steered clear of it after the failure of the European Political Community and Defence Community ideas in 1954. From accession through to the new century Britain found it easy to protect its own interests in foreign policy, opting out of common positions where it did not suit and ensuring that the system of diplomatic coordination remained firmly intergovernmental. Yet in this it did not stand out. Others too were content to retain their national foreign policies, indeed in some cases (like Ireland) to use the European brand to raise their profile.[32] In any case Britain was quite willing to see practical improvements and rationalizations of what was initially a basic and cumbersome set of procedures. The London Report of 1981 on reforming EPC owed much to Lord Carrington's impatience with the cumbersome nature of system of rotating Community presidencies as applied to foreign policy. The British were also pro-active over a secretariat to help foreign policy coordination (the ancestor of today's External Action Service) and to promote liaison between European embassies in third capitals.

Almost all foreign secretaries in this period, like their officials, were happy with the CFSP framework – which is why Eurosceptics accused them of going native. But their responsibilities on the Council of Ministers for a long term covered the *communautaire* side of the EU as well as foreign policy, which meant that the respect earned by figures like Sir Geoffrey Howe, Robin Cook and David Miliband conferred advantages across the range of their dealings with European colleagues. Howe's European policy turned out not to coincide with that of his boss, Margaret Thatcher, and ended unhappily for both of them, but at least their initiative to launch the Single European Market (SEM) had by then borne fruit, leading Germany in particular to assume that the UK would prove a solid partner (and counterweight to French *étatisme*) in the decades to come.

The general euphoria at the end of the Cold War meant that this hope was not immediately disappointed. It is true that the negotiations for the Treaty of Maastricht were often sticky, with the first signs of serious British doubts about the constitutional implications of the progress sought by others towards more integration. The UK obtained an opt-out on the Social Charter and prevented any moves towards majority voting in foreign policy.[33] But the argument that a united Germany could be best tied down within a stronger multilateral framework eventually won the day. In 1997 the Treaty of Amsterdam provoked a further bout of British angst, partly because it was by now evident that the integration process was progressing via a form of ratchet, whereby each treaty contained provision for review and further proposals not too far down the line. Further opt-outs were obtained from the new supranational provisions in the Treaty for internal security matters, including the incorporation of the Schengen system into EU law. Interestingly, in terms of what was to come, the new Labour government insisted on maintaining full control over UK borders, effectively forcing Ireland to follow suit. But none of this stopped the relentless march of EU treaties, as when the failure of the attempt to legislate for a 'European constitution' in 2005 simply produced the Treaty of Lisbon in 2007, introducing among other things a would-be EU foreign minister (the High Representative) and a permanent President of the Council. That led the UK in 2011 to hold up the adoption of around 100 CFSP declarations on the grounds that the HR was exceeding her powers in speaking for the 28 in various international settings.[34]

Suspicions in Britain about conspiratorial incrementalism were not entirely fair. Given the weight of change in Europe resulting from the end of the Cold War it was inevitable that there should have been a series of intergovernmental conferences (IGCs) working on institutional reform. Indeed, much of the work was required because of another area in which the UK was a prime mover – enlargement. John Major's Conservative governments of 1990–97 had seen the enlargement of the EU as important for geopolitical reasons in the new fluid Europe, to help the 'orphans' of the old Warsaw Pact. But it was also not slow to see the potential for future alliances around the table of the European Council.

The Blair administration that succeeded it was more idealist at first, seeming to wish to foster regional solidarity. Blair seemed like a breath of fresh air to his European colleagues. He addressed the National Assembly in Paris in French and presented himself as pro-European. Within a year of taking office he had even raised eyebrows in Washington through his joint initiative with France at St Malo to promote European defence cooperation. This in turn led to the creation of the European Security and Defence

Policy in 1999, and a series of military and civilian missions from 2003.

Over the passage of time, however, Blair's geopolitical concerns came to hold sway. New Labour was happy to see the path open towards a substantial expansion of the EU, from fifteen Member States in 1997 to 25 by 2007.[35] The reasons were mostly strategic, in terms of stabilizing the ex-Warsaw Pact region, but also politically calculating in that the new east European members were both more sympathetic to intergovernmentalism than supranationalism, and pro-NATO. After the Iraq War their accession also helped Britain to work its passage back to the centre of EU policy-making, after the damaging split with France and Germany.

Putting on the brakes

Thus Britain did at various times take positive initiatives with the aim of pushing forwards the European project in certain respects and encouraging other Member States to believe that in time London might be willing to accept a further deepening of the EU, if not to buy in to the federalism that some still saw as the desirable end-point. Yet these islands of cooperation, or endless 'false beginnings' as a contemporary saw them, were not enough to prevent the growing sense of irritation on the continent (and indeed in Ireland) over Britain's foot-dragging, sense of exceptionalism and what an expert French observer at the time called 'a strategy of minimalism'.[36] Although signs of Euroscepticism were beginning to emerge elsewhere as the new millennium arrived Britain was clearly both the most ideological opponent of integrationism within the EU, and its most formidable obstacle – given that constitutional change could only be achieved through a unanimous vote in the European Council. Within the UK a minority, but a growing one, was beginning to conclude that British interests and values might simply be incompatible with the direction the EU majority wished to travel, and that a parting of the ways was thus inevitable.[37]

These difficulties came out in a series of major disagreements. Right from the first days of membership in 1973 Britain had proved itself to be an 'awkward partner', despite its ten-year struggle to be allowed into the EC club. There is no place for gratitude in international politics. The terms negotiated by Edward Heath were deemed unacceptable by Harold Wilson's incoming Labour Cabinet, which judged (rightly) that renegotiation and then a referendum was the way in which to get the left and the unions to buy into the new venture. In practice, as Christopher Tugendhat observed, the new deal 'changed little of substance. Its real damage, however, came later'.[38] Overall, the two sets of negotiations had left several hostages to fortune. The agreed UK contribution to the Community budget had not taken account of the fact that it would get so little in return through spending programmes such as the Common Agricultural Policy. The effects of sacrificing the British inshore fishing industry, with its huge historical and emotional resonance, were also to be felt much further down the line.

After Wilson gave way to Callaghan as Prime Minister, the complaints began about the fact that so soon after entry Britain was about to become the largest net contributor to the budget. When Thatcher came to office she took up the cause with enthusiasm, embarking on the 'I want my money back' campaign that so irritated Helmut Schmidt and Valéry Giscard d'Estaing, the main players on the other side of the table. The personal pride of all three became implicated and matters escalated. To her officials 'The Prime Minister expressed impatience with the wish of other members of the Community to have more evidence that the Government was Community-minded', and even regretted that she had not demanded that Britain become a net beneficiary of the budget![39] The dispute disrupted EC business right through to the final settlement at Fontainebleau in June 1984.[40] The acrimony then shaped the Milan summit of 1985, where Thatcher found herself isolated. Both sides had dug in, with the British (who were certainly not the only ones at fault) increasingly perceived as hostile to the very project they had just joined. The dispute also, unfortunately, played into every stereotype of continental Europeans common in the UK.

There was inevitably collateral damage from this long-running stand-off. The Westland dispute of 1985, for example, nearly brought Mrs Thatcher down, and drove one of the most Europhile of her ministers, Michael Heseltine, out of the Cabinet. Ostensibly trivial, it centred on whether the British helicopter company Westland should become part of a European consortium, which would henceforth supply the armed services, or be taken over by the US firm Sikorski. It turned into both a struggle over both Cabinet government and the orientation of the defence industries. As it became clear that the Prime Minister was not going to permit a leaning towards Europe, especially on defence, Sikorski won the day.[41]

Right at the end of Thatcher's period in office came another episode of major divergence from majority thinking in the EC. This was over monetary policy, contributing first to the Prime Minister's resignation in November 1990, and then to Britain's humiliating exit from the European Exchange Rate Mechanism (ERM) on 'Black Wednesday' in September 1992. The preceding Labour government had decided to stay out of the ERM when set up as a way of reducing exchange rate fluctuations, but had in effect shadowed the system. This was done by keeping Sterling within its parameters and by contributing gold and foreign currency reserves to underpin the new 'ecu', a European Currency Unit based on a basket of national currencies. The policy continued under three successive Conservative Chancellors (Geoffrey Howe, Nigel Lawson and John Major), with Major eventually persuading Thatcher to join the ERM itself in October 1990, perhaps because other EC members were by then starting to envisage a genuinely single currency. The intra-Cabinet battles on monetary policy polarized views on Europe more generally and became entangled with other issues and with the politics of the European Council more generally. A case in point was Thatcher's Bruges speech of September 1988 in reaction to Jacques Delors' address to the Trades Union Congress. The Prime Minister's strident tone produced strong reactions, making it totemic for Eurosceptics and UK-sceptics alike for years thereafter. Either way, Europe remained essentially an issue of external relations, even if one that could no longer be pigeon-holed as 'foreign policy'.

The wounds left by these events meant that those in the UK who might otherwise have favoured participation in the euro, launched in 2002 after nearly a decade's preparation, tended to keep their heads below the parapet. This left the field open for critics of the concept of European Monetary Union (EMU), ensuring that Britain would remain outside yet another of the new EU's major policy areas, and widening the comprehension gap with its continental partners – who would have benefited from a more robust and informed debate on the euro. That the decision to retain Sterling now seems well advised, as indeed do many of the structural criticisms of the euro project itself, should not obscure the fact that the conflicts over monetary policy in the febrile years bracketing the end of the Cold War damaged Britain's whole relationship with the EU, and to an unnecessary degree.[42] It reinforced the view on both sides that the EU was indeed on track to becoming a federal union, and in Britain that the key attributes of sovereignty were at risk. It is worth noting that the first serious suggestion of leaving the EU was made in 1995 by Norman Lamont, the Chancellor turned by Black Wednesday into a thoroughgoing Eurosceptic.[43]

Between the Maastricht Treaty and the 2016 referendum there were three more major issues that worsened Britain's relations with the EU and helped to move the idea of an exit from the implausible to the possible. They were the Social Chapter, the Iraq War, and the divide over immigration. Of these the Social Chapter can be briefly dealt with. John Major had obtained an opt-out at Maastricht, which was opposed by Labour who then signed up to the Chapter on their return to power in 1997. This did not go down well with those parts of British industry that feared the effects on its competitiveness outside Europe, and which had got used to the freedom from trades union constraints achieved by Thatcherism.[44] Their opposition gave the Conservative Eurosceptics another arrow in their quiver so that by the time Labour lost power in 2010 the issue had become central to Tory critics of the Lisbon Treaty, which had further strengthened the language on Member States' social obligations to include full employment and 'social protection'. As the new Conservative/Liberal Democrat coalition could not opt out of the ratified Treaty retrospectively, this had the effect of ramping up the demands for a referendum on membership.

The Iraq War was not the first occasion on which Britain had disrupted European solidarity in foreign policy but it was the most serious. It also dealt a further major blow to Britain's attachment to the EU. On the right there was initially scorn for the unwillingness of France and Germany to join the US–UK action to overthrow Saddam Hussein, together with much *schadenfreude* at the inability of European foreign policy to reach an agreed position. That the war came increasingly to be seen as a dreadful mistake did not shift their view of the EU. For their part the critics of the war in the centre and on the left despaired of the ability of Europe to unite and in particular to stand up to Washington. The long wars in Iraq and Afghanistan between 2001 and 2014 focused attention on those European states with the military capacity to participate, for good or ill, and moved it away from the EU, whose 'battlegroups' turned out to be a dead letter and whose modest ESDP missions did not aspire to more than peacekeeping and election monitoring. Thus, while both Suez and Vietnam in their different ways gave a boost to European integration, Iraq if anything damaged it – by demonstrating once again that when it came to a big foreign policy issue the EU was left on the sidelines. The arguments that raged within the Member States over justifications for the war simply passed it by.

The issue of immigration has been bubbling away in British politics for decades but only began to have a European dimension with the Schengen system of borderless travel within the EU, from the mid 1980s. This led to successive governments insisting on opt-outs both from Schengen and from the wider area of Justice and Home Affairs.[45] After 2004, however, it came increasingly to the fore, cut across natural party lines and eventually catalysed the various elements of anti-EU feeling into the mood that produced a majority vote for Brexit. 2004 was the year in which, following a decision two years earlier, the Blair government allowed people from the ten countries entering the EU that year to have immediate free movement of labour into Britain, and not to delay the process for three years, as France and Germany did. The decision did not become an issue in the 2005 General election, as Home Secretary Charles Clarke had feared it might, despite the fact that it almost immediately led to large numbers of eastern Europeans entering the UK and to negative reactions from the local population in some of their main destinations.[46] Yet it combined with the loss of life caused by Islamist terrorists in the same period gradually to propel migration to the top of the political agenda – regardless of the fact that the atrocities that hit Britain from 2005 on were committed mostly by home-grown jihadists. The decision to allow Bulgaria and Rumania also to become EU members from 2007, which the Blair government had pushed hard for, eventually ensured that the numbers arriving in the UK from east Europe would become a very hot domestic issue.

One of the first consequences of this change in the political atmosphere was the rise of the UK Independence Party (UKIP), which soon focused its hostility to the EU on the immigration issue. Although the first past the post electoral system in Britain made it very difficult for the party to gain parliamentary seats, the proportional representation system of elections for the European Parliament compensated it handsomely. After the 2009 vote UKIP had as many MEPs as the Labour Party. Still, the main threat it seemed to carry was to the Conservative Party, which increasingly began to adopt UKIP positions in order to close the door to its right. From 2012 the opinion polling and by-election results showed UKIP gaining ground rapidly, to the extent of becoming the largest British party in the European Parliament after the 2014 elections. This so ratcheted up the pressure on Prime Minister Cameron that in 2015 he risked the fatal move of offering an 'in-out referendum' on Britain's membership of the EU.

The migration issue had become so central, and so toxic, that it affected Labour as much as the Tories, although the effects of the 2004 decision had been unforeseen by both parties at the time.[47] Once it was clear that UKIP was making ground in Labour heartlands, where working-class conservatism combined with fears about job losses, wages being driven down and cultural change, the party began to voice a *mea culpa* for the cosmopolitanism of the Blair years, and to tack to the right on immigration. It thus became caught between its old tradition of openness to new arrivals and the need to cover its flanks against the familiar accusations of being unpatriotic. This necessarily had the effect of cooling such enthusiasm as remained for European integration, given that the 'four freedoms' of movement (capital, goods, services and people) were the unshakeable pillars of the Single Market and of the Union's image of itself. It is clear that Labour's older supporters, at least, wanted the party to do something about immigration, that this fed into the instincts of Jeremy Corbyn, its leader from 2015, and that it conditioned the Party's lack-lustre support for the Remain camp in the Referendum that followed. That in turn may well have made the difference in the final, narrow, result in favour of Leave. Although the decision of the voters was shaped by many interacting factors, the immigration question, sharpened by the crisis of September 2015 when around one million refugees flooded north to escape the war in Syria (though very few to the UK), is likely to have tipped the balance.[48]

A retreat in mind and deed

The balance between enthusiasm and scepticism, between constructive initiative and foot-dragging, steadily shifted over the 43 years of British EU membership to the point where first a referendum, and then an actual vote to leave, became practical politics. The era of Heath and Roy Jenkins, of Kenneth Clarke and Shirley Williams, has passed. David Owen, once a convinced Europhile, is now just as trenchant on the other side of the argument.[49] The victorious Eurosceptics are not always as personally parochial as the views they espouse, or the attitudes they foster. Nigel Lawson lives permanently in France, Nigel Farage was married to a German, Boris Johnson loves travelling and indulging his talent for classical languages. But they have managed to exploit the fundamental ambivalence of the British over a project that not only qualified aspects of national sovereignty but also required a cultural openness that has not resonated with enough voters. This could change as the older generations die off. But perhaps it is just that Britain has a certain idea of itself, preferring its own version of internationalism in the form of an uneasy Anglophone multiculturalism, to that whose icons are Charlemagne, Beethoven and Jean Monnet. Euroscepticism is not without some deep cultural roots.[50] As part of this the British, having abolished their peasantry three centuries ago, have never appreciated the subsidies of the Common Agricultural Policy. For better or worse their preference since the repeal of the Corn Laws in 1846 has been for cheap food, sourced globally. It is revealing that when the mass British public finally got a taste for wine it soon became a major market for Australian, New Zealand and South African imports, despite the proximity of the European wine lake.[51]

It is paradoxical that British conservativism on Europe, expressed in both the two main parties, has become increasingly vociferous in its rejection of federalism during years in which the likelihood of a United States of Europe has become ever more remote. Britain decided to leave the EU at the point where its argument in favour of strong nation-states was being echoed elsewhere, by populist parties growing in strength and by some governments, particularly in eastern Europe. A further twist is added by the fact that the Brexit vote appears to have created more unity in the EU than existed before, and possibly to have re-ignited the belief in further integration. It might even prove to have been the high-water mark of populism in Europe.

The wave of British disenchantment does not, however, depend on the straw man of federalism. It has led to issues that had seemed settled on the basis of inter-party consensus being reopened for controversy. Thus, for some the European Court of Justice has come to symbolize unacceptable interference in national affairs, the common commercial policy is now seen as a straitjacket, and the benefits of the free movement of people to hundreds of thousands of British people living in Spain, France and elsewhere in the EU, have been outweighed by the threats free movement is thought to pose to the national way of life. The prosaic but useful process of European foreign policy coordination was for long relatively immune from such attacks, but even it has come to be stigmatized as a danger to NATO and to the independence of Britain's armed forces. Many Britons naturally do not subscribe to these views, but they have been endlessly ventilated by the tabloid press and had sufficient traction to produce a 52/48 majority in the decisive vote.

Revealingly, most people on either side of the argument would be unsure as to whether their debate is about *foreign* policy. On the one hand a large part of the country's problem is that 'Europe' appears to be alien, 'over there'. Britain in contrast is seen as unique, neither European nor Americanized. On this view dealings with EU partners are *ipso facto* matters of foreign policy, whatever the legal position. And when law and national politics clash the sense of frustration at the constraints on a country proud of its independence is heightened. On the other hand even those favourable to EU membership find it hard to see Brussels and the European Council as inherent to domestic politics, as is the case in Germany, Italy and many other Member States. They tend to oscillate between seeing relations with the EU's institutions or with the other 27 as normal and routine, and assuming that they are the business of diplomats, as specialists in 'abroad'. In this sense membership of the EU over four decades has done its work: the British are in two minds as to whether Europe does or does not provide the stable framework they need as a buffer against the chaos of events. In or out of the Union, this ambivalence is likely to continue.

3

Does Britain Need European Foreign Policy?

As we have just seen, part of the problem the British have with Europe is one of identity – whether Europeans are us or them, and ultimately whether Europe is a source of foreign policy, or merely its object. This is not wholly surprising, given the argument that has raged as to whether a European foreign policy (EFP) really exists. Realists inside Europe and among watching states have always been sceptical as to whether an organization of sovereign states could hold together sufficiently to pursue effective common policies towards the outside world. That the 28 do so in trade and competition policy is not thought relevant, since while these are certainly areas of vital interest they are not in the same league as the issues of war and peace. For their part liberals have often been disappointed at the failures of the EU to live up to its aspirations as a 'normative power' to improve the world. It can thus be argued that the Member States are no nearer to constituting one of the pillars of a multipolar world than they were in the 1970s, when their efforts at a collective diplomacy first got off the ground.

And yet, the failures of EFP must be balanced against real successes. Disunity does not always mean inaction.

The United States has come to value the division of labour whereby the EU does things that NATO cannot and that Washington prefers not to take on alone. European diplomacy has also survived six rounds of enlargement, from nine participants at its outset to 28 now, and it will almost certainly survive shrinkage to 27. It has steadily developed its administrative structures, to the point where – rather against the odds – it is now represented by a High Representative (HR) who acts as a foreign minister (albeit without a sovereign base) and whose status and perceived usefulness to third states has quietly grown during three incumbencies. It has managed to develop a role in the sensitive areas of security and defence, including the development of a satellite capability, while also liaising across bureaucratic boundaries on issues like economic sanctions and counter-terrorism where it can draw on the resources of the supranational aspects of EU business. In doing all this the legalistic arguments about whether a European diplomacy has been either too supranational or too intergovernmental have largely faded away. Even the UK has become more relaxed about the theology of foreign policy cooperation, while no serious observer would suggest that the Brexit vote occurred because the British people have doubts about the value of working with European partners on foreign policy questions.[1] Even in 2017 a Eurobarometer poll showed that only 37 per cent of UK respondents were against the idea of a common European foreign policy, with 50 per cent in favour and 13 per cent don't knows – and this was before the solid European support for Britain over the poisoning of Sergei Skripal in March 2018.[2]

The European foreign policy system

'European foreign policy' is, however, a vague term. What is meant by it in terms of structures and activities? The technical answer is that it is European 'political cooperation' on a voluntary basis between the Member States, and this (EPC) is how it was titled from its beginning in 1969. EPC was, with much fanfare, re-invented as the Common Foreign and Security Policy (CFSP) at the Maastricht Treaty of 1993 but, in truth, there was no qualitative leap forward then or at any other time – rather a slow process of incremental change, more often procedural than substantive, has taken place. It has now been operating as a system of coordination for nearly half a century. Rather than replacing national foreign policies it exists alongside them – although there are plenty of enthusiasts for integration who are impatient to see that change. The distinction between the Common Market and the Single Market provides a useful point of comparison: foreign policy has remained stuck at the 'common' stage and arguably still has progress to make there given that no equivalent of the common external tariff has emerged – Member States sometimes adopt the same positions, but not infrequently prefer to go their own way. They are still far from agreeing a single decision-making path.

Taking the long view, it can be seen that a certain amount of convergence has occurred between national foreign policies over time, although whenever new members join the EU club dilution inevitably takes place and the process needs revitalizing. If the system is to work it depends on socialization into the *acquis politique*, meaning the set of broadly agreed positions that provide the parameters for European diplomacy. This is a much less structured process than the *acquis communautaire*, which shapes the economic aspects of external relations and is anchored in European law, although non-specialists rarely understand the distinction – understandably, given that it is now blurred in both the language of the treaties and the political discourse of 'European foreign policy'. Academic debate rages over the extent to which the informal processes of convergence have led to 'Europeanization', and in particular over how far that might be irresistible and progressive.[3] In Britain some of the same sectors of opinion that are most critical of the EU also assert that UK foreign policy remains robustly independent of the CFSP, seeing no contradiction, but opinion in most other countries is relaxed about viewing

Europe as a necessary but loose framework for national strategies, which can achieve little by themselves.

In institutional terms Europe's foreign policy system is now sophisticated, if still intergovernmental. Foreign ministers meet monthly in a Foreign Affairs Council, and twice-yearly in so-called 'Gymnich' meetings without the presence of officials. Development and defence ministers can also appear, depending on the issue, and at times have their own configurations. The most important issues will also rise to heads of government level to appear on the agenda of the European Council, and to require ad hoc meetings, sometimes of a smaller number of states. On a day-to-day basis the system is run by the HR, currently Federica Mogherini, who is 'triple-hatted' in that she also speaks for the EU in international fora, and holds the office of a Vice President of the European Commission. In this last capacity she supervises the External Action group of seven Commissioners whose work looks to the outside world, viz: neighbourhood and enlargement negotiations, trade, development, humanitarian aid, climate action and energy, transport and migration.[4] In principle, this provides a wide array of instruments to deploy in foreign policy – assuming that the Member States agree, and that their use is compatible with the treaties. One of the EU's perennial and mountainous obstacles arises from trying to ensure the coherence of EU policy across the range of policy competencies, and in the face of national differences of view. Britain has come to see the value of coherence, after initial fears that it would lead to the 'communitarization' of foreign policy.

Finally, since the Treaty of Lisbon in 2009, the HR has been supported by the European External Action Service. This is run by staff in the Council Secretariat in Brussels and acts as an embryonic European foreign ministry, liaising with EU 'embassies' abroad, which in turn work with the missions of the Member states (where present) with the aim of producing common positions and 'joint actions'. Enthusiasts for the EEAS hope that in time the need for national embassies, and indeed foreign ministries, will fall away, leaving the EU free to conduct a single foreign policy. This remains, however, a distant dream, difficult to realize while nation-states continue to exist, perceive themselves to have distinct interests and regard foreign policy as the ultimate expression of their sovereign independence. The United Kingdom has been particularly sceptical about the EEAS but here too it has come to accept that there are some economies of scale to be had. Post-Brexit it might come to regret exclusion from the network.[5]

The point of it all

Beneath all the official activity, what is European foreign policy for? Over the decades there have been many grandiloquent statements espousing decent liberal values for a better world and the EU's intention to help bring it about. But the gap between aspiration and reality, rhetoric and action, has been so persistent and so obvious that it has encouraged widespread scepticism. The problem has been addressed, but largely through procedural reform on the one hand, and a firm belief in the value of strategic vision on the other. The first *EU Security Strategy* (ESS) appeared in 2003 at a time when the organization was being cleft in two by the Iraq War, and when its leaders were desperate to show the United States that they too were running a serious foreign policy operation.[6] Robert Cooper, a former senior member of the British Diplomatic Service with the ear of Tony Blair, had a major hand in its drafting in his role as adviser to HR Javier Solana.[7] But the ESS was an over-ambitious document. Although it focused attention on the purposes of EU foreign policy it did not live up to its name as a viable *strategy*. In 2016 it was finally replaced by the *Global Strategy* after exhaustive consultations, to the extent that almost every issue and bureaucratic interest is represented somewhere in its sixty pages.[8] This new version does set out principles and priorities in a way that recognizes the limits on what the EU might be able to achieve, but it is still far-reaching. Its publication was delayed until just after the Brexit decision, although that surprising outcome is not reflected in its scenarios. Security, prosperity and 'a rules-based global order' are its watchwords. There is a strong emphasis on unity, on regional partnerships and on peacebuilding, especially in Europe's unstable neighbourhood. It does acknowledge that fair words will mean nothing without hard choices, pragmatism and joined up policies.

The UK in EPC/CFSP

None of all this should be, or was during forty years of membership, anathema to the United Kingdom. In 1989 the Conservative Foreign Office Minister Lynda Chalker went so far as to circulate an EC booklet on EPC describing 'the European aspect of foreign policy that is of growing importance to the Government'.[9] The procedural improvements in the CFSP in the decade that followed were not light touch but neither were they intrusive. In fact, they have proved advantageous in that they facilitate rapid exchanges with like-minded states, short-circuiting much of the apparatus of bilateral diplomacy. They also provide access to a 'politics of scale' in terms of the weight of bloc voting in the UN system, and access to economic sticks and carrots far beyond the capacity of a single state. Finally, they provide political cover in the event that a Member State falls out with a major power, whether China, Russia, India or even the United States. It is easier to cite the need for solidarity with partners than to attract odium alone.

On the other side of the balance-sheet the UK has always been nervous about the emerging role of the EU in security and defence, fearing for a disruptive impact on NATO and not wishing to take on commitments that might tie down its own expensive, high-end, armed services. Yet, as NATO has become more of a forward 'defence' and counter-terror organization in Afghanistan, Iraq and Syria, so this argument has come to have less force. Furthermore, Britain has certainly not found the various CSDP missions too demanding – it is only the seventh largest contributor to them.[10]

It does occasionally find the views or even the values of other Member States to be at odds with its own, especially when they lean towards anti-Americanism or a reluctance to get tough with Russia, but the only damaging consequence of this is a degree of diplomatic isolation, which is in any case the logic of the *souverainiste* approach favoured by the Eurosceptics.

We shall return later to the obstacles, beyond the tricky area of defence, to Britain taking a more positive approach to Europe's role in international politics, but for the moment let us focus on its actual record of participation. Over the near half century of its involvement, this is the area of EU activity that the UK has found most congenial, and one of those – together with the Single Market and the drive for further economic liberalism – in which it has felt most able to be constructive. It is also true that if we leave aside the issue of extending the supranational method to foreign policy, where Britain has been firmly resistant, the country has been more active and effective as an agent of European diplomacy than any other single Member State. Indeed, it has sought to act as a leader in the system and has not infrequently been acknowledged as such by its partners – which makes it all the stranger that it is now seeking to leave the conference table.

Britain took to EPC in the first place because it was able to shape the process from the start, and because foreign policy cooperation was a voluntary matter, outside the Community's legal framework, making it easy to set limits to institutional growth. It was also the case that it did not have anywhere else to go. It rapidly proved useful, providing cover after the Middle East war of 1973, when the US policy towards OPEC seemed too belligerent, and during the negotiations for the Helsinki Accords of 1975 in which the Europeans showed surprising solidarity in pursuing their agenda of détente plus human rights in the face of contrasting pressures from Moscow and Washington. Britain played a leading role in the second of these cases, as it did when the Soviet Union invaded Afghanistan, just after

Christmas 1979. As EPC had manifestly failed to produce a rapid or united response Lord Carrington, then Foreign Secretary, initiated the creation of a crisis mechanism so as to make possible a flexible response on future occasions. He was also the driving force behind the Venice Declaration of 1980, which was the first occasion when Europe took an even-handed position on the 'Arab–Israeli conflict'. Although the Declaration has changed little on the ground, it remains a touchstone for both EU and British policy in its recognition of both Israel's right to exist and the need for a Palestinian homeland.[11]

Margaret Thatcher's period in office saw a slackening of this wave of British enthusiasm for European foreign policy, but not a fundamental retreat. European unity was crucial in achieving a UN Security Council Resolution condemning Argentina's invasion of the Falkland Islands in 1982. The Prime Minister's subsequent disappointment with President Reagan's behaviour over both Grenada in 1983 and the 1986 Reykjavik summit with Mikhail Gorbachev meant that she was careful not to dispense with the insurance policy represented by EPC – although the endless quarrels over money and integration within the EC proper were eventually to produce a fatal collision with other European leaders.

The end of the Cold War represented a triumph for European diplomacy, which had encouraged a democratic transition in the ex-communist countries, and was now in pole position to help them consolidate. Yet the Yugoslav conflagration that immediately broke out cast a dark cloud over this optimism and engendered divisions over how to respond. British policy first clashed with Germany over whether the seceding republics should be recognized, and subsequently (with France) became exposed through its willingness to commit troops on the ground. This failure of the new CFSP in the first half of the 1990s was partially redeemed by its ability to hold together as the new millennium approached in projects of post-war stabilization. The incoming Labour administration of Tony Blair was a leading player in this phase, not just in kick-starting the European Security and Defence Policy (ESDP) but also in diplomatic cooperation with its European partners – at least until 2002 and the looming shadow of a war in Iraq. As we have seen, Britain was particularly prominent in promoting the enlargement of the EU to the east – a major act of 'cross-pillar' foreign policy.[12]

The divisions over Iraq, at home and within the EU, made taking a constructive role in other areas of European diplomacy difficult, but not impossible. It was not that the UK had made a strategic decision to abandon the CFSP, but rather that Blair's specific choices over Iraq had damaged European unity and led to distrust. Even so, it should not be forgotten that other EU states, notably Spain and the new east European members, also sided with the Bush administration over Iraq, while France and Germany soon proved keen to mend fences with the UK. All three engaged in practical cooperation within ISAF in Afghanistan, together with most other EU members, in Europe itself after the start of jihadist attacks in 2004, and in the strategic attempts to reduce the North-South divide by bringing millions out of poverty. These efforts continued beyond the end of the New Labour period in power, not least because the presence of the Liberal Democrats in the Coalition government from 2010 ensured some pro-EU instincts. It was only once the Conservatives won power alone in 2015 that the Eurosceptic instincts of their back-benchers found full voice, dealing a blow to the idea of diplomatic solidarity by exploiting fears over Germany's unilateral decision to open the door to refugees, and the apparent prospect of Turkish accession to the EU (in fact remote).

This rapid trek through Britain's history in European foreign policy-making shows that its leaders have aspired to a leadership role. Even when the UK has preferred to plough its own furrow it has not wished to dispense with the system as such, finding it useful for both procedural and substantive reasons. Precisely because CFSP is not incompatible with the continued existence of a robust national foreign policy Britain has viewed it as a comfort-able and long-term framework within which to work. Yet there have been some persistent problems, quite apart from the conflict that occurs every time there is a suggestion of majority voting or some other supranational innovation being applied to foreign policy.

The first of these relates to Britain's wish for the CFSP to be an effective instrument of its own national policy. This is also an aspiration of the other large Member States, which thus compete in a zero-sum game. In short, if European foreign policy could be reliably harnessed to British foreign policy objectives, with the other participants falling in behind British leadership, even the most hardened sceptic might find it acceptable. But since this is in effect no more than a system of coordination that is just what cannot happen. As a result Britain has learned not to expect too much and to work in other fora. Even when agreement can be reached above the level of the lowest common denominator, the HR's need to get 28 states in line, and the complexities of the various Brussels bureaucracies, often make the EU less than agile in the processes of implementation.

The second problem British diplomats encounter is the EU's self-image as a 'civilian power' – that is to say, in itself the EU cannot deploy troops or fire missiles, and has no obvious wish to do so. If the reverse were to be true then the UK would already have opted out of the CFSP and the CSDP, so great is its attachment to making its own deci-sions in this area, but London is often exasperated by a tendency in Brussels and the more integrationist states to will the ends of foreign policy without willing the means – there is much impatience about high-flown rhetoric, and a tendency to lecture third states in the full knowledge that nothing will change.

This is a version of the US complaint that many Euro-peans do not want to do hard power, and certainly do not spend enough on defence. But the British go further, seeing themselves as exposed among the middle powers when it comes to risking lives and resources in the defence of common interests, being able to project military power only in conjunction with the French. The concern goes beyond troop deployments; in spending on overseas development aid (ODA) only Britain, Denmark, Luxemburg and Sweden currently reach the UN target of spending 0.7 per cent of GNI.[13] Most of the other EU 28 have never even come near it, letting the European Commission's budget do the work – to which most of them are not net contributors in any case.[14] Given that the UK's Department for International Development has become as significant an aid player as the Commission, and the increasing politicization of aid, Britain has little incentive to communitarize its activity.

It might be thought to follow logically that the UK would be content to see the EU taking on major responsibilities for defence and overseas aid, but this is not the case. Indeed the third issue for Britain is that Eurosceptics (and in particular the right-wing tabloid newspapers) keep up a relentless campaign of scare stories about Europe seeking to become a major power at the expense of traditional nation-states. To some extent this worry harks back to the traditional fear of a continental hegemony, but the analysis is rarely historically literate.[15] The usual tendency is to demonize the President of the Commission, or figures in the European Parliament, when they incautiously promote such things as joint battlegroups, or the rationalization of national defence efforts, at present chronically wasteful in the duplication of spending and arms production. This raises the spectre of a European army, which is for the foreseeable future a non-starter. On overseas aid the attacks are rather different: sceptics wish to see a reduction in spending, not an increase, and certainly not a loosening of national control over its distribution, since it has the potential to be harnessed for British trade in the context of the fierce export competition between Member States.

Taken together, these objections to what the EU might do present any British government with a significant problem. Even incremental moves towards consolidating the resources of the Member States are likely to be seen at home as damaging the national interest. They will also provoke suspicions of integration by the back door – calls like that of the Governor of the European Central Bank for a European *affectio societatis*,[16] which imply that regional projects have an emotional as well as a politico-legal rationale, seem alien even to moderate British opinion.

The fourth problem that European foreign policy raises for the UK is that of its closeness to certain non-European states. The concerns about betraying New Zealand sheep farmers may have faded quickly after 1975, while Washington has no more 'special' a relationship with Britain than with half a dozen other friendly states, but there are aspects of history that still inhibit the UK from fully committing to European diplomacy. Much of this has to do with perceptions, and vicious circles – as when southern Europeans vent their irritation by criticizing 'les anglo-saxons', or when the British hark back to the war-time days of fighting on alone in Europe, with only the empire for support. The hard facts of the present day, of a fragmented Commonwealth, resentful ex-colonies and a super-power ally whose policies cause as many problems as they solve, are not always acknowledged. This reluctance is in itself an indication of how difficult Britain finds it to accept a European destiny. If we add in the persistent nostalgia for a global power role, and the strong cultural connections to the United States, the lack of full-hearted commitment to EU foreign policy becomes more comprehensible.

The other participants in the CFSP have gradually learned not to expect too much of the UK. At one level there has always been a reliance on British experience in world affairs, a respect for its historical resolve and the capacity of its armed forces, and a hope that the foreign policy dimension would eventually reconcile the UK to integration more widely. Germany has been content for the two European members of the UN Security Council to lead in this area. Conversely, there has also been resentment at London's tendency to cherry-pick the areas of cooperation that suited it, even within the CFSP, and with France there is a traditional rivalry over leadership. The more overt British choices to align with the United States at the expense of European solidarity, as over the bombing of Libya in 1986 or the invasion of Iraq in 2003, have caused exasperation and resentment, evoking memories of General de Gaulle's talk of Britain as a 'Trojan horse' within the European Community. This is despite the US's support for British membership of the EC from the start, and the fact that over the years Washington has become more relaxed about the compatibility of the CFSP/CSDP to NATO. Its preference has traditionally been for Britain to play a leading part in European foreign policy – which flatters London but at the time produces suspicion in other EU chancelleries.[17] This has, however, weakened in recent years as US relations with Berlin and Paris have strengthened.

Cases in point

Foreign policy is subject to grand generalizations about the national interest, national character and geopolitics. But specific cases are needed if we are to understand the push and pull of the various factors, internal and external, which generate actual decisions. With that in mind this section looks at how Britain and its European partners have formulated foreign policy in three contexts and three time-periods: over the Balkan wars in the 1990s, in relation to humanitarian interventions in Africa from 1998 on, and during the negotiations with Iran over its nuclear programme between 2004 and 2016. They represent a range of different challenges and contexts. All three involved both Conservative and Labour governments. One represented the shocking return of war to Europe, the second relates to the balance of ethics and interests in a continent deeply affected by European colonialism, and the third was a long-drawn Middle Eastern crisis with the potential to destabilize the international system.

To begin with the Balkans and the impact of a collapsing Yugoslavia on the EU: the optimism engendered by the collapse of communism and the reunification of Germany was soon dispelled by the power grabs of Serbia and Croatia and the ethnic hatreds on display as the new republic emerged from the ashes of the Yugoslav state. The EU, which had signed a Trade and Cooperation Agreement with Yugoslavia on the death of Tito in 1980 in the hope of helping the country to hold together, initially attempted to resist the same tide of nationalism that they had encouraged among the Warsaw Pact states. Britain, together with France and Germany, were the leading EU actors, but the three soon diverged over whether fragmentation was inevitable. The so-called 'hour of Europe' rebounded to become a symbol of the inability of sovereign states to maintain unity in a crisis.[18] It had been trumped by domestic politics in that German opinion could not envisage the maintenance of an autocratic communist regime in Yugoslavia against nationalist revolts just when the rest of eastern Europe was liberating itself and when East Germans in particular were exercising their right of self-determination to join the Federal Republic.[19]

This left, in effect, Britain and France in the hot seat as responsible for attempting to restore order in the Balkans given that violence soon broke out over borders and ethnic cleansing, with Croatian and Serbian designs on Bosnia Herzegovina. German pacifism, together with strong local memories of Nazi occupation, ruled out a leading role by Berlin. The first half of the 1990s saw Europe's two main military powers struggling to exert influence by deploying troops under the UN umbrella – but solely in a peace making, not peace enforcement, role. This led to an impatient US finally imposing a peace settlement at Dayton in 1995, after the use of air power to bring Serbia to the negotiating table. The EU had been humiliated in its own backyard, while Britain had come under fierce criticism from its own public opinion for a 'realist' policy that had failed the Bosnian Muslims in their hour of need.[20]

Out of this furnace, and the world's failure in Rwanda in 1994, was forged the conviction that sovereignty needed qualifying on humanitarian grounds, leading to a number of interventions, often with the UK taking a prominent part. One of these was in Kosovo in 1999. Here the UK deployed the Royal Air Force as part of a NATO operation that eventually forced Serbia to concede de facto autonomy to the province. European foreign policy was supportive of the action but the EU, having no military forces of its own, was dependent on its bigger Member States – to say nothing of the US – to bring about the desired goal. In practice this state of affairs was convenient for the Union as while all Member States deplored ethnic cleansing and favoured 'a large degree of autonomy' for Kosovo, the prospect of full independence was not universally welcome.[21] Cyprus, Greece, Romania, Slovakia and Spain remain unwilling to recognize Kosovo.

Thus the CFSP has often provided the UK with the advantage of majority European support for a policy it was committed to, without having to wait for a unanimous vote. This is what the Treaty of Amsterdam called 'constructive abstention', or the right of a Member State to opt out of a common position but not to obstruct others from going forward (ToA Article J.13).[22] It is also true, however, that both the EU and the UN were eventually supplanted in Bosnian diplomacy (and then over Kosovo) by a 'contact group' of the powers – the US, Russia, France, Germany and the UK. These informal groupings are common in crisis-management, indicating the unwieldiness of the larger, established, organizations

On the longer term issues of peace building in the Balkans, the EU has been united and committed, making up for its divisions and weaknesses in the early 1990s. This is what Robert Kagan dismissively referred to as 'the Europeans doing the dishes' after the Americans had made the dinner.[23] In Bosnia stabilization efforts have continued through EU-UN cooperation, representing a vital barrier between the still antagonistic parties. Only this external presence, and supply of aid, has kept the Bosnian state alive. Neither British foreign policy alone, nor a joint operation with

France and Germany, could have provided the resources, the security, and most importantly the international legitimacy, to achieve that over a long period. The same is true of Kosovo, over which Tony Blair encouraged the emergence of a Stability Pact for South-Eastern Europe by holding out the bait of EU enlargement for the region, and where the EU Rule of Law Mission (EULEX) later took on responsibility for helping to prevent the new country from sliding into chaos. After 2008 NATO's KFOR peacekeeping force, to which Britain had contributed the biggest cohort, was scaled down, with civilian efforts through the EU taking most of the strain.

The second major area of foreign policy in which Britain and European diplomacy become entangled is that of sub-Saharan Africa, and to a lesser extent the Maghreb. In a detailed study Catherine Gegout has identified 14 countries or regions in the African continent in which European states variously took an interest between 1987 and 2016. She specifically analysed the motives at stake (usually mixed), finding that the UK intervened militarily in seven cases: Somalia 1992, Sierra Leone 2000–2, the DRC (with the EU) in 2006, in Ivory Coast (2004), Libya 2011 and 2015–16, and South Sudan in 2013. It did not intervene militarily in some areas that fell within what might be presumed to be its zone of influence (Uganda, Kenya, Lesotho and Zimbabwe) – although it was active diplomatically. It was 'symbolically involved in EU operations in the DRC (Democratic Republic of the Congo) in 2006, in Chad/CAR [Central African Republic] from 2008 to 2009, and in the CAR in 2014–15'. Of all these cases only three represented specific national concerns, namely the protection of British citizens in Sierra Leone, Ivory Coast and South Sudan. Others were explicitly related to the need to promote European foreign policy, or to Britain's role within it, namely the DRC in 2003, and Chad/CAR as referred to above. Two more predominantly involved support for France, the other major European power (Chad/CAR 2008–9, and Mali, 2013–), while a further six arose out of broad issues of international security of concern to both Europe and the wider international community (Uganda, 1987, Kenya on various occasions, Somalia, 1992–3, Zimbabwe, 2008, Libya, 2011 and 2015–16, South Sudan, 2013).[24]

This list overlaps with the various CSDP missions of the EU, which by definition Britain has helped to shape, and to a number of which it has contributed personnel. The most important of these is Operation Atalanta (EU NAVFOR Somalia) in the Indian Ocean, which has had some success in reducing piracy.[25] Operation Sophia (EU NAVFOR Med), which interdicts human trafficking off the Libyan coast, also has a significant UK presence. It should thus be clear that while the UK has exercised its sovereign right to pursue distinctive interests, many rooted in its past imperial possessions and its continuing Commonwealth links, its activity in Africa has increasingly involved multilateral cooperation, often European but not exclusively so. This is the nature of both modern international politics and of the country's reduced power position. Africa has had to become less of a priority for the UK, so that when particular challenges arise joint action – through any combination of the EU, the USA and the UN – is likely to be preferable to unilateralism. Zimbabwe is a striking case in point. President Mugabe's contempt for Britain's historical role in his country meant that he was impervious to expressions of concern over the expropriation of white farmers' lands. London was therefore reliant on EU support for a package of 'laser' sanctions on the Zimbabwean military and the political elite, because it both increased the potential impact and spread the burden of responsibility (not that it made any difference to Mugabe's policy).

It is clear that the European Union, impelled by France, has made Africa much more central to its foreign policy than seems necessary to Britain, whose (NATO-influenced) strategic priorities over the last two decades have lain in the Balkans, Iraq and Afghanistan. The majority of ESDP missions have taken place in African countries, while the UK's contributions in terms of personnel have been 'meagre'.[26] Yet the surface impression is misleading: the issues of migration and terrorism have risen steadily to the top of Britain's concerns, with it becoming evident that the flow of people from the African continent represents a major source of problems. The effort of DfID over the last 20 years to improve the flow of aid to Africa has been partly about poverty-reduction per se, especially among the very poorest, but it has also been geared to conflict prevention, and thus indirectly to forestalling irregular migration.[27] In both these goals the UK has influenced the EU's orientation while increasingly relying on joint efforts. There is, after all, much room for a division of labour. France and Britain needed each other to carry out the Libyan operation of 2011, and the UK supplied transport aircraft for France's intervention in Mali in 2013. Britain has made considerable efforts to help train officials and soldiers in various African states, but it lacks the armed policing capability that France and Italy, with the *gendarmerie* and *carabinieri* respectively, possess.

Beneath the level of high-end interventions lie a range of important issues on which 'effective multilateralism', as the EU terms it, is essential for all Europeans. The monitoring of the EU's external borders through FRONTEX is one, inadequate as it so far has been, and encouraging 'good governance' in fragile societies is another. A particularly powerful example is provided by the Ebola virus epidemic, which started in west Africa in 2014. The UK, Italy and Spain were among countries that experienced the spread of the virus, albeit in a very limited number of cases thanks to the collaborative measures, medical and administrative, which contained it. The World Health Organization of the UN led the response to Ebola, but it leaned on other international organizations with capacity in the field, including the EU. After a slow start the European Commission Humanitarian Office (ECHO), through its Civil Protection Mechanism, coordinated the deployment of emergency supplies and over time the EU provided nearly two billion euros to help west Africa manage and recover from the epidemic.[28] The crisis showed up weaknesses in the EU's response but also made it frighteningly clear how vital such international coordination is for disease control.[29]

Thus in Africa the UK has had to face the fact of its fading influence, even in collaboration with France, while the Commonwealth has proved too divided and intractable an institution for Britain to lead. In consequence Britain has limited its political activity in the continent, focusing mostly on aid and trade (although Africa only represents 2.5 per cent of the UK's overall trade). It is still capable of acting alone where absolutely necessary, as with the provision of security training in Tunisia after the 2016 atrocity against British tourists, but otherwise it has to work in conjunction with others, among whom the other EU states have to be prominent, given the facts of geography and history.

The third case of a foreign policy problem where UK and European foreign policies have been necessarily entangled, is rather different. Iran's nuclear power programme represented a potential threat to world peace, both as such – given the possibility of an Iranian bomb – and indirectly given the stated determination of Israel and the United States not to allow such a development in any circumstances.

Although relations between Iran and the West had been tense ever since the revolution of 1979, the nuclear issue only surfaced in the first years of the twenty-first century. George Bush's 'axis of evil' speech four months after 9.11 identified three countries as both sources of terrorism and in pursuit of weapons of mass destruction. One of those was Iran, although there was no evidence that it had had anything to do with the attacks on New York and Washington. Still, soon afterwards exiles revealed a clandestine programme of nuclear fuel enrichment in breach of Iran's obligations under the Non-Proliferation Treaty (NPT). The International Atomic Energy Agency (IAEA) then called on Tehran to suspend uranium enrichment and reprocessing activities, and to allow inspections. Somewhat surprisingly, after an initiative taken by European foreign ministers, Iran agreed – and after further haggling it signed the Paris

Agreement in 2004 committing it to suspend enrichment for the duration of talks to be continued with France, Germany and the UK.[30] A year later these talks were halted after Russia entered the game by agreeing both to supply fuel for an Iranian reactor and to take spent fuel back. As Iranian intransigence grew, and a serious crisis loomed, a new framework emerged from a combination of the European efforts and the involvement of the UN Security Council. This was the P5 + 1, later also known as the 3 + 3, referring in the first case to the permanent five members of the UNSC plus Germany, and in the second to the three great powers of China, Russia and the United States, together with the three leading European states.

What followed was an exhausting and tortuous process of negotiations with Iran lasting ten years, before the historic agreement was signed at Vienna in 2015. At various times different states were involved in trying to break the impasse, individually and collectively, including Brazil and Turkey. But the EU led the way with a persistent and delicately balanced combination of carrots (in the form of constructive diplomatic initiatives) and sticks (economic sanctions, in association with the US). The EU's High Representative, Catherine Ashton, who had been originally ridiculed for her unfamiliarity with foreign policy, became an increasingly useful conduit for the discussions, not just for the EU-3 but for the P5 + 1 – which had moved to centre stage, with the IAEA in support. Crucial to the unblocking of the final obstacles were the election of the moderate Hassan Rouhani to the Iranian presidency, and the announcement of the US and the European Union in 2013 that sanctions would start to be relaxed.

It will be clear from the above account that the United Kingdom was continuously involved in what was one of the major international problems of the time, predominantly by virtue of its own possession of nuclear weapons, its permanent membership of the UN Security Council, but also its leading role in foreign policy discussions within the EU. Without the first two attributes it would have had no claim to be a front-rank participant in the negotiations.

Without the third it might still have been an important player but would in any case have been impelled to coordinate with France and Germany, whose political and economic weight gave them the right to represent Europe (it should be added that Italy was also able to play a useful role at times).

The Commission, the presidency and the HR all made important contributions as time wore on, through maintaining collective solidarity within the EU, and dealing with the legal issues arising from sanctions, but without the engagement of the key Member States these institutions would have been irrelevant. On the other hand it was clearly vital for the sustaining of this major diplomatic effort that Europe as a whole was willing and able – in some form – to take the lead. The US, China and Russia would have been unlikely to have maintained a common purpose over such a long period, while no individual European state would have had the weight to keep the key parties at the table. The 28 as a group held together and provided a useful backing chorus for the big three Europeans.

Britain, like the EU as a whole, has a strong interest in preventing the further proliferation of nuclear weapons, and will take what measures it can to that end. But as has been evident during the similarly long drawn out stand-off with North Korea, there are limited options even for the United States in such matters, let alone for a middle-range power geographically remote from the focal point of conflict. Working towards an international consensus is the only option on the table if peace and the stability of the international system are desired, a point brought home by how outside powers have been drawn into Syrian civil war, heightening its slaughter and creating yet more hatreds for the future. Furthermore a trading state like Britain looks wistfully at the prospects for exports in the event of normal relations with countries like Iran and North Korea becoming possible.

Britain has been particularly exposed to hostility from Tehran as the consequence of its role in toppling the Mossadegh government in 1953, and its general association with the US, the 'great Satan' in revolutionary iconography. It has accordingly suffered various particular difficulties in bilateral relations, from the lack of Iranian gratitude over the SAS operation to end the siege of their embassy in London in 1980, through the fatwa on the life of author Salman Rushdie in 1989, to the temporary detention of British sailors and marines in 2007, and the attack on the UK embassy in Tehran in 2011, which led to a rupture in diplomatic relations for three years. The UK's move closer to Saudi Arabia, driven by defence sales, has added further difficulties.

It has thus been immensely useful for Britain to work with fellow European states, in a variety of fora, in the pursuit of its concerns over Iran. It has benefited from support when suffering hostility, and from cover when wanting to avoid too much exposure – which helped in resisting US pressure for retrospective trade sanctions during their own hostage crisis of 1980, just as it did when pressing Iran over its nuclear programme. European solidarity was also useful to handle Israel's wrath over Iran, when Tel Aviv's natural inclination was to try to get individual states to align with them, and if necessary to divide and rule the EU. In the end the European effort, led by the EU-3 but drawing on the CFSP and the common institutions, turned out to be a triumph for the much-maligned idea of a European foreign policy, and one on which British governments quietly relied. In the monitoring of the 2015 agreement the UK continued to work with France and Germany, as indicated by their joint statement in July 2017 (along with the USA) condemning the launch of an Iranian space vehicle, and again in 2018 in a joint disagreement with Donald Trump's decision to pull out from the Iran deal.[31] It is noteworthy that London has (at the time of writing) both continued to support the deal and has held fast with France and Germany in opposing the extraterritorial impact of US sanctions on Iran, which damage European economic interests but also raise important issues of international law.

Brexit, however, has the potential to weaken these ties. Berlin and Paris had already begun to issue joint foreign policy statements independently during the various Ukraine crises, producing what is known as the Normandy contact group (or Minsk process) with Russia and the Ukraine. Although the UK is consulted and occasionally involved it is not a prime mover in this process. Since Brexit France and Germany have sometimes acted without any reference to Britain, as in the heads of government letter sent to Vladimir Putin protesting against Russian vetoes on humanitarian convoys in Syria.[32]

The three cases examined above, of the Balkans, Africa and Iran, demonstrate that on major issues of its foreign policy, in three different continents and over the duration of the last 25 years, Britain has found it necessary not only to work in harness with other leading European states, but also at times to draw upon the procedures and resources of the European Union. This is unlikely to change for, as the French analyst François Heisbourg pointed out in the immediate aftermath of the referendum, 'geography is destiny'.[33] The terms of trade will certainly change, since even if British concerns will still be taken into account by the EU post-Brexit, they will no longer be factored into its decision-making from the start. London will constantly be keeping an anxious ear to the wall, and will not be able, as it has been up to now, to obstruct moves towards defence integration. Indeed the EU has already started to speed up its discussions on Permanent Structured Cooperation (PESCO) and to move to a Coordinated Annual Review on Defence (CARD) – proposals that have previously come to nothing, and may well do again, though more through Britain's absence than its ability to obstruct.[34] As the UK government's negotiating paper of September 2017 amply demonstrated, there is a wide range of things that Britain and its European partners can do together – if they so wish. The paper did not identify *any* foreign policy advantages of a British exit from the EU, thus tacitly admitting the extent to which UK foreign policy has become, despite itself, Europeanized.[35]

4

Britain's à La Carte Menu

The conventional definition of foreign policy has widened steadily over the years since the end of the Second World War – by when it had become obvious that experts like the economist John Maynard Keynes, the nuclear physicist Robert Oppenheimer and the general George Marshall were playing central roles in diplomacy. The emergence of the European Economic Community meant that the trend could go either way: either all relations within the EEC would become domestic policy, or the issues within its competence would move into the sphere of foreign ministries and become foreign policy, despite being largely economic in nature. The truth ended up somewhere in between. On the one hand, European law made foreign ministries central players, through the Council of (Foreign) Ministers, which sat at the apex of the various meetings convened for specialist sectors, notably finance and agriculture. The European Council, for heads of government, was not created until 1975 – which partly explains de Gaulle's suspicion of the relative freedom of movement enjoyed by the European Commission. On the other hand, it was increasingly difficult for professional diplomats to master the technical briefs of trade, finance, agriculture and transport, which the Treaty of Rome demanded of them. They had no option but to allow their 'domestic' ministry colleagues to play an increasing role in consultations, and eventually to hold posts in the national 'permanent representations' (effectively embassies to the EC) sited in Brussels.

This reality, of 'integration' consisting in practice of different issue-areas bringing competing bureaucratic interests into play, reinforced the divisions in British opinion towards the project as a whole. While the EC was merely a 'Common Market', hostility was limited to those concerned about Commonwealth preferences being lost, and to those darkly suspicious of the still remote prospect of a federalist outcome. But as new areas of collective activity emerged, from development aid through structural and regional funds to monetary harmonization, so political alarm bells began to ring, while the Treasury and other ministries started actively to defend their turf. This meant that the FCO, with both subjective and objective reasons for being sympathetic to European cooperation, became increasingly to be seen as Europhile, making it a target for the nationalists, who behaved as if only they knew how to define British interests. But even the pro-Europeans displayed some ambivalence about the direction of travel the country had embarked upon. Over time, this uncertainty hardened into first a form of political schizophrenia – enthusiasm for some activities but obstructionism on others – before settling into a more consistent intergovernmental approach.[1] This entailed a preference for freezing integration more or less at the point attained by the Maastricht Treaty – itself controversial inside the governing Conservative Party. Never a progressive Member State, by the time the Community had turned into a Union Britain had become a firm force for the status quo.

It should not be assumed that governments made rational choices about which specific areas of European cooperation to support and which to oppose. There was never a clear menu to select from given that the whole process was the product of complex political interactions between – but also within – states. No one could tell what the pace of integration, let alone its end-product, would be. Rather, competing ranges of possibility emerged in outline form. Debate in the UK swirled inconsistently around the issues, defined by which party (and/or leader) held power, and much influenced by parochial domestic concerns.

We know that wanting to lead Europe on classical foreign policy issues was the high mark of British commitment, and that antagonism to federalism represented the other end of the spectrum. In between these two points various important subjects have oscillated across the foreign-domestic divide, with the UK inconsistent over its willingness to engage. This chapter takes four of these grey areas, so described because while they have provided the UK with incentives to commit to further cooperation they have also generated red lines, which have made the country a frustrating partner for other Member States and for the Brussels institutions – rarely been given credit by British opinion for carrying out the work required of them by the treaties. The four areas are: monetary policy, enlargement, security and defence, borders and freedom of movement. In confronting them the UK gradually edged itself into a position whereby it enjoyed an exceptional number of opt-outs from common policies amounting to a preference for a 'variable geometry Europe', even if it was usually thought politic not to advocate this as a basic principle. Perhaps indeed politicians did not always understand the implications themselves. As a powerful Member State Britain essentially enjoyed special treatment and was able to fudge issues of principle. The longer-term consequence of its semi-detachment, however, was not (as one might have thought) political satisfaction, but paradoxically to increase dissatisfaction and finally to tip British opinion over the edge into a vote for Brexit. The resulting negotiations now seem to be as much about opt-*ins* as a clean break with Brussels.

Monetary sovereignty

Together with defence and diplomacy the most obvious symbol of sovereign independence is money. By comparison national airlines and other flag-carriers can easily be relinquished. It was therefore a dramatic and deliberate demonstration of their commitment to European integration when on 1 January 2002 twelve members of the European Union gave up their national currencies in favour of euro coins and banknotes stamped with images carefully designed to evoke both a shared culture and national traditions. Arguably the macro-economic motives of this change were far less important than the political and symbolic ends it was intended to serve. If that were true then it was hardly surprising that the United Kingdom should once again have preferred an opt-out to participation – although it is striking how it has led the way in an unsentimental preference for market principles over maintaining British ownership of traditional companies like Cadburys or GKN. Globalization tended to strike fewer sore nerves in Britain than did Europeanization.

Britain was hardly alone in being attached to its currency. There was much ambivalence over the euro elsewhere, especially in the big economies of France, Germany and Italy.[2] France calculated that it would be worth the painful sacrifice of the eponymous franc if it tied Germany into a system that would prevent it from roaring ahead into a new national assertiveness, given it was now clearly the biggest as well as the richest Member State. For its part the government in Berlin shared some of these anxieties, but saw the euro as a way of getting Paris to turn integrationist rhetoric into practical commitment. As for the Italians, their governments saw the euro as a useful 'vincolo esterno' making possible domestic monetary discipline.[3] But public opinion soon became nostalgic for the lira when it transpired that vendors were often rounding up prices on daily essentials like a cappuccino.[4]

Emotional attachments belied the problems that national currencies had always had in a world where competitive nation-states were ever more subject to transnational financial forces. The collapse of the gold standard after the First World War had inaugurated a period of volatility, which led first to its temporary restoration and then final abandonment under the impact of the Great Crash and the recession. The pressing need for economic revival and stability after 1945 made the US dollar into the new fixed point for financial transactions, with Sterling in support as a reserve currency. The result was the vulnerability of other capitalist countries to changes in the US economy, as occurred in the late 1960s through overspending on the Vietnam War, culminating in the 'Nixon shocks' of 1971, which unilaterally imposed an import surcharge and broke the link between the dollar and the price of gold. This ignited the European interest in creating a system that would allow exchange rates between member countries to vary only within limits against the dollar and against each other (the 'snake in a tunnel'). Speculation against the over-valued Pound had already forced its devaluation (in 1967), which in turn undercut Britain's ability first both to sustain a military role 'East of Suez' and then to hold Sterling balances for other Commonwealth countries (the Sterling Area).

Thus, even those most attached to the Pound in the last decades of the twentieth century were aware that sustaining and managing a national currency was a mixed blessing. Monetary discipline had obvious attractions, as a defence against speculators but also as a way of holding down inflation at home. Reference to various forms of unavoidable international obligation had, after all, been a common way for post-1945 UK governments to justify pay restraint and austerity. But monetary coordination brings its own problems, as the later rigidity of the Eurozone was to demonstrate. Even exchange rates which are only semi-frozen are difficult to sustain in a group of countries whose actual productivity and growth varies considerably. Fearing this Britain stayed out of the Exchange Rate Mechanism (ERM, set up in 1979) until joining in 1990, against Prime Minister Thatcher's better judgement. Yet it was forced out only two years later by a dramatic demonstration of the money markets' lack of confidence in Sterling – a situation that Britain had effectively encouraged through its drive to foster the City of London as an export earner. The City's 'big bang' in 1987, deregulating financial markets at a stroke, had paved the way for the widespread removal of controls on financial transactions, and the consequent era of 'mad money' 24/7, which was to culminate in the crisis of 2008.[5]

As the creation of the euro became an ever more serious prospect during the 1990s, spurred by the end of the Cold War and by globalization, so Britain retreated into prevarication. John Major's government, hobbled by its Eurosceptic wing, could do nothing. Its New Labour successor, with its large majority and progressive ideas seemed at first likely to take a positive view of the euro project. Certainly Prime Minister Tony Blair saw joining it as essential to maintain the UK's political influence 'in the wheelhouse of Europe'.[6] But a large obstacle loomed in the form of Chancellor of the Exchequer Gordon Brown and his Treasury officials. The economy was effectively Brown's *chasse gardée* as the result of the power-sharing deal done with Blair during their joint revival of the Labour Party. He and his officials were deeply sceptical of the euro, not just because it would reduce their own roles but because it would severely reduce the macro-economic levers at their disposal in the race to be competitive with Germany and with the rising powers of Asia.

New Labour consolidated the improving economy they had inherited from John Major's government, while Brown's team soon concluded that not only would there be significant risks attached to giving up Sterling, but that the claimed advantages were unlikely to be great. Inflation was under control, and the worst excesses of the 'stop–go economy' seemed to be in the past. Union power had been tamed by Thatcher, while Blair had convinced the Labour Party to abandon its commitment to the nationalization of key industries. External discipline was no longer so attractive – indeed, it could be a vote loser, as with Labour's need to turn to the IMF in the 1970s, which remained a painful memory. The ability of the Conservative Opposition to exploit patriotic sentiment over issues like defence and the

currency could also never be under-estimated. An increasingly angry tussle ensued between the Chancellor and the
Prime Minister, entangled with their personal rivalry and
with Brown's impatient wish to have his turn in 10 Downing
Street. Blair was effectively out-manoeuvred in 2002–3,
not helped by his own focus on Iraq or by the quarrel with
France and Germany that ensued. The Treasury produced
five 'tests' that would have to be met before entry to the
euro could be deemed feasible, with Brown asserting his
right to judge when and if they had been met. Only a few
weeks after the invasion of Iraq the Chancellor announced
a negative verdict, which in practice killed the chance of
Britain joining the common currency for a generation, given
the increasingly implacable Tory hostility and the rising
tide of Euroscepticism.

It must be added that the substantive arguments against
joining were also strong, especially in the circumstances of
New Labour having been re-elected in 2001 with another
large majority, and of an economy that was out-performing
its European neighbours – Germany struggling with the
costs of unification, and France apparently unable to adjust
to a fast-moving labour market and to technological change.[7]
Although those relativities changed over the decade that
followed Brown's decision – with the German economy
soon powering ahead again – little occurred to change
British views on the desirability of the status quo. Indeed
the crisis of the euro zone after 2008, when the original
design flaws of the project became all too painfully public,
confirmed the Eurosceptics in their hostility, and created
relief in others over not having joined at the outset.

Inevitably this mixture of hostility, intellectual opposition
and smugness spilled over into attitudes more generally
towards the EU, and served to inflate the growing numbers
of people for whom the term 'Brexit' was becoming the
new norm. The continuing difficulties of the Eurozone after
the referendum, with Italy an increasing source of concern,
mean that even were the UK to seek to stay in the EU, or
some close approximation of membership, relations with

the monetary bloc would continue to be a critical problem.
If deeper integration is to occur, then those countries retaining their own currencies will be excluded from the making
of economic policies that are bound to affect them deeply.
Alternatively, if the euro were to fail then the damage to
the Single Market and demand for British goods would
be severe. This catch-22 is hardly an argument for a hard
Brexit but it does illustrate the limited margins of manoeuvre
that UK pragmatism has actually delivered. No amount of
rhetoric about the country's 'place in the world', whether
from pro-Europeans or globalists, can disguise this.

Widening not deepening

The second area that reveals the uncertainty, the ambivalence – even at times the cynicism – of Britain's approach
to European integration relates to dilemmas over enlarging
the EU: how far should it extend and what might the implications be? The purpose of the European project has been,
for many in continental Europe, steadily to deepen the
commitment of the Member States to the point where the
creation of a federal system would seem the natural last
step. This scenario has appealed to very few British observers. But the integrationists have also never been able to
resist the simultaneous temptation to expand the Community/
Union geographically and numerically. The fact that other
countries wish to join is in itself a validation, while the
economies of scale associated with enlargement promised
a larger market, a bigger budget and the extension of
common policies into new areas. From this viewpoint more
Europe has always seemed a better Europe. There was also
always a geopolitical dimension, whether relating to the
attempt to consolidate fragile democracies emerging from
periods of autocratic rule, to the wish to entice liminal
states into the Western camp, or more generally to make
the terms Europe and European Union coterminous.

This presented Britain with certain specific dilemmas.
On the one hand there was a genuine wish not to make

collective decision-making too unwieldy – after all, right up until the referendum most British politicians and officials saw British membership as permanent. It was also understood that as most of the new accession countries would be net recipients of financial transfers the weight on net contributors like the UK would increase. On the other hand, the lure of new, expanding, export markets was considerable, while it seemed very likely that the larger the Union became the more difficult it would be to agree on great leaps forward in integration – for those new members with traditions of neutrality would be likely to hold back from defence cooperation, while the 'orphans' of the Warsaw Pact were bound to want to tie themselves into NATO, with its hard defence guarantee, rather than commit hopes and resources to the wishy-washy rhetoric of European security integration.

Britain may have had its particular reasons for prioritizing the widening of the EU, but this did not antagonize their partners who, for the most part, also took a positive view of the policy. In particular London made common cause with Germany, whose economic and strategic interests in eastern Europe combined to overcome any doubts about the impact on integration. France was much more dubious, but unwilling to endanger its special relationship with Berlin and unable to resist the moral and political bandwagon of enlargement. The three were thus able to get away with pursuing a policy that at least in part was Machiavellian, in that it served other purposes beneath those publically (and genuinely) subscribed to.[8] There was in fact a tendency to groupthink right across the EU about the value of incorporating the states of the ex-Warsaw Pact.

All the British political parties tended to want a bigger and looser Community than that originally envisaged, if not for the same reasons. The Liberal Democrats were always likely to welcome new adherents to the European ideal, while the Conservatives favoured the expansion of the Western camp whether through NATO or the EU. New Labour, for their part, were willing to see some further integration in relation to the market and social policy, while Tony Blair also took a personal initiative to unblock cooperation on defence. Yet care was still taken to maintain a pragmatic, largely intergovernmental approach to cooperation, with entry into the euro made unlikely through a promise to hold a referendum if it ever became feasible. Furthermore London's enthusiasm for enlargement – which had made possible the acceleration of the process between 1999–2004 – led it to press for reform of the costly Common Agricultural Policy, while in Blair's second term the foreign policy alignment over Iraq with both the United States and the countries of Eastern Europe produced paralysing divisions within the EU, which disrupted the attempt to achieve constitutional change in time for the coming 'big bang' enlargement. The decision to allow immediate free movement of labour into Britain for the 2004 accession countries from the outset also took the UK on a separate path from France and Germany while in due course fostering further Euroscepticism at home. When, in 2007, the Treaty of Lisbon was finally agreed its most visible changes, in the form of a new fixed-term President of the Council, and a High Representative and External Action Service for the CFSP, if anything reinforced the trend back to intergovernmentalism. Prime Minister Brown's failure to arrive in time for the signing ceremony was widely taken to signal British priorities.[9]

It was, however, the geopolitical argument that really drove British support for enlargement. As a leading member of NATO and the UN Security Council, as well as a close ally of the United States, Britain assumed a responsibility for European order over and above its other commitments. It thus saw EU enlargement primarily through the lens of foreign policy, with the useful added benefit of its effects in slowing integration. The possible economic gains lay in the future, with Germany in any case in a better position to take advantage. As a one-time accession country itself, Britain appreciated the strength of feeling of those on the margins looking in, but more especially the political vulnerability of those societies whose fragility seemed likely to be resolved over time by participation in a regional family.

That had been the case in the 1980s with first Greece, then Portugal and Spain, all three emerging from periods of dictatorship. Given NATO's wish to draw Spain in to the alliance, where Greece and Portugal were already members, the foreign policy case for allowing them into the EC seemed powerful, outweighing the negative implications for the EU budget, and thus the UK's net contribution. A decade later the arguments for accepting Austria, Finland and Sweden were even less problematic: three rich states willing to move quietly away from their various forms of neutrality represented just one more way in which the newly triumphant West could consolidate its international position at low cost.

This logic hardly applied to the decision to accept thirteen more countries in the years 2004–13, with the implication of more to come from the ex-Yugoslav republics. Given their economic backwardness they were all too eager to be accepted by the West and in particular to join the EU family. On the other hand they represented a leap in the dark for the Union, both economically and politically, not least in terms of the doubling of its membership. Yet for its part Britain would have found it difficult to rebuff countries newly escaped from Moscow's yoke, especially bearing in mind that in 1939 the UK had gone to war for eastern Europe only to acquiesce in Soviet domination at the war's end. It had also become embroiled in the 1990s in the attempt to stabilize the Balkans, albeit after an initial failure to resist the aggression against Bosnia. For this goal the carrot of future entry to the EU was a crucial instrument. Lastly, the small states of Cyprus and Malta were both located in crucial strategic positions in the Mediterranean, as well as being ex-British colonies. Their tendencies towards anti-imperial resentment meant that London was never going to risk excluding them from the main European family.

The United Kingdom, therefore, like the EU as a whole, took a gamble that this steady expansion of membership would have broadly positive international effects, but without ever confronting the issue of where the EU's final border might sensibly be drawn.[10] It did not seem obvious at the time that enlargement was capable of creating new problems as well as solving old ones. Even today, the orthodox view is that enlargement has been one of the main success stories of EU foreign policy. In practice, however, it has thrown up some difficult challenges, which have become steadily more apparent. Regionally, it has pushed the EU's frontier much further to the east, with the result that Ukraine, Moldova, Belarus and the countries of the Caucasus now expect to come under the EU's protective wing, with hopes of membership further down the road. This in turn has alienated the Russian Federation, already resentful over its concerns having been disregarded by the West in the 1990s. For their part the countries of the southern littoral of the Mediterranean, excluded on principle from accession, have had fewer incentives to cooperate with the EU.

That the UK found all this a complication too far is indicated by its muted (Libya apart) and inconsistent responses to both the Arab Spring crises of 2011 and the furore that erupted after the Russian interventions of 2014, when France and Germany took the diplomatic lead.[11] Given the long-running *froideur* of British–Russian relations London was bound to press for sanctions against Moscow, but it could well have done without a crisis whose origins lay in part in the way in which EU enlargement and Neighbourhood policy had drawn Ukraine westwards. Yet if the UK did not want to go east, Russia still came to the UK in the form of the crisis over the poison attack on Sergei Skripal and his daughter in 2018. Then the May government was profoundly grateful for the unprecedented level of EU solidarity shown (in marked contrast, for example, to that shown to Italy over the death of the student Giulio Regeni, studying in Cambridge and murdered in Egypt in 2016).

It is on the domestic front that the unanticipated consequences of enlargement have been most sharply felt. The disproportionately large movement of people, both workers and accompanying family, to the UK after 2004 arguably did not damage the economy overall; indeed it had some clear benefits. But it was undoubtedly seen in many parts of British society as having facilitated the gig economy of insecure jobs without benefits, increased the pressure on a struggling National Health Service and education system, and stoked up even further an over-heated housing market. Perhaps even more significant, although paradoxical given the way the country had managed finally to adapt to the years of Commonwealth immigration, was the negative reaction to the influx of new languages, shops and tastes, which to some seemed to be supplanting their traditional way of life. The main consequence of this set of changes at the political level was increased Euroscepticism and support for the United Kingdom Independence Party (UKIP) although anger over terrorism and a growing discomfort with the visibility of Islam in British society (neither of which had anything to do with the EU) were also key factors, the whole blurring together into a revival of nationalism (especially English nationalism) with distinct overtones of xenophobia.

Even if Brexit is achieved, and assuming that domestic concerns over immigration will subside because migration from the EU will be reduced, the UK is still going to be much engaged with the issue of enlargement. Since its concern for the stability of the regional order will not suddenly disappear, it will presumably wish to see states like Serbia and North Macedonia enter the organization that it will have just left, and will encourage the EU to develop supportive (read generous) relationships with the states in the Neighbourhood, whether Ukraine and Moldova to the east or the Maghreb countries to the south. Relations with Turkey will remain a preoccupation given that country's intrinsic importance, but also through Britain's historical concern with the eastern Mediterranean and in particular its role as a guarantor power in Cyprus. But London will not be a prime mover in decisions on these matters, having to rely on joining forces (assuming it takes the same line) with Washington to exert influence from the outside, or attempting to find sources of leverage on key Member States. It will be in the policy debate, but outside the principal institution framing it and making the ultimate decisions.

Security not defence?

Britain's pick and choose approach to European cooperation is epitomized by the problem of hard power. One common interpretation is that the UK has been dragged kicking and screaming over a long period into a minimal level of cooperation on security and defence. As Italy's leading think tank put it 'Great Britain's policy over five centuries has been to stop a preponderance of power building up on the continent, and this explains its opposition to a common European defence policy'.[12] There is some truth in this, in that without British opposition the attempt to create a European Security and Defence Policy would have started much earlier than it did, in 2001. But by the same token the ESDP would have been a frail enterprise without the weight of British capabilities, while it was only Prime Minister Blair's willingness to envisage the initiative at St Malo in 1998 that made the ESDP missions of the last fifteen years possible and military uniforms in the EU buildings of Brussels a common sight.

It would be more accurate to see the UK's relationship to European defence cooperation as one of fits and starts, even ambivalence. It is certainly true that Britain has opposed any development that might complicate the operation of the Atlantic alliance, let alone substitute for it. London has never had confidence in European willingness to spend the money, or to commit to the unity necessary to deter Moscow from possible aggression. Its number one strategic priority since 1945 has been to tie the United States into the defence of Europe, and that remains the case. Moreover, the concept of a European army – which in practice would only be possible with the kind of central command created by a

United States of Europe – is anathema to British public opinion, whose attachment to national military traditions as much as to sovereignty has necessarily set it apart from key states like Germany and Italy, as the defeated powers of 1945. There a reluctance over the use of force is now deep-rooted. In the 1990s it had begun to change towards favouring humanitarian intervention, only to settle back into scepticism after 2003.[13]

Still, this attachment to NATO and to national independence (two values held equally and thus in a degree of tension) has not led the UK to restrict its cooperation with EU partners to pure diplomacy. How could it? The purpose of foreign policy is to promote the conditions in which a state can feel secure and enable its people to prosper. On that basis it has to engage in a great deal of activity that is neither war and deterrence at one extreme, nor mere talk at the other. Thus it was not long after the start of European Political Cooperation that Member States gave themselves (at British instigation) permission to discuss 'the political aspects of security'. In practice, they had already been doing this in the Conference on Security and Cooperation in Europe, notably at Helsinki in 1975 where their solidarity in pursuit of détente and human rights had taken aback both superpowers.

The UK had therefore come to recognize both that NATO was inadequate as a forum for handling international politics (as opposed to defence), and that for the most part multilateral action would be more effective than going it alone. Accordingly, while still obstructing the French wish from the 1980s to make the Western European Union (WEU) into a European caucus within NATO, London did not impede the steady expansion of foreign policy discussions to include security matters – including terrorism. It was then logical at Maastricht in 1992 for John Major to agree to rebrand EPC as the 'Common Foreign and Security Policy', which immediately faced the major challenge of the collapse of Yugoslavia, and the ensuing wars. After 1995, however, the EU played an essential role in maintaining peace in the Balkans, in which the UK participated, recognizing the indispensability of collective action.

This recognition produced concrete results in the Franco–British St Malo Declaration of December 1998, followed swiftly by the creation of the ESDP and its institutionalization. It was evident that the UK now sought a force multiplier through European cooperation on defence, not least as a hedge against the US pulling back from the region, as it had done in the first years of the Balkan wars. After an initially hostile reaction to St Malo from Secretary of State Madeline Albright, Washington came to share Blair's view that a European 'pillar' would not undermine NATO, thus enabling the UK to proceed with a foot in both camps. In this way the conceptual distinction between security and defence became gradually less sharp, as it had done in the academic world, where the idea of 'human security' had been in circulation for more than a decade, widening the concern from state policies of defence and deterrence to include the direct needs of individual citizens and social groups. Widening – and blurring – the field of vision enabled the UK to support the EU's cautious move into the defence area without compromising its stand on NATO as the priority. Indeed, although British traditionalists were reluctant to admit it, there was a growing acceptance that the instruments of 'soft' security that the EU could deploy, such as election monitoring, peacekeeping, military training and policing might serve at least as well in the new international climate as the high-tech hardware of conventional armed force – to say nothing of a second-strike nuclear capability.

There continued, however, to be limits on how far Britain was prepared to go with Europe's defence project. As ESDP missions proliferated after 2001 one might have expected the two Member States most capable of force projection to have been the backbone of the enterprise. That was not the case for the UK, which has been only the fifth largest contributor to the military missions and seventh to the civilian missions. As we saw in Chapter 3 it has carefully chosen where to take a prominent role – particularly in the two naval missions, against piracy in the Indian Ocean and against people smuggling from Libya across the Mediterranean.[14] Its breach with France and Germany over Iraq imposed a major brake on progress, as did the consequential commitment of resources, human, financial and *matériel*, to the long-drawn-out wars in both Iraq and Afghanistan. Although other EU states also were drawn into these quagmires, it was within a NATO/UN framework, making it all too clear that the ESDP was still far from being capable of taking on a war-fighting role. This was one reason – the others being the traditional attachments to Atlanticism and to national sovereignty – for Britain's obstruction of the attempts to create an EU military planning cell independent of NATO, with the potential to become a fully-fledged operational headquarters.[15]

On the domestic front any talk of progress in the ESDP immediately produces an hysterical reaction in the conservative press against the prospect of a European army and thus the renunciation of the national capacity for defence, which both restrains the British government and frustrates its partners. On the other hand, the really major differentiation in the defence area between the UK and other EU states (apart from France) is the possession of nuclear weapons, which is not called into question by the ESDP and which the Brexit debate has barely touched upon. It has proved perfectly compatible with EU membership despite the fact that a majority of Member States are active supporters of various nuclear disarmament initiatives at the UN.[16] Although scenarios can be imagined where this might change, the most reasonable conclusion is that whatever problems British foreign policy might run into as a result of Brexit, the Trident deterrent is unlikely to be among them. As France is even less likely to consider relinquishing its *force de dissuasion*, it will retain an interest in aligning with Britain on nuclear issues, shielding the UK from possible criticisms from the non-nuclear majority and preventing its isolation, at least on this dimension.

Conversely, London will be anxious to continue working through the bilateral Lancaster House accords of 2010, which provide, among other things, for regular liaison on nuclear matters.[17] It also wants to remain part of the EU's *Galileo* satellite programme for a European global positioning system, critical for both civilian and military purposes and a source of lucrative contracts. But a non-member of the EU, even Britain, cannot take this access for granted.[18] On the purely civilian side it will be well advised to seek some kind of associate partnership, as with Euratom, which monitors the use of nuclear fuels and promotes research on nuclear energy, in which both the UK and France have been heavily involved. One fifth of British electricity comes from French nuclear power stations, while the French firm EDF owns Britain's nuclear plants and is contracted to build (with China) a major new one at Hinckley Point in Somerset.[19] In all, of the EU members' 130 nuclear reactors, 66 are in the neighbouring countries of Belgium, France and the Netherlands, making cooperation on nuclear safety a vital national interest.[20]

The very fact that Britain is keen to be prominent in both European and Atlantic camps on defence and its related areas indicates how its key strategic interests inevitably diverge from those of its superpower ally. How could they not, given the asymmetry of power and roles? Britain needs the US alliance, as do the other European states, all of them middle range or small powers. But it also shares with them an unwillingness simply to sign up to US foreign policy in all its range and directions. NATO represents a vital defence umbrella but even with the organization's tendency to extend its reach beyond the Atlantic area, it is not a forum for coordinating foreign policies.[21] To be sure the growing self-assertion of Russia under Putin has pushed Europeans and Americans closer together again. They also work together in the bombing campaigns against Da'esh and in the special forces operations in Libya. But the bruising experiences in Iraq and Afghanistan, and the dismaying chaos that has followed on the initially successful intervention in Libya,

have inoculated public opinion in EU states, including
Britain, against further small wars outside their region.
This restraint applies less to France, which remains com-
mitted to its anti-jihadist operation in Mali.

As a group, the Europeans have little option but to focus
on broad security policies with a view to conflict prevention and damage limitation. They cannot envisage power
projection outside the region let alone a significant war-
fighting commitment. This is the burden of the EU's *Global
Strategy* of June 2016, which the UK had helped to shape
before the referendum. Being outside the EU is unlikely to
lead to any great divergence on the British side from its
political and preventive approach to security – unless the
very absence of the UK leads to real progress towards a
single EU defence policy, which would create new anxieties
in London.[22] Indeed the Government's foreign policy position paper of September 2017 explicitly drew attention to
the similarity between Britain's Strategic Defence Review
of 2015 and the EU's Global Strategy.[23] It concluded that:

> The UK would like to offer a future relationship that is
> deeper than any current third country partnership and that
> reflects our shared interests, values and the importance of
> a strong and prosperous Europe. This future partnership
> should be unprecedented in its breadth, taking in cooperation
> on foreign policy, defence and security, and development,
> and in the degree of engagement that we envisage.[24]

It is hardly plausible for Britain to move away from EU
foreign and security policy wholesale. The alternatives are
limited to either associating itself with US positions, which
on issues like Israel, Iran or China seems unlikely to be
acceptable at home, or to a deliberate unilateralism, distancing itself from the CFSP – which would be simply perverse.

Migration and freedom of movement

The free movement of people has so far been at the heart
of the EU's principles, just as it was at the root of the

majority vote for Brexit in 2016. The rise of populism in the UK, but also more generally, has been in part a reaction against the numbers of new arrivals in European societies and in part a dislike of the changes they have brought to traditional ways of life. But there must be very few people who actually believe in stopping immigration completely. No society could survive economically like that, just as it would soon become culturally and demographically sclerotic. Much of the concern evinced in Britain, at least, has been over the *pace* of change, and over the cumulative impact of migration, which raised the population from 56.3 million in 1980 to 65.6 million in 2016 – a rise of 9.3 million, or 16.5 per cent.[25] Since 1945 the rise has been of nearly 20 million, or just under 50 per cent.[26] From these figures it can be deduced both that modern Britain has been an open society, and that the newcomers from eastern Europe after 2004 were less a problem in themselves than for what they represented – the accumulation of difficulties and the perception of over-crowding, given the country's relatively high population density. It is interesting that the population density of England – which was the most Eurosceptic region in the UK in the 2016 referendum – would be the highest of all EU Member States bar Malta and the Netherlands, were it to be an independent state.[27] Its already high figure rose by 11.7 per cent over the period 1981–2010.[28]

Thus the passage of time and the particular politico-economic context makes a difference to public reactions to migration. British society is not intrinsically averse to the movement of people across borders, as is indicated by the large numbers of its citizens who have emigrated, including within the EU – to France and Spain in particular. Its business sector is almost wholly welcoming, given its growing dependence on foreign labour, whether French financiers, Italian baristas, Polish builders or Romanian fruit-pickers. This would seem to make a nonsense of the reluctance to accept the free movement of people as a basic principle of the Single Market, on which the British economy has become so dependent. Is it then yet another example of the UK's attempt to cherry-pick from European public goods? The answer is 'yes, but only up to a point'. The country is divided on this issue as on so many, while it is more than plausible to argue that had the Blair government not decided to allow immediate entry for workers from the A8 accession countries in 2004, when France and Germany imposed temporary controls, the size and speed of the immigration flow would have been moderated, with less of a boost to UKIP and the Eurosceptic cause.[29]

If Britain's line is that 'we can live with freedom of movement, just not too much', this does not make its relations with its partners any easier given that the EU has no wish to manage internal migration, and does not possess any mechanism by which it might be done, apart from the 'emergency brake', which has already been deemed insufficient. Other Member States, notably the Netherlands, have had similar reactions to Britain's, but have so far decided that the benefits far outweigh the costs of taking a stand. The Dutch too are an open, multiculturalist, society with a high population density but their location and importance for trade to and from the continent make a difference. For Britain, despite the barrier represented by the Channel, it has seemed sensible to opt out of the Schengen system of open borders, to oppose common European policies on extra-communitarian migration, and asylum, and to refuse to take part in the quota scheme proposed by the Commission as a way of distributing the Syrian refugees fleeing from their country's civil year in 2015.

The British position is paradoxical if not hypocritical. On the one hand it is seen, not without justice, as an example of a country that has adapted to mass migration, and which has established a multicultural tradition respecting the traditions of the large numbers of its citizens with origins variously in the Caribbean, in the Indian subcontinent, and in sub-Saharan Africa. It has also absorbed in recent decades the large numbers of educated young Europeans, particularly from France, Greece, Italy and Spain who have been unable to find work at home. Yet the 1.7 million people settled in the UK from the 'accession 12' states (ie those admitted to the EU in 2004 and 2007) between 2004 and 2017 seemed to have represented the last straw for enough people to swing opinion against membership of the EU.[30] Unfortunately, the success of the Leave campaign unleashed a wave of xenophobic comment (and some nasty incidents) indicating that in some quarters resentment had been bubbling away on a range of issues, until it found an outlet in Euroscepticism, ultimately to find apparent validation in the popular vote.[31]

Another aspect of British ambivalence, division or perhaps just confusion, relates to the service industries, As even keen Brexiters would acknowledge, trade with the EU's large, integrated, market will remain important to the UK economy whatever new openings might appear globally. And central to that European trade is the service sector, which has rescued the balance of payments from the pit into which it was falling due to the decline in manufacturing. As Coutts and Rowthorn point out:

> In 1950, Britain was a leading industrial power with a trade surplus in manufactured goods equal to 10% of GDP. There is now a trade deficit in manufactures of 4% of GDP. Over the same period, trade in services has moved into substantial surplus exceeding 4% of GDP. No other large industrialized country has experienced such a large shift in the structure of its trade.[32]

Of this vital contribution from the service industries – that is, financial services, knowledge-based industries, sport, tourism, transport, investment income – exports to Europe in 2014 were worth £59.5bn, as opposed to £34bn to the Americas (and the UK has a positive trade balance in services with EU, unlike its massive manufacturing trade deficit).[33] Yet service industries depend on a flexible labour market and the closely related free movement of people across international borders, at all levels from delivery drivers to hedge fund analysts. Change is rapid, given the near

universal dependence now on information technology, and
on the ability to innovate in that and many other areas. The
top people are in demand globally, as in football, music or
higher education. Restaurants rise and fall faster than any
other kind of business. Transport by definition involves
much frontier crossing, so that airlines and shipping companies always have multinational staffs. They are also highly
time-sensitive and frustrated by checks and delays. In this
respect at least, therefore, the UK's wish to have a more
restrictive immigration policy, placing barriers before the
very Europeans who have become important to its society
and economy, amounts to cutting off its nose to spite its face.

   There is another side of the coin, however, which is the
security dimension. Here again, Britain (in practice mostly
Conservative governments) has wobbled over whether or
not to be fully committed to Europe-wide cooperation. On
the one hand the UK does not want to be in Schengen. On
the other it wants to share the Schengen Information System.
Similarly, during Theresa May's long tenure as Home Secretary, she initially withdrew Britain temporarily from the
European Arrest Warrant (EAW), which had been used
successfully to obtain a rapid extradition from Italy of one
of the perpetrators of the 2005 London bombings, only to
return to it not long before the Referendum. After being
appointed Prime Minister, however, with the responsibility
for negotiating Brexit, she and her Cabinet finally had to
take a stand on the matter. The *Future Partnership Paper*
on 'Security, law enforcement and criminal justice' makes
it as clear as it can be without using the words that the
aim is to keep the EAW, and many associated forms of
technical collaboration in the area of homeland security
– which is hardly surprising since the UK has a history of
such partnerships since 1976, when the Trevi group on
airport security was set up.[34]

   There has been a similar ambivalence as to whether the
UK should be a member of Europol. Apart from the question
of whether picking and choosing among the various aspects
of European cooperation on crime and counter-terrorism is

the best way to achieve the trust needed to ensure effective information exchange and crisis communication, it seems clear that the concern for sovereignty is highly selective. The UK is home to various major listening posts and centres of information analysis in which it shares data with the United States. Evidently some parts of the political and administrative elite – but not all, and not all of the time – do not consider EU partners to be on the same level in terms of usefulness or trustworthiness. This leads to mixed messages.

From club member to guest

Boris Johnson, in the period before the Brexit Referendum said that 'my policy on cake is pro having it and pro eating it'. This position, of taking the advantages of a relationship without any of the downside, is what any rational policy-maker would adopt – if it were feasible. Arguably indeed, British governments of all stripes have operated on this basis for most of the time the country has been a member of the EC/EU, and they have got away with it. Many exasperated continental observers of Brexit have asked 'what is there not to like' about the situation in which the UK enjoys access to the Single Market, the global weight of the Common Commercial Policy, and a leadership position in foreign policy, while at the same time being granted a whole range of opt-outs in areas not to the British taste. Now, however, the tide has turned. Those on the other side of the negotiating table have been pointing out that London is asking for continued close relationships in areas such as foreign policy, security and criminal justice, despite its desire to leave the Union – which amounts to 'wanting to be a member of the club without paying any dues'.

As Britain will continue for the foreseeable future to be a middle-range power of weight in the European region, and to serve on the UN Security Council, regardless of its exit from the EU, its cooperation is bound to be sought on various issues by its former partners. It will not be possible to cold-shoulder the UK completely, even were that the unanimous wish of the other 27 – which it is clearly not – given that states like the Netherlands, Portugal and France have good reasons for wanting close relations with the UK, to say nothing of the EFTA states that are part of the European Economic Area. The obvious strategy for an 'exited' UK is therefore to play on divisions within the EU, and to try to insert itself via proxies into the policy-making areas of major concern to it. This may well prove possible. But it would be wrong to assume that it will be a friction-less process. Enjoying an à la carte menu is going to be a much more costly exercise than ever it has been during full membership of the club.

5

Regional or Global?

The 'descent from power' and loss of empire in the 1960s betokened a geographical shrinking of Britain's foreign policy scope. The military withdrawal from 'east of Suez' confirmed the drift, following as it did two successive applications to join the EEC. The eventual success in 1973 of that increasingly urgent strategy led over the decades that followed to the re-orientation of trade towards Europe, to a meshing of gears in foreign policy between Britain and its new partners, and to an acceptance of the fact that the resources were not available to sustain a truly global role. It is worth remembering that the NATO alliance endured because of its specific focus on the Transatlantic area. It could not have functioned with a global reach because of the excessive demands, financial and political, which that would have imposed on its members, Britain included. Between the end of the Korean War in 1953 and the arrival in office of Tony Blair – leaving aside the various rearguard operations against decolonization – the UK participated in only two 'out of area' military operations. These were the retaking of the Falklands in 1982 (assisted by EC diplomatic support, and by secret intelligence from France and the USA), and the UN operation to expel Iraq from Kuwait in

1991. It avoided involvement in the Vietnam War, and declined the options (some would say the obligations) of military action when Rhodesia declared UDI in 1965 and when Turkey invaded Cyprus in 1974. From 1969 it was much preoccupied with counter-insurgency operations on the home front, against the Irish Republican Army.

The victory in the Falklands suggested to some that the limits of geography might not be so significant after all, leading to grandiloquent statements about Britain's importance, culminating in the claim that the United States had only resolved to contest Saddam Hussein's invasion of Iraq because of Prime Minister Thatcher's determination.[1] The underlying trend resurfaced soon after this first Iraq War, when John Major and Douglas Hurd acted so cautiously over the new Balkan wars as to be accused of cowardice and isolationism. Their successor, Tony Blair, in part reacting against such passivity, associated with the loss of many lives in Bosnia, and in Rwanda during 1994, picked up the torch of Thatcher's more ambitious foreign policy. He was also animated by the ideas of the globalization school, which subordinated geography and strategy to the dynamics of the market, mobility and information technology. The result was a revival of military action well outside the European theatre – in Africa (Sierra Leone, 2000–2), west Asia (Afghanistan, 2001–14), the Gulf (Iraq, 1998 and 2003–9) – but also in Europe over Kosovo in 1999.[2]

The strong reactions, public and professional, against the second Iraq War in 2003 did not prevent decisions to use the Royal Air Force in Libya in 2011 and Syria from 2014, but they did prevent the deployment of ground troops. These last two cases might be on the margins of Europe, but they still derive from a foreign policy that prioritizes Britain's own region and the problems of its immediate neighbours over crises further afield. Perhaps Britain would have been willing to bomb Zimbabwe had its citizens been in the peril faced by Benghazi in 2011, or to intervene in a civil war like Syria's if one had broken out in, say, Venezuela, but merely asking the question indicates the improbability of such scenarios. The logics of propinquity and regionalism tend to trump universalism.

At no point, however, was the argument about the scope of British foreign policy definitively settled in favour of regionalism. Evidently too much depended on the context and on the government of the day. In any case, acknowledging an apparent retreat in British foreign policy is asking for trouble with the nationalist press. We shall see later on in this chapter that competing claims on national resources, plus the rise of new powers, are imposing ever tighter constraints on the UK's freedom of manoeuvre in foreign policy, but since in a crisis leaders determined to put Britain in the front line can usually persuade the Treasury to find the money, further far-flung ventures cannot be ruled out.

It is undeniable that the Brexit decision has added a whole new dimension to thinking about Britain's international role, with the government left with nowhere to go but to puff up the notion of a 'global Britain' as the UK places itself on the margins of the European theatre. Leaving the EU requires strenuous efforts to create effective commercial partnerships, bilateral and multilateral, across the world. It must also entail, if only to avoid the humiliating image of a once-great country waiting in the wings for others to set agendas, a generalized diplomatic campaign to raise the British profile at all levels and in all quarters. But what that will mean in practice for the scale of the operation, for commitments to new politico-military partnerships, and for the redistribution of national resources, is unclear. British foreign policy is hardly back to square one, given its positions in NATO and the UNSC, but it has a new script to write on the basis of what are bound to be new and testing experiences.

If the United Kingdom is indeed to move back into a global posture in its international relations then that will be sustained by two pillars: the United Nations, and in particular its Security Council, and the Commonwealth. There are two other possible sources of support – bilateral strategic partnerships, and solidarity among the 'Anglosphere', but they are as yet nothing more than flights of fancy. What follows takes each of these four possible frameworks in turn, with a view to evaluating their potential as foundations for a post-regional foreign policy with the capacity to protect Britain's security, economic interests and status in world politics. That done, the chapter concludes with a capability analysis, so as to assess whether the 'global Britain' strategy requires a changed resource base from that associated with the European system of cooperation.

The United Nations

Britain, like France, has always been determined to defend its separate membership of the Security Council (not that it has ever been seriously threatened). It has also never conceded that it sits there to represent the EU, agreeing in the Maastricht Treaty (Article J.5) only to 'concert and keep the other Member States fully informed' and to 'ensure the defence of the positions and interests of the Union, *without prejudice to their responsibilities under the provisions of the United Nations Charter*'.[3] That said, Britain has for the most part worked well with its European partners, especially France and those (like Germany) which manage to be elected as short-term members. The problems have arisen on high dramas like Iraq and Libya where fundamental differences of view, especially about the use of force, simply could not be resolved. The idea of a single European seat, so often mentioned by others, has never been seriously pursued, not least because it would run into implacable resistance from both France and Britain, and would reduce the overall European presence in the UNSC.

In technical terms, therefore, Brexit has no bearing on the UK's seat in the Security Council. Even were a head of steam to be raised over membership reform, Britain's veto means that it can protect its status. What is more, France would almost certainly see it as in its own interest to maintain solidarity. In any case, this scenario is remote. For the time being the possession of nuclear weapons and a history (not unblemished) of support for the UN means that London can continue to count on a significant role in New York, where the skills of its diplomats tend to be highly respected – and often relied upon. Yet diplomacy cannot disguise the reality of Britain's limited power relative to the United States, China and Russia. The last vetoes cast by the UK were in 1989, and the total cast by the country since 1945 is only 29, compared to the USA's 80 and USSR/Russia's 110.[4] It is rare that a distinctively British interest surfaces there of the kind that produced Security Council support over the Falklands in 1982.[5] Most activity has been geared to working in perceived Western interests, often in harness with both the US and the Europeans, but at times more with one than the other. Exceptionally, as in the negotiations over Iranian nuclear power, liaison across all the P5 proves possible. Here Britain made an important contribution. But for the most part it is a follower, not leader, in the UNSC.

Brexit is likely to produce subtle changes over time in these dynamics, and probably not to Britain's advantage. The need for coordination with France, and indeed the increasing German and Italian presence, will remain. That can take place in New York between the national permanent representations, in London, Paris, Berlin and Rome bilaterally, and in Brussels through contacts with the High Representative. But the process will be more laborious than as an actual Member of the EU. It may be that special arrangements will be made to allow the UK continued access to the secure inner communication networks such as COREU, but this seems unlikely – at least on a formal basis – given the legal issues that arise over exclusive and confidential information sharing.

Whatever deal is cut, Britain will have a different, less intimate relationship with its erstwhile partners. Furthermore, in the UNSC itself it will lack the degree of cover that automatically comes from EU membership – that is, being able to cite a collective agreement when a position becomes embarrassing, while still retaining ultimate independence. It might thus be exposed to more specific criticisms, and indeed find its right to permanent membership more loudly called into question. In contrast France will become the only EU Member State with permanent status on the Security Council. It is unlikely to lose the chance to 'speak for Europe'.

So far as other parts of the UN system are concerned, where no veto or other privileges apply, the UK naturally has had less weight. As the General Assembly (GA) operates on the basis of one country, one vote, the essence of success is coalition-building. Without allies a state's views count for little, unless it is the United States or perhaps China. Britain enjoys a certain amount of goodwill, but that is counter-balanced by the post-imperial resentments that also linger. The UK's failure in November 2017 to secure enough votes to get its candidate elected onto the International Court of Justice, and the vote against it over the Chagos Islands, might be straws in the wind of the isolation that could follow Brexit.[6] The solidarity of the EU has proved useful in the GA in the past given that the EU 'is widely recognized as a major pole and important political group'.[7] As this is likely to remain the case the UK will have either to shadow EU positions, hoping to find some way of sharing in decision-making, while also trying to line up with its Commonwealth partners – fewer of which are likely to prove as 'like-minded' as its European neighbours.

In the specialized agencies, Europe's habits of coordination have become a reflex, but if policy were to change on, say, herbicides or genetically modified foods, then an independent UK concerned to keep onside with the US might find itself diverging from the EU in the Food and Agricultural Organization, just as difficulties and delays could happen in the World Health Organization's regional Office for Europe if the EU were to take positions on pandemics or the safety of medicines that the UK does not share. In this sense Britain would indeed enjoy the greater autonomy the Brexiters hanker for, but at the same time would have to work harder to build coalitions of support – which would be necessarily ad hoc and probably ephemeral. EURATOM is another case in point. IAEA Director-General

Yukiya Amano marked the organization's sixtieth anniversary by noting its longstanding cooperation on nuclear safeguards with the EU, remarking that 'the IAEA and Euratom have for decades applied safeguards jointly in Europe, including through joint team inspections'.[8] A post-Brexit UK will need to do its own liaising, with both.

Modern international relations are characterized by interlocking institutions with overlapping jurisdictions, making it a significant advantage to be part of a group of states able to caucus before meetings of a larger forum and to carry weight in negotiations with other groups. In the IMF and World Bank, for example, the UK has the fourth largest voting power, behind the US, Japan and Germany, equal with France. Were British policy gradually to drift away from that of the other Europeans, London would have to align itself with Japan and or the US to secure its goals.[9] This might or might not turn out to desirable. It is true that this might not matter much, given that the EU has not yet managed to play a major role in the international financial institutions, but if the Eurozone were to become more integrated, with its own external relations, this would affect the UK in a wider context than is currently imagined.[10]

The Commonwealth

As the UK consolidated its membership of the EC/EU so the Commonwealth faded out of the picture in discussions about the pillars of British foreign policy. True, there was still occasional talk of the 'three circles' and therefore of the connections that its imperial past confers on the UK. Equally, predictions about the demise of the Commonwealth, or of the UK's departure/expulsion, have always proved mistaken. Once established most international organizations prove surprisingly durable, and the Commonwealth is no exception. Moreover the Commonwealth Secretariat was, and remains, based in London, with the Queen as its head. The end of empire had led to a graceful acceptance that the term 'British Commonwealth' would thenceforth be inappropriate, but this was a necessary act of diplomatic accommodation. Its interests might now be pursued more subtly, but the UK is still probably the single most influential Member State.

All this said, there is no chance that Brexit will inaugurate a period in which the Commonwealth will become a major, or even a significant, framework for British foreign policy. It is too loose and diverse an organization, with common positions rarely achievable across the whole membership. 'Imperial preferences' of all kinds are long gone with nothing from the Commonwealth to replace them. Even small group solidarity within the organization is elusive, with the more advanced economies just as wary as the UK of seeming to place themselves apart from the still developing countries, among whom India and South Africa in any case seem to prefer their new status as BRICS.

Clearly the UK will not be able to afford to neglect its Commonwealth membership once detached from the EU. There is support for it across all political parties, while the organization's unusual mix of states from both North and South, fifty-three in all, plays into the renewed wish for a global orientation, and also helps to provide cover against complaints about British neo-colonialism. Given the loss of a relationship with the ACP group (the African, Caribbean and Pacific States with which the EU has signed special association agreements) it also provides a cross-regional home for Britain's remaining small overseas territories – thirty-one Commonwealth members have a population of less than 1.5 million. Absence from the ACP group, however, will allow French influence, historically strong, to grow even further in its three zones. Since Paris has resented Mozambique and Rwanda, as non-Anglophone states, having the chance to join the Commonwealth this would be an opportunity for France to respond in kind. What is more, the redistributive elements in the Lomé/Cotonou agreements, while often criticized, are still much more attractive to developing countries than anything on offer through the Commonwealth.[11]

The Commonwealth will continue as a useful set of privileged connections for the UK in both general diplomacy and the UN's General Assembly and specialized agencies, but it is no substitute for the highly institutionalized consultations of the EU28. Most states seek some form of diplomatic shelter in a regional group, such as MERCOSUR in South America, ECOWAS in West Africa and ASEAN in Southeast Asia. These do not rival the EU in ambition but they help with external profile and political cover. Britain will now have to do without a regional bloc and to gamble on the benefits of flexibility that might bring. The Commonwealth, however, is only a marginal asset in that regard. Notwithstanding the lack of legal constraints on sovereignty it has often proved a difficult forum in which to conduct British foreign policy.[12] In the past even issues that seemed designed to produce Commonwealth solidarity have opened up fault-lines – as in 1968 when India and Pakistan refused to take the Asians Idi Amin was expelling from Uganda, or in 1983 when the United States invaded Grenada.[13] It is also the case that when Queen Elizabeth II, the much respected Head of the Commonwealth (and head of state for sixteen of its members), finally leaves the scene the glue holding the organization together might turn out to be surprisingly thin. The UK has succeeded in getting agreement that Prince Charles will in time become the next Head, but that was largely the result of the wish to show respect to his mother for her commitment and longevity.

The Anglosphere

The idea of a group of countries acting together in international relations on the basis of a shared history and language is common enough. It is what is meant by *la Francophonie* and it led to the creation of Germany in the nineteenth century. The Warsaw Pact was an attempt to engineer such a system under Soviet tutelage. But it has been most prominent in the case of the 'English-Speaking peoples', the romantic phrase used by Winston Churchill as the title of his four-volume history.[14] Churchill saw British history in terms of the long defence of liberty, a torch to be taken up by the United States. With some insouciance he saw the British empire as the global embodiment of the principle – although his account stops before the colonies' critical role in defending the mother country in two world wars. The widespread reverence given to Churchill, not least in the USA itself, gave his concept some respectability, especially in conservative circles. It fell into disuse during the years of the UK's Europeanization, but has revived in parallel with the growth of Euroscepticism, and with revisionist historical accounts of the empire, in the form of the 'Anglosphere'.[15]

The right wing of the Conservative party, never in love with the European Union and its association with Franco–German restrictions on free market capitalism, needed to find an alternative grouping if it was to advocate Britain's departure. It is revealing that pure unilateralism was never attractive, but that the strategy that emerged was the Anglosphere is a comment on the severe constraints on Britain's post-EU options. Even in its more limited incarnation of CANZUK (Canada, Australia, New Zealand and the UK) the idea is bizarre. As Duncan Bell has observed 'it envisages integration as if geography does not exist'.[16] The other three members find their respective regional roles sufficient and cannot understand why Britain does not feel the same. Indeed, they have persistently favoured British membership of the EU. Gareth Evans, the experienced ex-Foreign Minister of Australia and not a hostile observer, has noted that 'if Britain steps away from Europe, thinking it can compensate by creating an influential new grouping of its own, it will find itself very lonely indeed'.[17] He also noted, more provocatively, that while the Five Power Defence Arrangements (Australia, Malaysia, New Zealand, Singapore and the UK) were still valuable, 'the truth is that the United Kingdom has brought nothing of significance to the region's defence since the fall of Singapore in 1942'.[18]

It is the larger group of CANZUK plus the USA that the Anglosphere enthusiasts tend to focus on, given the need to shelter under the superpower's umbrella. These states constitute the 'Five Eyes' intelligence group, which is undeniably a functioning network of some importance, and one which irritates the excluded European powers. It is essentially a relationship of trust and privilege that necessarily sends a message of relative distrust to those outside the charmed circle. Yet it is a sub-optimal relic of war-time days, which can hardly correspond to the practical needs of coordination against global terrorism, which for Britain must mean working with a far wider group of neighbours and allies. Furthermore, it is never going to be an 'action organization' in the sense of formulating joint foreign policies, let alone an alliance. Nor is it a natural trading bloc along the lines of the EU or NAFTA.

The Anglosphere is a non-starter for many reasons, including rather crucially, as Evans says, that none of the possible members is 'likely to have the slightest interest in joining it'.[19] In Britain itself it would be difficult to find serious advocates of such a bloc, not least because of the unpleasant haze of historical and racial superiority hanging over the way the notion of English-speaking peoples is interpreted. They seem mostly to be white and living in developed countries, despite the importance of English in India, large parts of the African continent, and elsewhere.[20] Boris Johnson, with typical carelessness, has even raised the ghost of the 'kith and kin' argument associated with Ian Smith's white regime in Rhodesia fifty years ago.[21]

Strategic partnerships

If the Anglosphere is a nostalgic fantasy then what of the forward-looking notion of 'strategic partnerships' so popular in contemporary foreign policy planning? The EU made much of them in its 2003 'Security Strategy', only to row back in the 2016 revision labelled 'A Global Strategy'. British foreign policy has been aspiring to them since at

least 2003, when a keynote paper written for the first ever
conference recalling UK ambassadors to London prioritized
'Building strategic alliances with key bilateral partners'.[22]
Still, while the New Labour governments of that era talked
increasingly about the importance of 'strategy' and 'strategic
priorities', their international paradigm was essentially that
of globalization, networks and multilateralism. It was only
when the Conservatives entered government in 2010, with
their mix of Euroscepticism and a desire to resuscitate bilateralism that the idea of national strategic partnerships took
off. An agreement with that title was signed with Romania
in 2011, while Prime Minister Cameron met Turkish leader
Recep Tayyip Erdoğan to sign another in 2012. Three years
later, on the occasion of the visit of Xi Jinping to the UK
Cameron was happy to hear China's leader talk of a 'comprehensive' UK–Chinese strategic partnership. In the same
year Britain and India started to talk about their own bilateral strategic partnership, following Cameron's decision to
make it a top priority.[23]

The attempt to pursue such partnerships in parallel with
the two rival rising powers of China and India exposes the
problems with the approach. Political life is full of slick
concepts like this whose emptiness is soon exposed, especially through overuse. In this case the more partnerships
are hailed by a given state, the less exclusive and less valuable they will seem. If the habit then spreads widely through
the state system the problem is compounded. Bilateralism
is an inevitable and necessary part of international politics,
giving substance to the cumbersome procedures of international cooperation. But the diseconomies of scale and
the competitive nature of the search for special relationships
makes a reliance on multiple bilateralisms as a substitute
for multilateralism wholly implausible. By definition, a
'privilege' can only be granted to a few.

The 'global Britain' aspiration requires new friends to
be pursued relentlessly, particularly in trade. Contrary to
some expectations that would amount to virtually the reverse
of the Anglosphere idea. For whatever the attractions of

Australia, Canada and New Zealand, they are not in the same league as the states that have either large populations or significant domestic markets, combined with political potential. Apart from the USA, and leaving aside the EU, the other states in that category are Brazil, China, Indonesia, Iran, Japan, Mexico, Russia, Saudi Arabia and Turkey. Relations with Nigeria, Pakistan and the Philippines are also likely to be important for the UK. While there might be liberal qualms about getting close to some of the governments of these countries, the strategic partnerships approach is essentially realist in that it stresses Britain's independence but also its vulnerability as a *demandeur* in international relations once out of the EU. It will not have the luxury of picking and choosing, or the cover provided by a regional organization. Policy will have to target the key economic and political powers, regardless of their ethical standing.

The trouble with a hard-headed realist approach is that it cannot make solidarity claims on other states. They have to see cooperation as in their own interests, with clear incentives provided. Given this, which other players outside Europe might have good reasons for welcoming a closer relationship with the UK, and what added value might a 'partnership' bring to either side? Of those listed above only Russia currently is on antagonistic terms with Britain. Even that could change if Her Majesty's Government decided to sup with the devil with a long spoon, as Churchill did with Stalin, this time in the interests of securing export opportunities and secure supplies of crude oil and petroleum products. Vladimir Putin and Sergey Lavrov might welcome a prudential decision in London to back away from what they present as a British campaign of Russophobia.[24] This is not a likely change of policy at present. But once out of the EU a more isolated UK might not have the luxury of rebuffing major states over a long period. Conversely, if the powerful energy and commercial interests of other European states were to produce an EU rapprochement with Russia Britain would have a hard choice to make.

Of the other possible partners of significance the UK can hardly hope to get closer to Japan, Saudi Arabia and United States than it already is, at least without sacrificing the very advantages of independence that Brexit is supposed to create. Iran is a very different kind of case; like other European states Britain is anxious to see the nuclear deal hold and commercial opportunities grow. But geopolitics and the inevitable difficulties that arise from dealing with a theocratic regime, to say nothing of the difficult post-revolutionary history between the two states, place strict limits on where this relationship can go. There is also the element of zero-sum game when pursuing relations with Saudi Arabia and Iran at the same time, given the two states' current enmity.

China is another special case – one with both potential and dangers for the UK. On the one hand the relationship, between a state of 1.4 billion people soon to be the world's largest economy and a post-industrial society with a population of 65 million, is seriously asymmetrical, whatever flattering rhetoric Chinese leaders occasionally employ. On the other, China is *the* major market into which British trade could diversify, even if by the same token opening the home market further will create problems for manufacturing industry and for the balance of payments. Inward investment is also a two-edged sword, in that however welcome the injection of capital, whether into nuclear power stations or professional football clubs, issues soon arise about durability, and indeed sovereignty – albeit in a different way from the concern about EU membership.

Such problems are not insurmountable, but it would be idle to assume that China represents a major pot of gold for an outward-looking Britain, especially given the uneasy political relationship with a country whose human rights record British governments are bound to criticize and whose maritime policy is on a collision course with the United States. Indeed, even for a more realist Britain seeking partnerships where it can find them, China embodies the difficulty that it will not be easy to be on friendly terms with a range of different kinds of states, some of which will be at odds with each other. Choices will be unavoidable.

This leaves the rising powers of Brazil, Indonesia, Mexico and Turkey, together with states like Nigeria and Pakistan, also with large populations and unrealized economic potential but as yet hampered by chronic internal problems. Of these Indonesia is an intriguing possibility. The world's largest Muslim state and fourth largest national population, its economy has steadily grown to the point where it is the sixteenth largest in the world – although in terms of per capita income it is in the lower middle income (ie poor) group, along with countries like Egypt and the Philippines. Yet as Indonesia is relatively stable, with a high literacy rate, while it does not indulge in costly foreign policy adventures, it has clear potential for growth. It is the only G20 member from southeast Asia. The Department of Trade warns, however, that doing business in Indonesia requires much patience.[25] The UK is the country's seventh largest investor but not among its leading importers – who mostly come from the region. The head of Indonesia's Investment Board has already accepted that its forthcoming trade deal with the EU could be adapted to the UK but pointed out that 'of course the UK would be in a much weaker bargaining position outside the EU, so we would expect much more favourable terms of trade against the UK post-Brexit'.[26] UK exports to Indonesia are at such a low level (less than half those to Greece and 1/28th of those to Ireland) that the only way is up, but even if substantial gains are possible this will take a very long time.[27] At the political level cooperation will continue on counter-terrorism and maritime issues but that will hardly add up to a privileged relationship.

The same is broadly true of the other candidates referred to above. Brazil and Mexico have been talked up for decades as representing major economic opportunities, but British trade with Latin America has never risen above modest levels. Only 1.4 per cent of British exports go to the region.[28] Exports to neither country figure in the top 25 of our leading export or import partners. Exports to Brazil are about one seventh of those to Ireland, for example, and those to Mexico are half those to Brazil. Again, the low numbers suggest potential, but the competition means that the UK will struggle to achieve much. Investment is a different story, as British finance in Latin America has traditionally been significant. Yet in an age of tax havens and multinational shareholding it is always difficult to be sure what benefits flow back to the supposed mother country. The political level is no more promising. Britain can hardly expect to have particularly close relations with either Brazil or Mexico, given distance, the role of the US in the Western hemisphere, and the sheer lack of concrete shared interests.

Turkey is a particular case given that it too is sited on the geographical and political margins of the EU. It represents a moderately important economic partner with both exports and imports figuring in the top 25 of the UK's bilateral exchanges. It is also a fellow member of NATO, and one that should be well-disposed towards a country that has been consistent in supporting its eventual accession to the EU. On the other hand it would not make sense for the UK to keep pushing this argument once it has departed from the Union, quite apart from the difficult issues of President Erdoğan's increasing authoritarianism and the imbroglio in Syria. Furthermore in the still festering dispute over Cyprus Britain's role as a guarantor power means that it can only act as an honest broker. A strategic partnership is not feasible for this reason alone.

If the trope of a global Britain rests on the assumption of a developed set of bilateral relationships, replacing the single template of regional system, then its aspiration is for the country to be 'the most networked state'.[29] This concept has its origins in Foreign Secretary William Hague's inaugural speech of July 2010.[30] Although in many ways consistent with Tony Blair's talk of being a 'pivotal power' and 'thought -leader', as it is with David Miliband's conception of Britain as 'a global hub', his detailed and wide-ranging set of prescriptions also heralded the enthusiasm

for the concept of a global Britain, which emerged during
the referendum campaign and took off thereafter.[31] This
was not surprising given Hague's personal history of Euroscepticism, although interestingly he became much more
positive about the CFSP during his term of office in King
Charles Street. The speech talked of developing 'a distinctive British foreign policy that extends our global reach
and influence, that is agile and energetic in a networked
world, [and] that…builds up significantly strengthened
bilateral relations'. This was because '[t]oday influence
increasingly lies with networks of states with fluid and
dynamic patterns of allegiance, alliance and connections
including the informal'. Thus UK diplomacy must be sufficiently innovative 'to create our own criss-crossing networks
of strengthened bilateral relations'.

Is this a realistic aspiration? Leaving aside vainglorious
claims about primacy it is certainly true that Britain has a
long-established and extensive set of international relationships, spread across all the world's continents. While some
of these are difficult, through ideological hostility or the
scars left by history, most have the potential for growth.
Britain is still widely respected for its past achievements,
for its domestic stability and civility, for the excellence of
its universities and for the creativity of its artistic and media
communities. Its financial and legal sectors are of global
importance. The UK's military power, although reduced,
is still to be reckoned with given the skill of its armed
forces, while its status on the UN Security Council and its
extensive network of diplomatic missions ensures a high
diplomatic profile. In short, it still disposes of significant
reputational assets.

Resources

When considering what resources the UK has to underpin
a global rather than regional role we need to start with a
capability analysis of these assets and of their functionality.
The main indicators here are the diplomatic service

(including membership of international organizations), the armed services, overseas aid, and soft power in its various forms. Let us examine these briefly in turn.

In terms of diplomacy, the UK currently operates from 225 posts world-wide, of which 149 are embassies, 55 consulates/consulates-general, nine are permanent representations to international organizations, and twelve are other types of mission. This equates to seventh place (fourth by number of embassies) in a league table of the 62 G20 and OECD member countries.[32] Table 5.1 provides the points of comparison. It is worth noting that the UK has significantly fewer posts than France, whose service was judged 'best in the world' by an FCO advisory panel in 2012, and fewer missions to key international organizations than France, Germany and Spain – all of which also have the benefit of being able to use the External Action Service, from which Britain is about to cut loose.[33] The order of size – France, Britain, Germany – has not changed over forty years.[34]

Thus, governments in London will have to plough resources into the diplomatic service if it is to rise to the challenge of providing a high-profile global network and of meeting the objective set by William Hague of overtaking France – of which little has been heard since.[35] The embassies already have to provide homes and support for 108 Department of Trade offices, 41 DfID offices and 43 Science and Innovation Networks. Now they also have to go flat out to convince their host states that Britain's position in the world will not be diminished, and indeed that it merits privileged relationships. This is despite the fact that ever more demands have been made on a limited budget in recent years, especially through the creation in 2015 of the cross-departmental Conflict, Stability and Security Fund (CSSF). Headed by the National Security Adviser, this targets the countries of most interest to British security objectives – a laudable aim, except that ten regions and seventy countries are identified as needing help, on a budget of £1.1 billion of which the FCO contributes £695.5 million from its annual allocation of less than £2 billion.[36]

Table 5.1 Top twelve diplomatic networks by size among the group of OECD and G20 countries

Country	Total posts	Embassies/High Commissions	Consulates/ C-General	Permanent missions to IGOs	Other representations**
USA	273	167	90	9	7
China	268	166	90	8	4
France	266	160	89	15	2
Russian Fed	242	143	87	10	2
Japan	229	134	62	9	14
Turkey	229	134	81	12	2
United Kingdom	225	149	55	9	12
Germany	224	149	61	12	2
Brazil	221	137	70	12	2
Spain	215	115	89	10	1
Italy	205	122	75	5	3
India	181	124	48	5	4

** Representative offices or delegations where there is formal diplomatic relationship, but which are headed by a dedicated home-based head of mission.

Source: Lowy Institute, Global Diplomacy Index 2017.

The result of the June 2016 referendum led to a rapid recognition of the need to 'beef up' key embassies within the EU as well as those vital for a global Britain strategy – quite apart from the demands of the Brexit negotiation itself. Membership of the EU's multilateral diplomatic system, with its economies of scale, had led to pressures to cut back on missions. Now the engine of state has been thrown into reverse gear, with the move to multiple bilateralisms inevitably requiring significant extra resources – of personnel, estate, and therefore money.[37] In 2018 the prestigious embassy building in Bangkok was sold for £420m in order to pay for improvements in thirty to forty missions elsewhere.[38] Diplomacy has thus been expected, by Number 10, by the Treasury and by the National Security Council, to do ever more with resources, which have been at best static over the last decade and even now are only growing by small increments. The FCO and Diplomatic Service staff numbered 4,678 in 2007–8 as against 4,499 in 2016–2017, while spending over the same period has increased from £1.736 billion to £1.997 billion – the increase probably being accounted for by new CSSF activity.

As for the armed services, at $52.5 billion Britain has the fifth biggest defence budget in the world, just behind Russia and Saudi Arabia but ahead of France (47.2) and Germany (38.3). All are dwarfed by the expenditure of the US (604.5) and China (145.0).[39] Yet the UK's spending went down by 1.6 per cent in 2015–16. This is because the country is struggling between new commitments and stretched resources. The government has undertaken to spend more than two per cent GDP on defence, proudly setting an example in NATO. It has sent 800 troops to Estonia, special forces to Libya (with Royal Navy vessels stationed off that country's coast), while it has also stepped up its contribution to the air war over Syria. Britain provided air transport support to France in its Mali campaign and, like that country, has had to divert significant resources into countering terrorism at home and abroad. It has two state of the art aircraft carriers coming slowly into service, but could not agree the interoperability with France, which might have led to shared costs. It also does not yet have the planes to fly on the carriers. It is vocal about the threat from Russian submarines to transAtlantic cables but has not had an airborne submarine monitoring capacity since the retirement of the Nimrod patrol aircraft in 2010. The Boeing P8 replacements do not come on stream until 2019–22.[40] All this is in competition with the costs of the renewal of the Trident strategic nuclear deterrent, which Parliament approved in 2016. Arguments continue as to whether Trident should be removed from the defence budget to relieve the pressure on conventional equipment spending. In January 2018 the National Audit Office produced a damning report on the MoD's Equipment Plan for 2017 to 2027, which concluded:

> The Department's Equipment Plan is not affordable. It does not provide a realistic forecast of the costs of buying and supporting the equipment that the Armed Forces will need over the next 10 years.[41]

In other words, the defence budget, which is approximately twenty times that of the FCO, will either come under great pressure or will export the squeeze into other departments and other areas of external policy.

It is thus apparent that whatever geopolitical image is to drive UK foreign policy in future – global, regional, networked or issue-based – it is unlikely that the country will have a higher profile in terms of the projection of military power than it has at present, and it may well be facing a further reduction in its capacity. The Falklands should still be defensible once the new aircraft carriers are available, but a new attack would expose once again how thinly stretched are Britain's resources. Between 2001 and 2009 Britain fought two wars in parallel, in Afghanistan and Iraq, with unhappy results both on the ground and for the reputation of the armed forces.[42] That kind of over-extension is unlikely to be tried again. Indeed, despite the

confidence among the enthusiasts for Brexit in Britain being
a major power at the global level, the historical record
shows an inexorable decline in operational capacity since
1945. Apart from the 1982 war against Argentina the Royal
Navy has only been engaged in battle once (in 1991, with
the USA against Iraq), while its size has shrunk from 202
vessels in 1960 to 70 in 2015.[43] The Army has been far
more active. Since the Cold War ended it has seen action
in the Balkans, in Sierra Leone, in Afghanistan and Iraq.
But its size is notably down too. In 1989 (when the UK
spent 4.09 per cent of GDP on defence) the regular army
amounted to 155,500 troops, with 255, 200 in reserve. In
2016 it consisted of 86,700 with 59,200 reservists.[44] Even
allowing for the post-Cold War 'peace dividend', technological advances and a leaner, rationalized, outfit this is still
a big reduction given the actual increase in war-fighting
and range of tasks that the army has had to face over
the last quarter century. Regardless of Brexit something
is going to have to give, in expenditure, in personnel, in
equipment, in commitments – or in all of them – although
extended global ambitions will certainly sharpen the contra-
dictions.[45] A House of Commons Report on North Korea
has recently epitomized this ambivalence over the scope of
UK foreign policy. It concluded that Britain was unlikely
to be a specific target of North Korean aggression, and
would have no legal obligation to help if another state were
attacked.

> Yet in the event of North Korean aggression against South
> Korea and/or against the United States, it is unlikely that
> we would stand aside' (Summary) … and
> Any UK military involvement in this theatre is not going
> to be decisive. However, the UK might be able to provide
> significant offensive cyber-capability or relieve US forces
> from commitments outside the region, should the need arise.
> (Paragraph 99)[46]

It does not follow that issues of over-stretch will force
British foreign and security policy to fall back on regional
cooperation with the EU and its Member States. Political

will is an important variable as it has been in the past in defying straitened resources. But it is plausible to think that they might. Prime Minister May's speech at the Munich Security Conference in February 2018 paid lip-service to 'an independent foreign policy' but in its detail virtually pleaded for the status quo in foreign and security policy to continue.[47]

In contrast the use of soft power has no geographical restrictions. Its very rationale is to allow the individual nation-state to project itself on the world stage, in the hope of improving its image wherever its signals can be received. In Britain's case the country disposes of significant resources of soft power, through the British Council, the BBC, university system, entertainment industry and the other, less institutionalized forms of cultural relations. It is increasingly trying to mobilize these, so as to attract other states to its products, its way of life and its values – in other words, to start wanting the same things as we want.[48] The hope is that new, cooperative, relationships will thus be fostered.

Whether all this amounts to a platform for reviving the country's global role, and for substituting the assets relinquished through leaving the EU, is another matter. The problem with soft power is that it is mostly generated by civil society, with little at the state's disposal for effective use in international relations. Indeed, when a government attempts to exploit culture, science or even private business its efforts are quite likely to be counter-productive. The state can hope to build up external influence over the long term by investing in universities, the arts and infrastructure, but it cannot hope to see immediate results. Even then the commercial benefits will be restricted to tourism, education and the other service industries, which are already among Britain's strengths, and some will be raked off by multinational companies like Sky or the US hotel chains.

Competition from other societies – for example in the spread of university courses taught in English, broadcasting rivals to BBC World, or the development of information technology hubs like that in Bangalore, India – also places limits on the gains to be expected from an official branding and networking strategy. Even the English language is a double-edged sword, given that appealing to outsiders means understanding the languages and cultures of others, not just drawing them towards your own. Yet as a society Britain has been turning away from the world in certain respects, independent of the Brexit decision. The negative balance of trade in student movements, and in particular the catastrophic decline in the teaching and acquisition of foreign languages, has begun to affect even official levels of expertise.[49]

One further constraint exists on the global impact of soft power: governments, and particularly the Treasury, have become reluctant to spend money when they are unable to see tangible benefits – that is, generally within the five-year life span of an elected government (although defence procurement is inevitably an exception). Thus, the British Council is now expected to earn its keep through commercial educational programmes and projects like Erasmus (EU-funded). It only receives 15 per cent of its income from the FCO grant-in-aid. At the same time the FCO sees the Council as a key instrument of its soft power strategy, pressing it to target countries and themes of only incidental profitability, with the aim of aligning it with government objectives and promoting 'a friendly knowledge and understanding' of the UK. It might prove possible in the long run to achieve this through the Council's commercial activities alone, but as a global educational provider it is hardly in the same league as Britain's universities and in particular the University of London's highly successful external degree programme, in operation since 1858. The Council's strong reputation has been gained over 75 years by an eclectic interpretation of 'cultural diplomacy' and of British society. Continuing to project the richness of British society, as opposed to government policy, in the one hundred plus countries of the Council's outreach will be tough without a significant injection of public resource, just as the BBC would be lost without the licence fee. Both organizations provide international public goods from which the UK benefits enormously, if indirectly and often intangibly. If expected to behave like private businesses the range of their activities would shrink.[50] No doubt their glorious pasts and national origins would continue to bestow some aura, as it does for the now privatized British Airways, but this would fade over time.

The last resource available to the UK as it confronts the need to revive its global role is official development assistance (ODA) to poor countries. In this century the country has taken ODA increasingly seriously, as evidenced by reaching in 2013 the UN's target of spending at least 0.7 per cent of GNI on aid, and in particular by Parliament passing the obligation into law two years later. The Department for International Development has become a major player in both the UK's external relations (causing envy in the FCO), and in the global development regime. The upgrading of ODA in large part derived from a genuine desire to reduce poverty world-wide and to emulate the Netherlands and the Scandinavian countries that had blazed the trail. That was accompanied by such other milieu goals as helping young people in poor countries to stay at home rather than become irregular migrants, managing climate change and stabilizing fragile and combustible hot-spots. All these are evidently in Britain's interests, even if the dividends only become apparent over a period of years.

More immediate aims, such as using aid to secure lucrative contracts and export orders, are inhibited by the Acts of Parliament of 2002 and 2006, which limit the purposes of aid to the welfare of the recipient peoples.[51] But it would be naive to think that commercial factors are wholly absent, and they are bound to be more prominent now that Britain has to hustle for new trade opportunities worldwide. In any case, foreign policy has crept back into development policy by the back door, through impatience over liaison problems with DfID, and the pressure to access its budget for wider goals than strict poverty reduction. The emphasis

on good governance and friendly relations as conditions
of receiving aid have led to a conscious effort to restore
coherence – and the primacy of politics – to Britain's relations with the developing world.[52]

The connections between aid policy and the UK's particular concerns must become stronger after Brexit, and
not just because governments will be bound to see it as an
instrument of national policy.[53] At present, 36 per cent of
Britain's £13.4 billion of ODA spending goes through multilateral channels, of which one third (i.e. c. £1.5billion) is
a contribution to the European Commission's development
funds.[54] That could be available for bilateral redistribution
in due course, but the long lead times of programmes already
agreed, plus attachment to the good practices achieved in
the area, are likely to persuade London to continue participating in some form. The very nature of what has become
a development-diplomacy complex, involving states, international organizations and NGOs, entails a multilateral
bias, so that even monies not disbursed through the EU
might end up committed to UN or other collective endeavours. Over a third (34%) even of Britain's own national
aid disbursements cannot be identified as being given to a
single country or region. It is also worth noting that the
top ten recipients of UK ODA are (understandably) not
countries with much potential either as markets or as strategic partners for the UK in the coming decades (see Table
5.2). Of the rising powers, India and South Africa have
been taken off the recipient list – although Germany and
Japan still make India a priority – and China now only
gets limited non-DfID assistance with a few research projects. Only 4 per cent of the budget goes to the Americas
and of that hardly anything to Brazil.

All this means that, although Britain does a great deal
of good in the world and benefits in a general sense from
a reputation as a generous and progressive country – going
a fair way to counter accusations of neo-colonialism – there
are likely to be very few specific payoffs in terms of trade
or political influence. To be sure, the prioritizing of Pakistan

Table 5.2   Top 20 recipients of UK bilateral aid 2016 (in millions £)

Pakistan	463
Syria	352
Ethiopia	334
Nigeria	320
Afghanistan	235
Tanzania	186
Jordan	175
South Sudan	161
Sierra Leone	154
Somalia	152
Bangladesh	149
Kenya	134
Congo, Dem Rep	130
Yemen	127
Lebanon	124
Iraq	119
Uganda	111
Burma	107
Nepal	103
Malawi	103

Source: see note 52.

as a recipient, despite its massive corruption, makes sense in terms of counter-terrorism, while Kenya and Nigeria are potentially important players for the future of the rising African continent. But otherwise, ODA is quite properly concentrated on poverty reduction, an approach that seems unlikely to change – unless the radical right comes to power in Britain.

Geography and foreign policy

An insistence that Britain must make a clear choice between a regional and a global role would be based on a false antimony. The boundaries of the European region are notoriously contested. Its concept of neighbourhood certainly includes western Russia, and parts of Turkey. Given the problems of migration and terrorism British interests extend into north Africa and the Sahel, while the 'great sea 'of the Mediterranean has been the cradle of European history.[55] So, a narrow interpretation of the region is simply impossible. In any case economics compels Britain to engage closely with China and other growing economies, while humanitarian and legal commitments require a focus on the least developed countries. The functional activities of the UN's specialized agencies, in areas like health and climate, are of major importance, to say nothing of Britain's responsibilities as a permanent member of the UN Security Council. Taken together these things give the UK a global outlook and set of engagements.

A global orientation, however, is not the same as a global power role – which would entail a country freed from the constraints of EU integration and geography undertaking a range of new activities and commitments world-wide. All strands of opinion agree that on any significant issue the UK needs to work in harness with others. The question is, with whom? For the reasons surveyed in this chapter the Commonwealth and the Anglosphere do not represent feasible alternatives to the sophisticated patterns of interaction developed by the EU, while Britain's ability to lead or even shape UNSC initiatives is strictly limited. Some new economic and strategic partnerships might emerge, but the number of plausible candidates eager to work closely, let alone exclusively, with Britain is vanishingly small. The concept of the UK as hyper-networked, revelling in multiple connections and cross-cutting memberships, is superficially attractive given its history (although there is also a downside to that) but in the internet age it is difficult to conclude that Britain is uniquely placed to profit from them. It might be possible to pursue cooperation on an ad hoc, issue-related, basis but by definition that is impossible to plan ahead for, and to be sure of support.

Then there is the issue of resources. The UK is a rich country by world standards, which probably can continue to afford a strategic nuclear force and a welfare state if it wants to, just as it should be able to fund top-class armed forces while also working for social peace in our increasingly diverse society. But it will not be easy, and compromises will have to be made in all areas. What will certainly not be possible is a reversal of the historical decline in Britain's international ranking, relative to both its own past and to the roles of other states in the changing balance of power. To put it bluntly, no one seriously thinks that the UK any longer has a significant role in the Americas, in the Asia–Pacific region, or in most parts of Africa. The wars in Iraq and Afghanistan exposed the limits of British power (for those who still held on to some illusions) in the Middle East. To be sure, the existing resources of both soft and hard power mean that Britain can make useful contributions on an ad hoc basis, but only in conjunction with other states and with regional groupings – which brings us back to the EU …

Whether governments and public opinion like it or not, Britain's major influence is confined to the broad geographical area of Europe and the north Atlantic, however widely its concerns and aspirations range. Its foreign policy will have little clout, whether on Russia, North Korea, China, the United States, Zimbabwe or almost any other case that comes to mind, if it is not coordinated with its ex-partners in the European Union. Even the EU struggles to act as a global power, but at least it has the status of a bloc in a multipolar system. Alone, Britain would no longer even be in the game.

6

A Tale of Two Special Relationships – Paris and Washington

Cutting across the regional–global debate is the reality of two deeply entrenched bilateral relationships. One – with the United States – has been deemed 'special' ever since the Second World War, but the other – with France – goes back just as far, and is equally important to modern Britain. Neither country can be disregarded, but it would also be wise not to pile too much weight of expectation on what they can do for the UK in a world of sovereign states where even friends put their own interests first. The United States did not go to war for Britain in either 1914 or 1939. The French government chose to make peace with Germany rather than fight on in exile after the blitzkrieg of 1940. For its part although Britain made France an extraordinary offer of complete union it also kept back its fighter squadrons and withdrew its army for its own defence.[1] It might seem extraordinary in this context that Paris and Washington have remained the two most important capitals for British diplomacy over the last three quarters of a century, but put in a wider context it becomes obvious that there has been no alternative since 1945. Germany, Italy and Japan have not aspired to the role of major powers, while Russia and China have been adversaries. There have been inevitable tensions in Britain's relations with France and the USA, but these have been mitigated by the development of international institutions, in which the three have become embedded. This very fact, however, raises the question of whether the three sets of bilateral relations, and the balance between them, will be destabilized by Brexit. What follows examines the problem first through the concept of a 'special' relationships, then through an analysis of the interactions between these three allies of such different political cultures, before focusing on the two dyads of UK–France and UK–US.

Special relationships

The anthropomorphic language of international relations, referring to friends, enemies, passions, memories and so on, has often been criticized by realists and others who think that states possess only legal personalities. But states are run by human beings who are influenced by culture, tradition, public opinion and the many other ways in which sentiment and a sense of the past colour present policies.[2] Thus, although professionals yawn cynically at references to the UK–US 'special relationship', politicians still use the cliché when it suits them to send a signal or to press a particular emotional button.

From an analytical point of view it is clear that some inter-state relationships survive for longer and in better shape than others. The existence of a formal alliance both indicates a commitment and helps it to endure – the days are past when states issued and broke their words as a matter of course, even if Donald Trump is trying hard to falsify the proposition. China's break with the Soviet Union in the 1960s, or Anwar Sadat's reversal of Egyptian hostility towards Israel were extraordinary and untypical events by today's standards, where alliances usually develop institutional complexity and bureaucratic inter-penetration, making 'voice' and 'loyalty' more likely than 'exit'.[3] Britain's decision after 43 years to abandon the EU is certainly an anomaly in the practice of democratic statecraft. But at the same time the locked-in nature of its relationships means that the volte-face is bound to be superficial in many respects – which is why purist Brexiters have become agitated as the difficulties of disengagement have begun to dawn. The UK has multiple close ties with the EU and with individual Member States, however ambivalent it might be about them. This is partly because its bilateral ties are nested within many multilateral organizations, quite apart from the EU. In Europe alone Britain and France share membership in the Council of Europe, the European Space Agency, the OSCE, the OECD and NATO. At the global level there are the key fora of the UN, the G7 and the world financial institutions. Given geography, history and their aspirations to take on international responsibilities this creates not only a 'coordination reflex' but also pressures to agree common positions on matters of substance.[4]

Such proximity and entanglement does not automatically make for a 'special' relationship. After all, the list above applies to almost all European states, while for Britain and France harmony has not infrequently been interspersed with episodes of antagonism. States routinely talk up a particular connection for the purposes of an official visit or to influence decision-making in the other party. There is often also a deliberate blurring of the nature of relations between peoples (that is, at the personal and cultural levels), between states, and between particular administrations. If the two countries involved are broadly equal in power and status then the genuineness or otherwise of the partnership will probably be transparent, but if there is an asymmetry then the weaker partner will be prone to exaggerate the tie in the hope of consolidating it, while the stronger might indulge in the same rhetoric for a particular gain, but prove less than constant over a longer term.

'Special' is such a loaded term that it is best avoided. The implications of inclusion/exclusion and of a league table of friendships give too many hostages to fortune, quite apart from the tendency to lose credibility by making claims, which events can all too easily expose as wishful thinking. Yet some bilateral ties do turn out to be more long-standing and substantial than others. Of the three countries that make up the subject of this chapter the relationship between France and the United States has been important but rarely one of trust. It has, however, survived some serious breaches, as over Iraq in 2003. That between the UK and the US has been steadier, but often overblown, particularly in Britain. That between France and the UK has been uneasy, with moments of open conflict, but never one of indifference. What are the underlying factors that might, in principle, foster enduring closeness despite the inevitable periods of difficulty?

Geographical proximity is neither necessary nor sufficient, as France's ties to Africa, and the US's to Israel, demonstrate. On the other hand, since neighbours cannot ignore each other they inevitably become entangled in some form, if only antagonistically, as with Poland and Russia. A shared definition of geopolitical interests is a powerful centripetal force, although as this is not immutable it cannot be taken for granted. The US's threat of a pivot to Asia might in time weaken NATO, just as Britain's entry into the Common Market loosened its ties to Australia and New Zealand. The perception of a shared history, especially where it involves significant sacrifice, will lead to states giving each other the benefit of the doubt, and only fades over a long period. It is likely also to connote significant cultural links between societies. Such things as war-time cooperation, inter-marriage, and economic interdependence. These things do not make a sense of political affinity or common destiny unshakeable, but they do dispose towards it.

An inter-allied triangle

On the criteria just described it is not surprising that France, the UK and the US should have connections that go beyond the normal in international politics. Although there were various outbreaks of violence between them in the late eighteenth and early nineteenth centuries over territory in north America, over the last century they have been allies in two world wars, followed by cooperation in an enduring multilateral alliance. Each is a significant trading and investment partner of the others. In terms of symbolic bonds, France and the US look back to the cooperation that helped the latter gain its independence from Britain, to the French gift of the Statue of Liberty in 1886, and to D-Day 1944. Britain and the US, having overcome the colonial trauma, share attachments to Winston Churchill, to the English language, to the family ties created by GI brides and to the fusion of popular music traditions in the 1960s.[5] France and Britain have learned to put behind them Napoleon and Mers-el-Kébir, because they also remember the shared tragedies of Verdun and the Somme, de Gaulle's broadcasts in exile from London to France after 1940, and the joint ventures of Concorde and the Channel Tunnel.

These familiar episodes may seem little more than fuel for a certain amount of sentimental and manipulative rhetoric, but they do represent subtle inhibitions on the worsening of tensions beyond a given point during the spats that even allies are prone to. A common commitment to capitalist economics and to liberal democracy is also important, but that is no less true of Japan and many other Western states with whom these lines of least resistance do not exist. Without them a major effort has to be made to overcome the weight of history, as France and Germany have succeeded in doing – most remarkably – since 1963. Britain's excessive attachment to its 'stand alone' picture of a glorious past has been a factor in preventing a close partnership of its own with Germany, and therefore also the formation of a 'big three' group, which might have made for more effective leadership of the European Union. As it is, France is unlikely to abandon a security relationship with the United States even in the interests of a European defence community, while Britain badly needs to continue working closely with France even after Brexit. For its part the US, whatever impatience it regularly shows towards the old continent, is fully aware that the European members of the

UN Security Council still represent its most effective allies
in a crisis, and in 'defending the liberal order'.[6]

An isosceles triangle has two sides of equal length, rising
from a shorter base-line. This is an inexact metaphor for
the relationships between the three countries under discussion, but the US does provide the foundations of security
for Britain and France, two countries of similar size and
profile in international affairs whose great power days are
behind them. As a result the three have been embroiled in
an important triangular interplay since 1945. This can be
demonstrated by a brief survey of the series of key historical moments in the foreign policy of each state individually,
usually with significant consequences for wider international
politics. The history will then provide the platform for an
analysis of the dynamics of this distinctive three-player
game.

One line of continuity in this history has been the United
States' support for the project of European integration.
Indeed, it was the midwife – if not the progenitor – of the
process at its start.[7] This has put it at odds from time to
time with the UK, which first stood back from the EEC
before making an application under the shadow of both
the Suez fiasco, in which US opposition signalled the death-
knell for European empires, and Acheson's famous speech
about Britain needing to find a new role. In the 1960s de
Gaulle's new Fifth Republic found its identity in part through
foreign policy. Its obstruction of US-backed British entry
to the Common Market, and the General's vocal opposition
to the Vietnam War, created tensions with both London
and Washington, not least through forecasts of Britain acting
as America's 'Trojan horse' once admitted to the EEC.

In 1973 the kaleidoscope settled into a different pattern.
De Gaulle having left office, Britain finally joined the European project at the third attempt. The Conservative Prime
Minister Edward Heath then joined forces with France in
criticizing the United States over the latter's unilateral ending
two years before of the Bretton Woods arrangements on
dollar convertibility, and over Secretary of State Kissinger's

patronizing demand for a 'Year of Europe', in which the Europeans would help to renew the Atlantic alliance.[8] In the same year the two Europeans also opposed the US attempt to set up a consumer cartel to fight OPEC's use of oil as a diplomatic weapon after the October war in the Middle East. This was the beginning of Britain's realization that European foreign policy cooperation provided a way for it to distance itself from the US without endangering NATO, but also to put a brake on French interest in a 'third force' in international politics between the two superpowers.

The year 1982, however, was to bring home to the UK that it needed hard power support from its allies, whatever the intricacies of triangular diplomacy. Ostensibly on its own in overturning Argentina's invasion of the Falkland Islands, in fact it received secret intelligence from both France and the United States. Political differences re-emerged for a short period over the issue of German unification, which Washington favoured in the teeth of initial scepticism from London and to a lesser extent Paris.[9] Strategic cooperation quickly returned, however, in 1991 over the end of the Cold War and when the three countries led the UN force to expel Iraq from Kuwait. In the decade that followed the pattern of divergence and re-alignment continued, with unease over the whiffs of US triumphalism and tensions over the Balkan wars arising from the breakup of Yugoslavia. In 1998 Tony Blair and Jacques Chirac decided that it might be best not to rely so heavily on the US to solve European security problems, and so launched European defence cooperation at St Malo, much to the irritation of US Secretary of State Madeleine Albright. Yet only four months later the three Western states were leading NATO's *Operation Allied Force*, the air campaign that forced Serbia to withdraw from Kosovo.

Al Qaeda's attacks on the US on 11 September 2001 produced strong reactions of solidarity in both France and the UK, but the rush to war over Iraq soon detached France. In an indication, however, of the transience of both quarrels and alignments between these sovereign democracies, by 2007 Nicolas Sarkozy had authorized France's return to the military command structures of NATO, initiating a period in which Paris became seen in Washington as an ever more important defence partner, in some ways more critical than the UK (because less easy to take for granted), to the chagrin of British devotees of the 'special relationship'. Not long afterwards, possibly in reaction, the British initiated discussions with France, which culminated in the bilateral Lancaster House treaties of 2010 on defence cooperation, touching on rapid reaction forces, procurement and even nuclear deterrence.[10] The very next year the two states took the lead in the air war in Libya that led to Colonel Ghaddafi being overthrown. This was apparently a demonstration that Europe, in the form of its leading military powers, could act decisively in its own neighbourhood, although in practice it was a NATO operation with significant US support and capabilities in the background.

This major joint action did not turn out to be a precedent for the ongoing Syrian crisis. In 2013 President Hollande of France expressed himself disappointed at the failure of Prime Minister Cameron to get parliamentary authorization for air strikes after the use of chemical weapons by the Assad government – a failure that led the US in turn to back away from one of its supposed red lines. That Britain then did join the other two states in the air war over Syria a year or so later did little either for events on the ground or for solidarity between the allies, given the lack of clarity over targets and war aims. Its purpose was largely to play catch-up, and to avoid appearing side-lined. Even Donald Trump's election and erratic international behaviour during 2017 did not succeed in cementing Franco–British foreign policy cooperation. By then the UK had voted to leave the EU and Emmanuel Macron, as new French President, had skilfully managed to keep open channels of communication to Washington without alienating his EU partners – in contrast to Prime Minister Theresa May's constant difficulties.

The history of the relationship between Britain and the two states to which it is closest is one of turbulence within limits. How are we to understand the dynamics of these relationships? Does the triangle work, as a kind of diplomatic triumvirate? Do some sides of it work better than others, and in what contexts?

Three-way cooperation has occurred at times, as we have seen, but mostly in the major security crises of the first Iraq War, Kosovo, 9.11 and Libya. It tends to fade quite soon because, although such fundamental values as commitment to NATO and opposition to aggressive war are shared, there are too many differences of interest and outlook to sustain a triple entente of solidarity across a broad front. Bilateral relationships suffer from the same malady but endure better by the sheer logic of having fewer moving parts. Of the three dyads possible, that between France and the US need not concern us. It is Britain's balancing act between the other two that is important for its foreign policy before and after Brexit. The separate relationships with France and with the US ties are analysed in more detail later in this chapter. The point here is simply that each affects the other however much politicians try to compartmentalize. The shadow of the world's only superpower inevitably hangs over whatever the two European states attempt to do together – as over Suez in 1956, or at St Malo in 1998. Conversely, the UK's assertion that it has an inside track with the United States has often been complicated by France – either in terms of British policy being perceived as sycophantic towards Washington (as over Vietnam, or support for the Palestinian cause), or of Paris obstructing a joint US–UK position (as with the first two British attempts to join the EEC, or over Iraq in 2003).

The underlying dynamic of the triangle is that the US wants Britain and France to collaborate, as a way of encouraging Europe to take on its share of responsibility for upholding the liberal international order, so long as that does not get to the point of undermining US leadership. Had Britain, for example, joined France in opposing George

W. Bush's war on Iraq that could conceivably have stopped the plan in its tracks. More recently, solidarity on climate change measures has ensured President Trump's diplomatic isolation – although it has not made him change course. The American President's capacity to hit back can place serious strain on European solidarity, as over the Joint Comprehensive Plan of Action (JCPOA) over Iran. Thus the two Europeans factor in the United States' probable reaction on virtually all foreign policy decisions, not least their degree of bilateral cooperation – which is more likely if smiled upon by Washington. US criticisms or impatience, on the other hand, do not necessarily drive Paris and London further together. They cause frictions, embarrassment and domestic doubts, as during the Bosnian wars of the 1990s. After all, the fracture lines down the English Channel are near the surface; they open up all too easily. Britain has used closeness to the US as a shield against demands that it be more truly European, while it takes little for French suspicions of 'les Anglo-Saxons' to surface. Each middle power is, in effect, pulled between its leading role in Europe's politico-military affairs and its desire to remain close to its superpower ally. Brexit will provide a new context for this tension, but it will not remove it.

The French connection

The historical turbulence of the Franco–British relations over many centuries has been well-documented.[11] As late as 1898 at Fashoda in the Sudan the two states were close to war. Even in the century or more since the Entente Cordiale inaugurated a broadly cooperative relationship there have been many difficult clashes. A similar trajectory of slow disengagement from empire, and adjustment to loss of great power status, has not necessarily produced similar responses – indeed at times the process has been sharply competitive. Crucial moments of joint action, such as the liberation of France in 1944, or Libya, still generate resentments, given that no initiative ever goes unpunished.

Differing approaches to the management of Europe's international order, and especially towards integration, have led
to regular periods of estrangement and mutual incompre-
hension – such as Britain's 'empty chair' stance in the early
1990s and the recriminations over the Iraq War from 2003.
The upsurge in British Euroscepticism over the last decade
caused both bafflement and anger in France, particularly
when it found an echo in the rise of the Front National
under Marine Le Pen. The eventual referendum vote for
Brexit has both exasperated French political opinion, tired
of the time and energy that the British problem has taken
up, and created a sense of opportunity, over the final lifting
of a burden from the European project. On the British side,
the divisions of opinion – and hope – are even stronger.

  Whatever the predictions, and feelings, about Brexit
forcing a parting of the ways, facts on the ground box in
governments on both sides. For one thing the two countries
have very similar *characteristics*. Their populations are both
around 65 million (although France has twice the land

Table 6.1 France and the United Kingdom: selected socio-economic
indicators (2017 unless stated)

Indicator	France	United Kingdom
Population	67.1 million	64.8 million
Median age	41.4	40.5
Life expectancy	81.9	80.8
Birth rate	12.2 births/1000 population	12.1/1000
Size	643,801 square km	243,610 sq. km
GDP per capita	$43,600	$43,600
Unemployment rate	9.5%	4.4%
Exports as % GDP	29.3	28.3
Imports as % GDP	31.2	30.3
Reserves	$146.8 billion (Dec. 2016)	$135 billion
Defence spending	2.26% GDP (2016)	2.2% GDP (2016)

Sources online: CIA: *The World Factbook*; OECD.

area), they are both located on the western shores of their continent, and they rank closely together on most socio-economic indicators.

Their international status is remarkably similar, since they both have permanent membership of the UN Security Council, are both nuclear weapon states, both have far flung remnants of empire for which they are responsible, and together represent Europe's only effective capacity for projecting conventional military power. For each, there is no other state in the international system that as closely resembles it as does the other.

A positional analysis is valuable but says nothing about the character of the state inside its external shell. Probing domestic culture and politics exposes the main differences between France and Britain. Beyond the cheap stereotypes about national character it is still true that the Republican tradition and Code Napoleon on the one side, and constitutional monarchy plus common law on the other, make misunderstandings all too easy.[12] Furthermore, while its capital city is key to each state, France is far more administratively centralized than a United Kingdom that has devolved powers to representative assemblies in three of its four constituent nations. This in part explains the contrasting approaches taken towards ethnocultural minorities. Britain celebrates multicultural diversity. France insists on civic integration to the point of not even collecting statistics about religion or ethnic origin. Beyond this, intellectuals have more status in France; British newspaper readership is higher; the French culinary tradition is one of the world's greatest; London is an incomparable global arts centre.

And so one could go on. The only importance of such differences from the point of view of foreign policy is when attitudes and domestic pressures start to impinge on mutual relations, which they do not infrequently, the Brexit decision being the prime example. Others would be Britain's unwillingness (citing legal impediments) to extradite individuals wanted in France on terror charges after the Paris Metro bombings of 1996–7, and demands from the Pas

de Calais region for Britain to be pressed to provide more
funds for the migrant camp close to the Eurotunnel ter-
minal (although the French government has so far shown
no sign of wanting to abrogate the Le Touquet agreement
of 2003, which effectively sites the UK border in Calais
rather than Dover).

Brexit represents a potential rupture in Franco–British
relations going well beyond the skirmishes of recent decades.
The European project is central to the history of the Fifth
Republic, as is cooperation with Germany. Neither of these
countries would abandon their commitment to the principle
of 'ever deeper union' unless compelled by domestic rebel-
lions. For France the idea of integration is still seen as the
way to 'rescue the nation state', even if the implicit contradiction means that the pace has to be slow. The Brexit
view – that the EU represents either a form of intrusive
empire or a ramshackle failure that it is best to cast loose
from – is wholly alien to their elites, if not to their rising
populist parties. Thus the fact that the UK has declared its
wish to depart represents a philosophical parting of the
ways, even if in truth there had been divergence right from
the outset of British accession.

The practical consequences of the Brexit decision have
already created turbulence in bilateral relations given that
France is not going to break the unity of the 27's negotiating position just to show friendship to Britain. In the longer
run, Paris may find ways of preserving a cross-Channel
closeness, but that will have to be balanced against the
wish to make the EU stronger and in particular to maintain
the special relationship with Berlin. In assessing the possibilities much depends on one's view of institutions: do
they socialize states and lock them in to particular patterns
of behaviour, or are they little more than weak bonds,
easily sundered by the powerful forces of international
politics? If the former, then we should expect France gradually to diverge from Britain as its activities become ever
more concentrated in the EU. If the latter, then the EU is
unlikely to come between the distinctive common interests

that the two countries share in relation to the world outside the region.

Against this background we need to weigh the fact that the UK – and not just the current government with its weak bargaining position in the leave negotiations – will be desperate to maintain a close relationship with France. It is far more important to the UK than are the traditionally anglophile European states, even collectively. French policies will be central in determining both the EU's future trajectory and its long-term relationship with Britain. Because of the symmetry between the two countries' international positions, as outlined above, to say nothing of geography, it is also a natural foreign policy partner in relation to the world outside the Union. On any given issue if France and the UK are in alignment then that immediately doubles the weight of each state by comparison to acting alone.

Such rational calculations of advantage cannot be made only by reference to the chessboard of international politics; they are inevitably affected by membership status. Being divided by the EU's political frontier changes what was a relationship of equality into one where the UK is more often a *demandeur*, while France has increased leverage. This will, however, vary according to the issue-area, not least because France itself has good reasons for still hugging Britain close.

The most obvious reason relates to the UN Security Council. On the face of things the notion of being able to speak for the EU, as its only permanent member, seems attractive to a country for whom international prestige is a key value. But French decision-makers know that it will remain easier to work with British colleagues in New York than with those from the rest of the P5, while Germany (however close a partner it is) does not yet have the will or the status to enter into commitments during major international crises – as its 2011 abstention on the decision to act in Libya demonstrated. France is unlikely to press the argument that the British right to a veto is undermined by its inability to represent the EU. Since the 2003 Iraq crisis the voting records of the UK and France have come to align closely in the UNSC, while they are both keenly aware, at least in principle, that they will be less exposed to pressure on an issue from the great powers of China, Russia and the USA if they are united.[13] Furthermore, while either country might lead on a possible military intervention, which for the Europeans would only be feasible in their 'neighbourhood', with a possible extension into sub-Saharan Africa (as in Mali in 2013), neither could act without at least tacit support from the other – or without the legitimation provided by a UN Resolution.[14] Lastly, London and Paris have identical positions on the possible reform of the UNSC – favourable in principle to the Council's expansion, but not to the creation of new veto rights or to any debate on the rights of the existing P5.[15]

Closely tied to the UNSC question is the status of being a nuclear power, which the two European states show no sign of foregoing. Equally there is no question of a joint deterrent, whether Franco–British or European, even were that to be imaginable in terms of decision-making and sovereign independence. As the EU has no competence here, or even remote aspirations towards being a nuclear super-power, Brexit will have no bearing on the matter. On the other hand, the two states have long skirted around issues of technical cooperation in this area, in which they do have shared interests. Since the signing of the fifty-year Lancaster House treaties of 2010, one of which dealt with nuclear cooperation, discussion has proceeded on joint weapons test simulations and delivery technology. There is also a wider shared interest in cooperation on the enormous costs of all defence procurement, without which national champions are unlikely to be competitive with US firms – not that this has been easy so far, or will be in the future, with or without Brexit. Competition over industrial capacity and exports is still sharp.

Cooperation in defence, which since Lancaster House also involves planning a joint expeditionary force, army secondments at deputy commander/brigadier-general level, and regular ministerial meetings, does not mean that motives and long-term objectives are the same.[16] Of course, both states' underlying concern is for the peace and security of their region, implying the abilities to deter and respond to any threats it is faced with. But Britain's priority is to work with France in order to strengthen NATO and reassure the US of European commitment to defence, with an ancillary motive of stopping EU defence cooperation from becoming a rival to the Atlantic framework. France, on the other hand, wants the Common Security and Defence Policy to succeed precisely so as to avoid over-dependence on the reliability of the US security guarantee – however valued that is – and to ensure that the Europeans have other choices than that of simply falling in behind US foreign policy.

In recent years, with Europe not having been one of President Obama's priorities, followed by Donald Trump's blowing hot and cold on every issue, this instinct has strengthened in Paris. Since the 2016 referendum, Britain's different approach has become more exposed to the glare of daylight because London at first crudely attempted to use security as a way of strengthening its overall negotiating hand, only to back-track and make fulsome noises about the vital importance of continued closeness to its European partners. France and Germany, meanwhile, with the British brake removed, lost no time in pressing ahead with the CSDP, via 'Permanent Structured Cooperation' and the launch of a 'European Defence Fund'.[17] This will probably not revolutionize the European security environment, but since Britain has sought for three decades to limit and control the process from within its new status as a bystander is bound to cause anxiety in the Ministry of Defence.

Concern will also be evident in the Home Office, and among the police and the security services, if the UK ends up on the margins of European cooperation on internal justice and security matters. The security establishment has lobbied effectively for the value of the European Arrest Warrant. Indeed, as the Brexit negotiations have got under way it is clear, as with foreign policy, that this is an area where the government badly wants to preserve the status quo. As sovereignty and money are not in question here the priority is not to end up excluded from critical functional networks in which Britain has traditionally played a major part.[18] A French defence ministry adviser said that the bilateral relationship in his area amounted to 'a lock of mutually entwined interests' that any government would 'find hard to pick'.[19] This is likely to apply even more to counter-terrorism activity, where failures to share information or to make procedures compatible can have the gravest consequences – a fact accepted on both sides of the Channel since the London attacks of 7 July 2005. The British Government's 'Partnership Paper' of late 2017 stated that:

> It is through pooling expertise and resources with EU partners that the UK has been able to develop some of the world's most sophisticated cross-border systems and arrangements in the fight against crime.[20]

'Crime' subsumes terrorism, cyber attacks, and human trafficking as well as the more familiar activities of the international mafia, sex offenders and money launderers.

Bilateral arrangements with states like France with similar problems are more important than the looser and often frustrating operations of large organizations like Europol, although they in turn rely on the sophisticated EU-wide Schengen Information System (SIS), to which the UK belongs despite having opted out of Schengen proper. This enables the real-time tracing of people movements on a large scale, with police forces being alerted simultaneously right across the system. It works well both because most states have a strong interest in mutual cooperation on crime and because those that choose to work more closely together can do so in ways that do not undermine the collective approach. The same is true of Prüm, an EU system that from 2008 has encouraged sharing of the fingerprint, DNA and vehicle registration data of criminal suspects.

One area where Britain and France do not work as closely together as they might, however, is the related issue of migration. This is because it has become highly contested domestically, leading to significant differences of national interest. The problem is not the hundreds of thousands of French and British people who have crossed the Channel to live and work in each other's country. It consists, rather, in the fact that France is not only a destination for many Africans and Maghrebians seeking a better life, but also a transit country for those from all parts of the developing world seeking to reach Britain. Over the last twenty years this has led to a succession of squalid camps at Calais, Dunkirk and some other points along the Channel coast, creating pressures for action from both the local communities and NGOs trying to relieve human suffering. The situation would not have arisen had the UK been willing to participate in the Schengen agreement on open borders – although in that case the sharp rise in the numbers of people entering the EU would have produced a much earlier domestic crisis. As it is, France has struggled to cope with its own growing population of irregular migrants at the same time as fulfilling its treaty obligations to Britain. This has led to governments in London agreeing to pay for ever more stringent security measures at the ports, and intermittent demands from French politicians – by no means all from the far right – to move border controls back to Dover. British Brexiters show no enthusiasm for this particular form of 'taking back control'. Were it to happen there would be short-term chaos in the Kent ports and a substantial increase long term in the numbers of migrants using France as the means to enter Britain. If Britain then 'closed the border', as France itself has often done at Ventimiglia on the Italian frontier, that would cause a crisis, for Paris would be faced with allowing back in ferry passengers not allowed to disembark in Dover. If, on the other hand, the French government continued to honour the Treaty of Le Touquet it would incur political costs at home from those asking why the UK should enjoy special privileges given that it had left the EU.

The last external policy area where Brexit must have an effect on Franco–British relations is that of economics. In this context that does not mean trade, where whatever exit deal is done will have some, if as yet indefinable, impact on the two countries' export competitiveness. It refers to the more structural question of the fate of the Eurozone. This is itself connected to the issue of integration; if the Eurozone is to develop, or even survive, it will do so on the basis of a greater element of supranationalism, which will automatically boost integration across the board. In that scenario France and Germany would move even closer together, making it ever more difficult for the UK to act in harness with either. Sterling might still remain relatively strong but the euro would be far more significant on the international money markets, with corresponding pressures for financial transactions in the common currency to move from London to the continent. On the same assumption, there will probably be pressures for the EU to play a greater role in the international financial institutions and the G8, with Britain more marginal because unable even to exert the limited influence on the Eurozone that it has as an EU Member State. Conversely the Eurozone could collapse, throwing the Union as a whole into crisis. Even this would be less likely to push France and Britain closer together than to generate a return to integration among a smaller group, like the original Six of 1957.

Hugging the US closer?

The UK might need to engage as closely as possible with France post-Brexit but to many the relationship with the United States looks even more indispensable. Even if we clear away the rosy mist from what has often seemed to be more a sentimental alliance than a true congruence of interests, it remains true that much of British external policy is entwined with its US equivalents. Most observers these days eschew the phrase 'special relationship' – because Washington flatters many of its partners in that way, and because it implies an across the board symmetry that simply does not exist. Rather, it is said, the unusual degree of trust and cooperation that does exist between the two is centred on the armed forces and on the intelligence services. Yet this is not the whole story. For one thing if a foreign power proves itself reliable in defence and security, critical areas for any state, that is a considerable asset in international politics, not to be sneezed at. Secondly, even in the area of trade, where the EU looms large, the US is still Britain's largest national export market. Thirdly, despite the differences of size and power between the superpower and an island state of 65 million people that accepted its loss of primacy eighty years ago, in some areas a rough balance of interests does exist. The United States appreciates the fact that it can generally rely on the UK to support its foreign policy priorities – or at least not actively to oppose them – especially in the UNSC. Of more concrete value are its listening posts and remaining bases in the UK, together with the data and expertise supplied by GCHQ (Government Communications Headquarters) in Cheltenham. In the same category are the British bases in Cyprus and in Diego Garcia, although the latter was effectively transferred over to the US for exclusive use in the 1970s, disregarding the interests of the indigenous Chagos islanders, to the UK's shame and eventual embarrassment.

This last example, however, brings us to the issue of the imbalance between the two parties. On the face of it the weaker state should benefit disproportionately from such a relationship. Certainly the UK currently enjoys a number of things seen as central to its security. Its second strike nuclear weapon system is only nominally independent, given not only the reliance on US missile technology and satellite guidance, but also the extent to which it is locked into NATO command systems.[21] The main perceived advantage is the ability to shelter behind the US security shield, both nuclear and conventional, against Russia and/or rogue states. As for all NATO members this guarantee has not been seriously called into question since the Intermediate Nuclear

Force controversy of the 1980s. Secondary advantages are the presumption that the UK will be given US support, or at least the benefit of the doubt, when non-NATO issues arise, as it was over the Falklands in 1982, or over the Litvinenko murder in London of 2006.

On this basis, Britain would suffer the most were there to be a serious breach in the relationship – although a counter-argument is that any gains have to be set against the price of being committed to unnecessary conflicts and undesirable bloodletting through acting as Washington's wingman. In recent years, indeed, before the troubling emergence of Donald Trump, even establishment opinion had shifted towards accepting that the UK should not automatically shadow American foreign policy. Apart from the strong popular reaction against the Iraq War there had been too many examples of the US seeing the world in a different way, from internment at Guantánamo to Barack Obama's Asian pivot. In this context, it is doubtful that the transatlantic relationship could provide a sufficiently safe harbour for the UK after Brexit.

In trying to analyse dispassionately the prospects for relations with the United States once Britain leaves the EU, two starting points seem clear: first, that solidarity cannot be assured given the separate rhythms of domestic politics in the two countries; second that the long-established pattern of cooperation between London and Washington sets limits to how far a quarrel between the two can go, especially in public. The regular disagreements, whether Grenada in 1983, Bosnia in 1994 or climate change in 2017, have never led to the unravelling of the wider political partnership. Looked at another way, an assumption of amity is not the same as having fully compatible interests, let alone acting consistently together. The UK might, for the most part, be able to rely on the US not actively opposing it but its diplomats are well aware that on a range of difficult issues, from Iran through Palestine to China and Russia, priorities are bound to diverge independently of who is occupying the White House or 10 Downing Street. It is also easy for Britain to get sucked into following US initiatives, which then blows back with consequences that cause the smaller ally more problems than the superpower – Iraq and Syria being recent examples. That was why Harold Wilson resisted the severe pressure on him to follow Lyndon Johnson into Vietnam, despite domestic criticism from those who felt the 'special relationship' demanded a gesture of solidarity.[22]

History and culture help to ensure the durability of an alliance but they are not sufficient to counter strategic necessity, differences of geography and sheer asymmetries of power. Fault-lines inevitably open up from time to time. When that has happened over the past four decades Britain has benefited from the 'cover' provided by membership of the European foreign policy system, so as to distance itself adroitly from US policy and to dilute the impact of American criticism. Without that to fall back on, Britain will face starker choices over following the vicissitudes of US policy, standing alone – or associating itself with the EU as an outsider. The country may rejoice in its newly found independence but it will find that in the contemporary international system that is an uneasy position to be in. If there is no default setting of agreement with EU positions, the same must apply to the United States. The inevitable consequence is alignment on an ad hoc basis, which risks offending both sides without influencing either.

The British elite likes mechanical metaphors to express what it sees as the country's distinctive political roles within the Western alliance. The UK has been variously claimed to be on the cusp of three intersecting circles, a bridge between Europe and the United States, a balancer within the EU, and a global hub in a networked world.[23] As recently as 2015, Robin Niblett envisaged Britain as needing to work within two concentric circles of which Europe represented the inner ring, with US–UK relations being the outer one. He predicted that 'if it leaves the EU, Britain will find itself truly the junior and dependent partner in an unbalanced security relationship with the US'.[24] This scenario is now coming to pass, ruling out the roles of balancer within the EU and of unique player in the three groupings of the Atlantic, Europe and the Commonwealth. This leaves two images intact: first the super-networked global hub aspiration (examined critically in Chapter 5), in which relations with Washington would presumably become less important as Britain diversified its connectivity; and second the belief that the UK can act as a bridge between the US and Europe.

This last idea not only lacks content but risks complete self-deception. The English language no longer needs any translators, given the fluency in English of most European professionals, while the notion that the United States still needs Britain to interpret continental cultures to it is risible – if anything, the reverse is true. What then might the metaphor mean? Certainly the Francophones often refer to 'les anglo-saxons', with the implication that Britain represents simply a nearer, more approachable, version of an essentially alien culture. More significant is Britain's possession of a welfare state, and opposition to both guns and capital punishment, all of which put it closer to the continent than to the US. Arguably the British people are divided down the middle between those who feel more comfortable with the United States, through language, popular music and cuisine, and those who identify more with continental Europe. So at this level the UK does have a foot in both camps.

At the foreign policy level, however, matters are more complicated. After Brexit, Britain will have no choice but to stress even more its central role in NATO. Since the alliance is critical to the security of all Member States, including those outside it, that gives London a potentially important role in helping the EU and NATO to work together. Yet, as discussed at various points earlier, that can cut both ways. Britain has an interest in trying to obstruct progress on European defence cooperation, which could set it on a collision course with France, Germany and Italy in particular. And if the CSDP does progress

Britain will be driven closer to Washington, which has a deeply ambivalent approach towards European defence cooperation – it demands more effort and spending, but also sees any institutional or policy divergence as a threat.

There are only a few other issues of general importance on which Britain might have privileged access to Washington. One is Ireland, where the problems have been seriously exacerbated by Brexit. The EU does not want to see relations between a Member State and its departing neighbour deteriorate, but rather than wait for the UK to bring in the United States, with its deep interest in things Irish, it is more likely to use its own channels to encourage US pressure on Britain on the hard border question, with all its risks for security, smuggling and community relations. For the rest, were sharp transatlantic quarrels to develop, whether on protectionism, climate change, Iran or China, it is conceivable that a post-Brexit Britain might have some mediating role, but this would be very limited. The bigger EU states, in liaison with the Commission where necessary, are perfectly capable of treating with the US themselves. In any case, if Trumpism continues to shape US trade and foreign policy then the UK might find it impossible not to align with the EU. Only where war is on the horizon will London's voice and channels of access to Washington continue to be critical. This might be thought to be a rare occurrence, but the belligerent noises from both Moscow and Washington are not encouraging. Cyber war in particular is on the increase and here Britain's capabilities in intelligence and communications make it a central player for both the US and the EU.

No longer indispensable

Since the end of empire, British foreign policy has been about balancing Europe with the Atlantic partnership, so as to avoid having to choose between the two. This has sometimes been a tricky balancing act, but for the most part it has succeeded. The UK has been important to the

US for its influence in Europe, and to the EU as a leader in foreign and security policy. After Brexit it will be even more anxious to establish close working relationships with both sides, which in Europe means primarily France, its analogue state. But this will not be at all easy to achieve. The British decision to opt out from the whole EU package, only then to seek privileged access to key areas like foreign policy naturally causes irritation inside the EU and bewilderment outside it.

So far as France is concerned, Brexit has sharpened the UK's desire for a partnership at the same time as reducing its leverage. Yet, because Paris is well aware that Germany is not about to transform itself into a heavyweight security player, it will be reluctant to see Britain float away into the distance from the rickety European armada. It also has a need not to be isolated on major international issues like the Middle East, non-proliferation and the fragility of regimes in the Maghreb and sub-Saharan Africa. It does not wish to rely too heavily on the US or to encourage talk of a single European seat in the UN Security Council. France will thus continue to cooperate with the UK and probably not allow trade or migration issues to get in the way. At the same time this cooperation will be more on French terms than in the past. The UK will not get access to informal consultations with EU foreign ministers or with the Commission's External Relations group if France does not wish it. London may hope to use access to other EU Member States to glean information and to get its views across, but the more it plays that game the more it will alienate the one power whose cooperation it most needs. Britain has little option but to rely on France.

As for the United States, its orbit will prove a powerful pull once Britain's independence from the EU is achieved, even when an unappealing president is occupying the White House. For many years British foreign policy revolved around the conceits of enjoying a 'special relationship' with the US and of being a bridge between the two sides of the

Atlantic partnership. The first has had a hollow ring for the last half century, while the second – to the extent that it exists – is now being dismantled by the UK itself. The United States did place particular value on Britain's role in the EU, which is why it supported membership in the first place and opposed (too publicly as it turned out) the idea of Brexit.[25] As Wyn Rees has said, '[w]hen EU initiatives in defence caused palpitations in Washington, it was the United Kingdom that assuaged those fears'.[26] This is not now an option. Rather, Washington may well have to spend time trying to persuade the Europeans to allow Britain within their foreign policy tent.

A specialist in US politics has observed that 'over the medium to long-term Brexit will make the United Kingdom a less appealing country to the United States economically, diplomatically and even in terms of sentiment'.[27] In practice that appeal has come to rest on ever smaller foundations over the years, reduced to areas of defence and intelligence. That in turn has created anxiety in London, distorting the priorities of UK foreign policy, limiting its solidarity with EU partners and reinforcing the belief, in the words of the Chilcot Report, that 'the best way to influence US policy towards the direction preferred by the UK was to commit full and unqualified support'.[28] If that has been true even during Britain's membership of the EU then the pressure to align with Washington will be even stronger in the future – while a decision to resist without the cover provided by the CFSP could leave the government exposed,.

Thus the United Kingdom, which perhaps never was as indispensable a partner to either France or the US as it imagined, will find after Brexit that if it wishes to sustain these two crucial diplomatic relationships it will have to make most of the running. It is one of the many paradoxes of the Leave campaign that its leaders tended either to look for friendship with a global superpower, with whom any relationship is bound to be unequal, or towards the chimera of the global role that Britain was forced to relinquish fifty years ago. The one country most similar to the UK in terms of its international situation is that which seems to incite most suspicion, and even nationalist resentment. Yet just as France continues to protect British interests in Calais and to leave the door open for a change of mind on Brexit, so in the long-term, it might prove to be the UK's most indispensable partner. But the benefits will not be there just for the asking.

7

Nothing Good Out
of Europe?[1]

Whatever the formal position post-Brexit (assuming it
happens) the UK will continue to have vital interests in the
international politics of Europe, both because the actions
of the EU and its members will affect it, and because there
are clear limits to what the UK can achieve on its own in
foreign policy.[2] Conversely, Britain will not have 'regained
control', or taken back sovereignty, because in foreign policy
it never lost them in the first place. The Common Foreign
and Security Policy is an intergovernmental process based
effectively on opt-ins to Common Positions, and with only
trivial elements of majority voting in relation to aspects of
implementation. Moreover, Britain and France, as permanent members of the UN Security Council, have never been
bound to follow agreed CFSP lines in New York.

One real consequence of Brexit, however, is that London
will no longer participate in a systematic, semi-domesticated,
process of coordination between partners. It will have to
revert to conducting 'foreign' relations proper with the
Member States of the EU, with all the freedom and constraints thus implied. Indeed, a greater effort will be required
to liaise with the former partners, both collectively and individually, to ensure that Britain is as close to their thinking

as possible, making diplomacy in Europe a higher priority than it has been since the fall of the Berlin wall. Britain will find itself experiencing what the USA has done for many years: wanting a seat at the CFSP table but being excluded by virtue of not being a Member State. Washington has found various ways round this by using its power and unique ability to create special relationships. Britain will have to try the same tactic but, as a country that has damaged the EU by the decision to leave, and as a mere middle-rank power, it will be more difficult. Indeed, having been part of a de facto leadership group in the CFSP with France and Germany it is already finding itself excluded on occasions from the new 'big two' (or three on occasions, with Italy).[3]

It is true that this is a two-way street, in that Britain's withdrawal will hurt the standing and effectiveness of European foreign policy. The UK is one of the few countries to meet both the UN target of 0.7 per cent of GDP spent on ODA, and NATO's 2 per cent target for defence spending. It is a nuclear weapon state and it is still willing to project military force beyond its frontiers – as Germany and Italy remain reluctant to do. The CFSP will carry less weight without British diplomacy at its heart – and without British diplomats, who have a high reputation among their peers. As a result it is possible, even likely, that the EU will take more refuge in symbolic rather than substantive foreign policy actions. If a more coherent European defence community were to emerge it would still rely on NATO for actual defence, and thus to a significant degree on Britain. Equally, the EU will miss Britain's Department for International Development more than vice versa. On the other hand, Britain's absence should finally force other key Member States to break cover, either by accepting significant foreign policy responsibilities or by acknowledging publicly their unwillingness to do so. In similar vein they will also no longer be able to hide behind London's opposition to majority voting on foreign policy. If they fail to come up to the mark the very aspiration to a European foreign policy

could fade from view, weakening the EU in the world –
which is not in British interests.

Half in, half out

The referendum decision represents a strategic decision
about the country's role in the world, and represents one
of very few occasions in which the British people have had
the chance to have a voice on a foreign policy matter –
although not many saw the choice in those terms. Yet taking
a broad view it seems likely that whatever departure deal
is negotiated, the main changes the UK will experience will
be felt at home, in relation to economics (that is, via changed
patterns of trade and wealth-generation), to regulatory
frameworks, and possibly to immigration. These represent
the significant effects of a structural shift in external relations but are not central to the high politics of international
relations. On foreign and security policy it is quite possible
that the country will end up in a 'same difference' situation
once its departure from the EU has been achieved – half
in, half out.

This view rests on two propositions. First, that the United
Kingdom has effectively been a semi-detached member of
the Union for many years. It has retained full freedom of
movement within the CFSP, and has only the vague obligation to defend Common Positions as part of its national
diplomacy. It has explicit (if rather unnecessary) opt-outs
from the comatose process of defence integration, and has
been able to prevent an operational military headquarters
being set up by the EU. It has obstructed even the discussion of common migration and asylum policies and it has
been able to choose how much or little of its overseas
aid effort to channel through the European Development
Fund. It is out of both the euro and the Schengen system
of open borders.

The second proposition is that where it suits its perceived
interests, the UK can enjoy significant benefits, and low
costs, from the EU's system of intergovernmental foreign

policy cooperation. It has found the Union's standing, instruments and resources indispensable in major issues like the attempt to stabilize the Balkans, sanctions against Russia and the negotiations over Iran's nuclear programme. It has at times promoted European defence collaboration as its own hedge against the dominance of US firms and Washington's occasional periods of detachment from the region. DfID has come to share many aims and projects with the European Commission, just as the Home Office and security services have become reliant on the various joint information systems now in place to counter organized crime and terror attacks.

Thus, even as a current EU member, the UK can be said to be in practice either half out or half in, depending on the viewing angle. Projecting to the years beyond the transition period of Brexit, due at the time of writing to end in December 2020, the May government has already made it clear – after a short period of trying to use British security assets as leverage – that it regards close cooperation with the EU and its Member States as essential for the country's international role going forward. The FCO has pushed this argument strongly even though, as one of its senior staff on the Brussels circuit acknowledged, 'about a third of our diplomats world-wide hardly notice European foreign policy anyway'.[4] As the future is unknowable, one should never rule out the possibility of dramatic change, but it seems highly unlikely that any government is going to want to diverge strategically from the EU in the foreseeable future. If, as a recent Permanent Under-Secretary to the FCO says, it is now not possible to think outside the US, China and the EU as the 'structural sources of global power', then the Europeans have to represent a major part of our external environment, not least because 'they live near us and look out on a similar world'.[5]

A very important issue for the future of British foreign policy is that of the resources it is able to deploy, and to access. The nuclear deterrent has a last-resort function, and it also undeniably bestows a certain kind of status in

international relations. But it is otherwise unusable. The
UK's conventional armed forces are of high quality, despite
cuts and setbacks in the field over the last fifteen years.
They are firmly located within NATO command structures, but have also become used to working with their
French equivalents in ways that would have been regarded
as unthinkable during the Cold War. If the Ministry of
Defence is decidedly less Europeanized than the FCO it
has still come to recognize the benefits of EU missions
like Operation Atalanta in the Indian Ocean, as it has the
various forms of bi- and mini-lateral cooperation within
the European neighbourhood. It will be keen for its major
command centre at Northwood still to have some part to
play in European missions – but that will depend on the EU.
If exclusion occurs from the *Galileo* satellite programme
in which Britain has already invested that will be a blow.
There will also be a wish across government not to let the
dismantling of the UK Permanent Representation to the
EU (UKREP) lower the UK's profile in Brussels. UKREP
will have to be replaced by an embassy to the Union that
could in theory also be accreditated to NATO, but without
enjoying the current inside track to both organizations –
via the double-hatting of its Military Representative in
the Military Committees of NATO and of the EU. It will
need to be sizeable and staffed at the highest levels in
order to monitor the EU effectively from the outside – or
perhaps, on an optimistic view, with one foot keeping the
door ajar.

Beyond the military dimension, unseen by most of those
not professionally involved, are the resources needed to
back up diplomacy, sometimes through exerting leverage,
to contribute to peace-building in particular zones, and
generally to promote a rule-based international order. These
involve both soft and hard power, as the latter is constituted
not just by the military arm but by all means of pressure.
Both the United Kingdom and the European Union possess
important assets for such purposes. The UK has, for example,
a globally respected legal system, an extensive diplomatic

network, and still sufficient politico-economic weight to have its views taken seriously even by the powerful states.

Taken together, however, the EU and its Member States possess markedly more clout, and thus represent an attractive way of amplifying Britain's voice assuming their messages are compatible. The EU will continue to sign up to a range of trade and association agreements, which cannot be ignored whatever the UK manages to do bilaterally. As a far bigger player the EU will always figure more in the thinking of third parties. Its economies of scale in foreign aid, reconstruction, election monitoring, sanctions policy, fisheries, voting in the UN General Assembly and many more things, create a higher profile than a single middle range power could achieve, even allowing for the EU's divisions and inconsistencies. Even more important is the Union's power of attraction, meaning that neighbouring states are drawn into close relationships with many aspiring to accession. Enlargement has slowed down in recent years (with Brexit it will go into reverse) but any future decisions on the remaining Balkan outsiders, or on Switzerland or Norway, to say nothing of the Ukraine and Turkey, would be not only a massive issue for British foreign policy, but also hard to influence from the outside. This would be a bitter pill for London to swallow given its leading role in successive rounds of enlargement from 1981 on.

The fact is that the EU's external relations, indeed its very existence, will continue to loom large for British foreign policy-makers, requiring them to make continuous efforts to stay abreast of the activities of the Commission and the Council. Assuming that feelings of false national pride do not get in the way, governments will find themselves often needing to associate British foreign policy stances with those of their European neighbours. This will particularly apply when money, personnel or diplomatic solidarity need to be deployed – or when they must be denied, as in cases of sanctions short of war.

It also goes without saying that in the efforts to combat transnational crime and terror any state needs to cooperate closely with as many like-minded actors as possible. Migration and terrorism have shown in recent years that the distinction between internal and external politics is blurred and complex. Trying to ensure the safety of the homeland inevitably involves dealing with outsiders. This can be done on a global scale, as via Interpol, but the bigger the group the slower the process and the less secure the data-sharing. This is what makes the EU a near-optimal group for coordination on security and justice issues, given its regional cohesion and institutional sophistication. It seems likely that a symmetry of interests will ensure that here, at least, Britain will be able to remain more inside the tent than out, as other European states will be keen to access its technical and police cooperation. For its part, the UK will continue to need cooperation on extraditions, airport security and counter-terrorism, even without the formal security agreement it is seeking.

For Britain no less than for France, Italy or Spain, the EU's 'freedom, security and justice' issues are inextricably connected to foreign policy. For example, if Western states engage in further interventionist policies in the Middle East or in the Sahel there will probably be blow-backs at home, added to the turbulence in the region, which will make differences between Member States and non-members seem immaterial. Yet that would also bring national foreign policies and bilateralism to the fore, given the weakness of the CFSP when faced with having to go beyond words into the realm of action. This is a reassuring scenario for Brexiters, who can argue that Britain will still be an attractive partner when it is a case of high politics and variable geometry foreign policies.

The issue of bilateral relationships is going to be very prominent for the UK over the years ahead. France in particular is a key imponderable. In many ways foreign policy binds London and Paris together, as the only two European nuclear weapon states and permanent members of the UNSC with global security responsibilities – if not the capacity to live up to them. The two states have had a special – if limited – defence relationship since St Malo in 1998, reinforced by the Lancaster House treaties of 2010. Equally importantly, both have struggled to cope over the last half century with the end of their extensive colonial empires, and with the ties and resentments that still linger. Local geography will also still play an important part, given the likely border issues over trade and migration, together with the vulnerability of Britain to accidents in France's extensive network of nuclear power plants – or simply to disruptions in electricity supplied from them to the UK.[6]

These facts provide an opportunity for the UK to bypass the formal procedures of the CFSP, making up to some degree for its exclusion. Given that France will be, for the foreseeable future, the continent's leading foreign policy player, a close relationship with Paris, cemented by the economies of scale the two states can achieve by acting in tandem, would keep Britain at the heart of Europe's international presence. This possibility has not been lost on either the May or the Macron governments. London has taken the initiative by making every effort to court Paris on foreign and security policy issues. The French government has been cordial in response, but has preferred to compartmentalize the issue, away from the central difficulties arising from the Article 50 process. It has been able to do so because the other side of the coin of bilateralism is that it confers considerable leverage on France, as the state playing on both chessboards – the CFSP, plus bilateral relations. Indeed, while continuing to stress the value of the Lancaster House mechanisms, France has worked with Germany to re-energize the CSDP through the mechanism of a Permanent Structured Cooperation (PESCO) among 25 Member States.[7] It is also now in a strong position finally to take over the position of Deputy SACEUR in NATO from Britain, given the latter's detachment from the EU. As the holder of the post also coordinates ESDP Missions that will have a very practical effect.

The UK may not have a breadth of options but it can play on French ambivalence about Brexit. France will be the EU's only permanent member of the UNSC even if this will not change much in the substance of foreign policy. It will still need to work with Britain in New York. On the downside, it is irritated by the opportunity costs of Brexit, while its new leadership opportunities in European foreign policy will be counter-balanced by more being expected of it once its analogue country has departed. In particular, it could be more exposed to criticism within the EU as the only nuclear weapon state in a group committed to non-proliferation.

France might, therefore, be willing to help the UK associate itself closely with European diplomacy whatever the outcome of the rest of the exit negotiations. For its part the UK cannot afford to distance itself from France, both in terms of the latter's influence over European integration and as the only state with whom it can act in harness – the Balkans in the 1990s, and Libya in 2011 being cases in point. There will not be much leverage in going cap in hand to Washington for a restoration of the US–UK 'special relationship', and little domestic support for that in any case. But a country that aims to substitute bilateralism for collectivism will have to court not just France but also Germany, as the most powerful Member State, able to shape the terms of the eventual Brexit and with a slowly rising willingness to accept a higher foreign policy profile. On Ukraine Britain was outflanked by French and German diplomacy long before the referendum vote. Denmark, Italy, the Netherlands, Poland and Spain, are also obvious targets for a sustained charm offensive.

There are two other motives for Britain avoiding a hard Brexit on the foreign relations side, both of them intractable – Ireland and Gibraltar. The first has become the most significant single obstacle to an overall settlement. It is so because the border between Northern Ireland and the Republic is not just a technical or commercial problem; it has major internal ramifications for the United Kingdom, as the Unionist parties resist any suggestion of their region becoming decoupled from the mainland. But the most important reason for preventing the opposite outcome – that is, a 'hard border' – is to forestall any collapse of the Belfast Agreement on peace in the Six Counties, which would cause turmoil in Northern Ireland and a deterioration of Britain's relations with the Republic. It would be a disaster if the Troubles were to restart, especially in the context of the security problems represented by Jihadist terrorism and an ever more assertive Russia. The issue of a united Ireland, which has been so carefully downplayed on all sides for the last twenty years could easily rear up again with unforeseeable consequences. For that reason (and others) responsible politicians in Dublin and London have a shared interest in emerging from Brexit with an agreement on the border that blurs the distinction between outside and in, from both UK and EU viewpoints.

As for Gibraltar, like all the leftovers from empire, it seems to be at once a minor anomaly and a powerful symbol of identity. The small population of the Rock identifies as British but it also overwhelmingly wants to remain within the EU's Single Market, not least as its economy depends on workers and visitors coming from Spain. In turn, the Madrid government would like, ideally, to bring Gibraltar under its jurisdiction, which Britain would certainly not permit without the agreement of its people. At an early stage, Spain claimed a veto on the overall Brexit negotiations to which some other Member States were sympathetic, although the rhetoric was soon toned down. Whatever agreement is reached, it is clear, as in the Irish case, that it will have to satisfy all three parties to some degree. Britain and Gibraltar must accept in this instance not only that the EU matters, but that they are heavily dependent on it, as indeed on Spain – a country with strong economic links to the UK and an important potential partner after Brexit. The current uncertainties open up risks but also possibilities in relationship to a new deal over Gibraltar, which would satisfy Spanish pride while keeping the inhabitants of the Rock inside the EU to all intents and purposes. With the appropriate spirit of compromise on all sides it could end up as both a British territory and an EU enclave via its close connection to Spain.[8] The similarity to the Northern Irish question is obvious. As both will be hard nuts to crack, it is possible that either or both will end up on the wrong side of a hard border, in which case their future stability cannot be assumed.

The policy process is the area where the day-to-day realities of Brexit in foreign policy become evident to professionals – if not to the public – and will hit hardest. Some practical and pragmatic choices must be made on both sides about the extent of consultation and participation. The EU's treaties, together with the shape of the final exit agreement, will determine the formal scope of British access, but there will be much scope for informal, even undeclared relationships. Intergovernmentalism among the 27 is inherently subject to leaks and to individual Member States breaking collective discipline. This is how the United States has been 'present in one way or another in every EU foreign policy decision', according to one senior European adviser.[9] Britain does not carry the weight of the US, but it will continue to be a neighbour, an experienced ex-participant in the CFSP and a potential support for any European initiative. So the chances of it being able to enjoy what the UK's *Future Partnership Paper* envisaged as 'regular close consultations on foreign and security policy issues, with the option to agree joint positions', are reasonably high.[10] The paper went on to talk about the 'ambitious new partnership' extending to work together on both the 'mandate development' and 'the detailed operational planning' of CSDP missions, in which the UK could still participate.[11] Indeed, the May government, then at least, seemed keener than any of its predecessors to participate in every aspect of European foreign policy-making. The former Conservative Foreign Secretary Lord Hague went so far as to suggest that Britain should seek to remain a member of the EU's key Political and Security Committee (PSC), if only as an observer, while seconding various experts to the European External Action Service, something that his government had been distinctly lukewarm about in its early years.[12] Much of this is little more than whistling to keep spirits up.

The new policy process will have its own challenges, however it turns out. As Sir Peter Ricketts, one of Britain's most experienced diplomats of recent years, has asked: 'with all the effort needed for the multiple sets of negotiations arising from Brexit, will the Government have the band-width for an active foreign policy as well?'[13] This is partly a matter of psychological and political distraction – the Brexit project has turned the UK inwards, plaguing it with severe internal divisions that are likely to continue for some time to come. But it is also a question of personnel. There has been an urgent move to recruit the large numbers of trade negotiators and the other civil servants who have not been needed these last four decades because of the EU's competence in commercial policy. The government is thus desperate to use all those in its administration – i.e. not just the Diplomatic Service – who have the ability to liaise with Brussels and with Britain's ex European partners. They are needed to work on the huge complexities of disengage-ment from the EU, on negotiations with third countries and on reputational damage-limitation world-wide. The tasks will last at least until the end of the transition period in December 2020 and probably well beyond it. Evidently many British people still view Europeans as foreigners; now those acting on behalf of the state will have to make the same assumption. All this will draw resources away from new international initiatives and 'global responsibilities', which will fall to the bottom of the list of priorities.

In terms of other international organizations, particularly the international financial institutions (IFIs) and the UN, with its committees and specialized agencies, Britain will retain its standing and ability to work with other European states. But unless a special deal can be agreed it will suffer from not having direct access to the EEAS and its growing portfolio of EU 'embassies' around the world, which have a high profile in most capitals where they are established. Moreover, if the Eurozone were to make progress, leading to the EU having a formal presence and voting rights in the IMF and the World Bank, Britain would inevitably seem marginalized, however healthy Sterling might be. It simply does not have the economic weight to deal on equal terms with the EU or the US.

Taking all the above issues of sovereignty, resources, partners and logistics into account, it seems likely that Brexit will not make such a huge difference to the substance of foreign and security policy, although it will amount to a major change in the policy-making process. Yet, if the UK ends up remaining 'half in', this will not be precisely the same as being a Member State half out. And being half in will only happen on certain conditions, viz: (1) the UK remains content to be semi-'Europeanized' in foreign policy – as it was relieved to be during the March 2018 crisis over the Skripal poisoning; (2) The EU plays ball by giving the UK special access to the CFSP mechanisms; (3) the development of the CSDP does not create tensions over the impact on NATO; (4) the external economic relations of the EU do not lead to a diverging of interests in the G7 and the IFIs, or over their use for political sanctions. This is a more significant point than it might seem. It would be a mistake for the UK to assume that foreign policy is only formulated in the PSC; COREPER and the Commission are arguably just as important given their management of the resources of the Union.

The givens of UK foreign policy

The fall-out from the 2016 referendum has been hugely distracting at all levels of British politics and policy. Eventually the dust will settle, as it always does, but leaving open the question of continuity with the past. A central part of that is the relationship with the EU, but equally important are the substantive aims of British foreign policy. Through history, sunk costs and long-established patterns of behaviour, we can identify the 'givens', or slow-changing characteristics of the UK's situation, which might endure despite the shock of Brexit. After all, the British outlook on world politics has now been stable for nearly half a century, accepting that the Euro-Atlantic region was its 'area of concentration', as the Duncan Report put it in 1969.[14] Any activity further afield would be exceptional, as in the rapid defeat of Saddam Hussein (largely by the US) in 1991. It was only the over-confidence of the Blair years that led Britain back into war in Mesopotamia and Afghanistan, difficult terrain even at the height of the empire. Now, the balance between the two legs of the structure has been thrown askew by the popular rejection of Europe. It may turn out to be remediable, as foreign policy elites in the UK and the EU almost certainly hope, but that is going to take a great deal of effort, stamina and finesse.[15]

A central issue for many is that of Britain's status and power in the world. Cases here are made on both sides of the Brexit argument. On the one hand, it is argued that being outside the EU is bound to leave the country marginalized in international politics; on the other is the view that it will free up the UK to return to a free-ranging global role, unhampered by a sclerotic, failing, European project. Only time will tell, although it seems certain that other states will be asking questions about the ability of the UK to exert influence by itself, or through shaping EU positions from the outside. More interesting perhaps is the sociological, even philosophical, question about the impact of Brexit on the attitudes of the British themselves – will there be a gradual lowering of expectations as to the country's importance in the world, or could expectations even rise? Will the view that being a great power is 'part of the habit and furniture of our minds' survive the loss of the platform that was intended to ensure continued international status after the end of empire?[16] Will there be a further move away from the values and interests of Europe, in favour of like-minded but more far-flung societies?

Who are 'the British' in this context? Apart from the obvious divisions between elite and mass, and between Leavers and Remainers, there is the generational divide between older citizens who may have had little experience of continental countries, and younger people more comfortable with a European identity through the great increase in educational, work and leisure mobility over the last two decades. But in a population of 64 million there are also large minorities from many countries, European and beyond. This multiculturalism creates, by definition, many global links, and some entrenched differences of outlook. Some derive from EU Member States, such as the sizeable communities from France, Italy, Poland, Spain and Romania; but these are relatively recent arrivals with few yet eligible to vote in UK elections. The same is likely to be true of some of the African diasporas, such as the Nigerians or Somalis. They will not have much of an influence on the political orientation of the UK in the world one way or the other, More established, however, are those with their origins in Pakistan and the Indian sub-continent. After forty years or so these are mostly fully integrated as British citizens, but they are also 'post-migrants', i.e. those into their second and third generations, with significant remaining attachments to their forebears' homelands. In comparison their experience of continental Europe and connections to its culture are flimsy. The EU project may seem just as remote to them as it does to traditionalist British nationalists. Insofar as they have political influence therefore, they will be inclined to encourage an outwards turn towards the wider world – not the Anglosphere, to be sure, but not incompatible with that set of ties either.

Any orientation is bound, however, to be affected by power and any changes in it post-Brexit. At the level of perceptions it seems inevitable that the UK will be seen by those outside the European region as less important simply because it has cut itself off from the world's biggest trade bloc and one of the poles of an evolving multipolar world. With nearly half the country dismayed, seeing the decision to leave as an historic act of self-harm, that is hardly surprising. But this impression might turn out to be ephemeral, especially if Britain emerges from the transition to show signs of renewal. Critical here will be the attitudes of the three major powers of the international system – the United States, China, Russia – and the relationships that a post-EU Britain manages to establish with them. It is not easy for an upper middle range power with a relatively small population to deal with such behemoths, which was one of the attractions of EC membership for Britain in the first place. Going into the conference chamber alone – if not naked then certainly without its usual protective coat – will be a big challenge.

It is a given that the UK needs to engage with these three powers. But what can be realistically expected, without the shelter provided by the European group? The United States will remain a key ally, and become even more important to London unless there is some unforeseeable upheaval. At the same time, because the asymmetry of the relationship will be more pronounced, caution will be needed when views differ, whatever the pressures of domestic opinion or economic interests. The United States is at once a saviour and a problem for all its allies, creating dilemmas of dependence that are best managed collectively. For its part, Washington's preferred approach is to pursue a soft form of divide and rule through bilateral dealings, while encouraging the key players to exercise leadership along its preferred lines. Once outside the EU, Britain will not be able to play the European leadership card, while it will also be more exposed to US pressure. Its habitual claim to represent a 'bridge' between the two parts of the Atlantic community will necessarily fall by the wayside.

No one has ever argued that Britain can achieve a 'special' relationship with the People's Republic of China, although David Cameron did talk about a 'golden era' in bilateral relations during the visit of Xi Jinping in 2015. Furthermore, the two states' signatures to the 1997 Treaty on the status of Hong Kong does bind them in principle to some shared responsibilities. But it is all too evident that Britain lacks the strength to prevent China from gradually squeezing the life out of democracy in Hong Kong, while its own commercial interests there and on the mainland inhibit any tendency to fall out with Beijing. China's huge market can no more be ignored by an independent Britain than can Saudi Arabia's, while the benefits to be had from its tourist and student visitors, or from inward investment, mean that political objectives, say on human rights or on the uses of Chinese military power, are unlikely to take front rank. Beijing is well aware of the limits of British power in east Asia. The UK is not alone in this; the European economies all compete with each other for commercial advantage in the Chinese market, and even the EU acting together is not able to exert serious pressure on China in the political–military sphere. But whereas EU membership confers some strength in numbers against both China and the United States – and the possibility of standing aside if the two were to clash – Britain will be exposed. In difficult circumstances it would need to shelter under either or both of the European and American diplomatic umbrellas, at whatever price might be demanded.

These are scenarios for the future, but in the case of Russia the United Kingdom seems already to have been subject to an attempt to exploit its new uncertainties. During the 2018 clash over the poisoning of Sergei and Yulia Skripal in Salisbury, the Kremlin clearly thought that the strong British reaction would not be supported by other European governments. It received an unpleasant surprise when the European Council not only gave Prime Minister May unanimous support in her condemnation of Russia as the culprit, but sent a further strong signal by withdrawing the EU's Ambassador to Moscow 'for consultations' – the first time this kind of state-like action had been taken at the collective level. This seems to augur well for a country that wants to leave the Union but still enjoy the solidarity of the European club in foreign affairs. On the other hand, the circumstances at this point were very particular. Russia seemed guilty of an outrageously contemptuous disregard of national sovereignty, while the EU-27 quickly saw the advantage in a friendly gesture towards Britain at the precise moment that the Brexit negotiations were entering their decisive phase. Where in 2016 the May government had threatened to withdraw British security cooperation if the EU were to be difficult on other matters, now the boot was on the other foot. Having received vital diplomatic support against Russia, the UK might find it more difficult to stand firm on all of its red lines in the exit negotiations to follow.

The Putin regime has shown its hostility towards Britain with increasing frequency, with the two countries often engaged in an escalation of rhetoric, leading occasionally to tit-for-tat diplomatic expulsions. It is difficult not to see the Skripal poisoning as a case of Moscow assuming British weakness, or at least as a test of its resolve in its new circumstances. As the UK is hardly the only state to be at odds with Putin this could lead to a standoff with the West in a form of Cold War revival. If so, then being outside the EU will matter little. But British governments will have to handle relations with Russia carefully so as to avoid becoming detached from their allies in a conflict that could ratchet up spending on defence and security without obvious ways of reining in the kind of indirect aggression that is now Russia's preferred *modus operandi*.

Relations with the three major powers will thus remain a central part of Britain's foreign policy landscape, but decision-makers will have fewer instruments to manage them. They will also not be able so easily to play the game, routine for the bigger EU states, of switching between unilateral measures and collective diplomacy as suits them. The same is true for the deeper partnerships that the UK must seek to build with countries outside Europe as it seeks to rethink its place in the world, initially driven by the need for trade agreements. These third parties will gain some leverage on foreign policy matters in proportion to Britain's economic interests in them. Given the Commonwealth network, Australia, Canada, India and New Zealand will be prominent, representing a poignant reversal of their role as petitioners when Britain was negotiating to join the EC in 1970. Other key states that British diplomacy will have to court, thus inherently demonstrating its increased weakness, are Brazil, Japan, Mexico, South Africa and South Korea.

The main trope associated with the new policy of outreach is that of 'global Britain'.[17] Together with the more parochial idea of the Anglosphere, this was savaged by critics before it had even got off the ground, as 'a slogan masquerading as a policy'.[18] A Report from the Foreign Affairs Select Committee of the House of Commons pointed out the lack of strategy behind the aspiration.[19] Such scepticism arises first because in a world inter-connected on multiple levels it is no longer plausible for Britain to present itself as uniquely qualified to act as a hub between differing regions and groupings. Second, a country that chooses to detach itself from its own region inevitably loses some plausibility. Third, Britain is already struggling to find the resources to support foreign and defence policies. Fourth, the inability to live up to the claim to be a global player will create a credibility gap and further reputational damage.

At one level it is a given that Britain must have a global *perspective* and look for profits wherever they might be found. Moreover, as an ex-Ambassador to both the European Communities and to the UN has observed 'Britain has been a global country for about 500 years. It did not become less so when it joined the European Union, and it will not become more so when we leave.'[20] Yet an admirably outward-looking identity plus the desire to find substitutes for dependence on the EU do not translate straightforwardly into a new world role or a sustaining set of new relationships worldwide. At the very least such a change will be long drawn out and hard won; at the most it will prove a will o' the wisp, leading governments astray. In the pol-mil sphere at least the idea of global Britain has little content.

One foreign policy given that causes the more populist Brexiters difficulties is the fact that Britain cannot do without multilateralism in some form. Leaving aside the EU's own networks the UK is entangled in a web of overlapping international institutions of which the most notable are

NATO, the Commonwealth, the OECD, the G7 and the G20, besides the elaborate UN system. None of these raises the spectre of a loss of sovereignty that so many dislike the EU for, and all are compatible with a 'global' outlook. They are sure to remain part of the pattern of British international relations. Their cross-cutting nature provides plenty of scope for ad hoc, issue-based, coalitions. This could be important for actions like economic sanctions – Britain can hardly impose them on its own, and when the EU is reluctant its options will be restricted.

Coalition-building is also inherent to the pursuit of 'milieu' goals such as the management of climate change, where global agreements are indispensable. At the same time Britain is likely to continue being a candidate for the various Quads and Quints that exist as shadowy contact groups, cutting across the formal institutions on security matters. The 'Five Eyes' intelligence grouping is a prominent case in point. Still, none of these groups engages in foreign *policy-making*, let alone constitutes an enduring diplomatic system to rival that of the CFSP, for all its rickety nature. What is more, since Britain's primary security interests are regional and not global, it has to fall back not only on NATO for defence, but also on the EU as the political and economic stabilizer of Europe and its neighbourhood. The UK's residual multilateralism is therefore essential for economic and functional cooperation, for peacekeeping under international law, and for cultural links, but it represents more a set of overlapping frameworks than a platform for relaunching a world role.

European despite itself – the limits of Brexit

Brexit was only indirectly about foreign policy, even if many saw the European Union as a foreign intrusion into British democracy. Foreign policy in the sense of a role in the world was also at stake in terms of the image of the country having an 'independent voice' and perhaps a degree of nostalgia for links to Commonwealth countries. But the debate that raged before the referendum, and continued after it, focused mostly on migration, economics, sovereignty and Northern Ireland. There has been little discussion of what the UK should be doing in the world, of the scope of its influence, of the main challenges to its interests or of the best ways of protecting them.

There can be little doubt, however, that these issues are at stake, not just in the negotiations over British departure, but for the future of the country outside the Union. Theresa May's government soon came to realize this, taking a strong line in urging the EU to accept a close and special partnership on foreign and security issues that resembles very closely the status quo of membership.[21] It is revealing that those in favour of a hard Brexit did not train their sights on this, perhaps realizing the lack of serious alternatives. Yet this is a major moment of historical change, when the traditional British approach of gradualism and the avoidance of choice has to be put to one side. The decisions taken before the end of the 'transition period' have the potential to shape the orientation and impact of UK foreign policy for the next half century, as did those after the last application for entry in 1969.

Much will depend on how far Britain wishes – and is able – to stay closely aligned with its erstwhile partners in the formulation of foreign policy, both pro-actively and under crisis conditions. Richard Whitman has identified three broad options: integrated player, associated partner, and detached observer.[22] The first would entail achieving special status as a member of the key EU bodies, the Foreign Affairs Council and the Political and Security Committee, which would amount to successful 'cherry-picking' by the UK, and at least in this area the softest of soft Brexits. In contrast, the 'detached observer' position is conceivable if negotiations with the EU turn sour, and/or a British government decides that it does not like the positions being adopted in the event of a more coherent and effective EU foreign policy. Neither of these scenarios seems very plausible.

The most likely outcome is that of some form of bespoke partnership, which would be consistent both with the EU's insistence that associates cannot enjoy the full fruits of membership, and with the facts on the ground of Britain's many shared interests with its neighbours. This too would avoid a revolution in UK foreign policy, but it would place a huge onus on the FCO to ensure that the British voice was still heard, despite being outside the corridors of power and discussion. Britain has now been participating for 48 years in Europe's system of diplomatic coordination. The system has proved conveniently loose; often dysfunctional but still ultimately indispensable as a multiplier of the resources of individual states, especially those like Britain trying to slow their descent from power. It enables collective action on critical issues like the Iran negotiations and the use of the EU's considerable economic and technical resources for both sticks and carrots. The prospect of London standing aside while the majority of Europeans confer on matters from Algeria to the Ukraine, from North Korea to the Israeli settlements, is both bizarre and dismaying. But that is the logic of Brexit.

International relations is a realm where change is slow until some thunderbolt – say 9.11, Brexit itself or the election of Donald Trump – arrives from a clear blue sky to overturn conventional thinking. So, although at present it seems that Britain has nowhere to go if it floats away from the European foreign policy system, it is still possible that new scenarios will emerge. One radical possibility, seen as likely by some, is the eventual implosion of the EU.[23] If that happens the nation-state might be strengthened, but it might equally be weakened. Military power might become critical if shadows descend once again over Europe, or the opposite could happen, whereby economic strength and soft power in a 'neo-medieval' set of cross-cutting networks, could turn out to be a society's greatest assets. Britain has held onto its nuclear weapons and still has more powerful conventional forces than most, while it disposes of a wide range of soft power assets. On the other hand, although still a rich country it seems likely that its economy will come under ever greater pressure to remain globally competitive in the decades to come.

The trouble is that policy has to be made in the short term, and on the basis of no more than medium term planning. The only commitment made on the basis of remote and theoretical contingencies is to the nuclear deterrent. Given this, the United Kingdom has to make some serious choices about its foreign policy needs, which in turn will affect the whole tenor of the Brexit negotiations and their eventual outcome. And the decisions will not be the UK's alone. The 27 EU Member States will not make things easy for the UK, even if many of them recognize its value as a foreign policy partner.

The underlying choice is a technical but also a cultural one: does Britain as a society feel ultimately more comfortable being independent within the wider group of Western democracies – the OECD world? Or does it still identify with its regional community to the point of accepting the need for diplomatic solidarity in an uncertain and at times dangerous external environment? This is the question that has been overlaid and confused by both Eurosceptics and integrationists, who insist on debating ultimate ends. Left to its own devices it is unlikely that the UK will compensate by increasing its spending significantly on its resources for external policy, particularly in the hugely expensive area of defence. British relative power in the world will decline, robbed of such economies of scale as are currently available to it. Indeed, if the EU – or its inner core – ever does succeed in becoming a major foreign policy player then Britain would finally have to face its worst historical nightmare: that of a united continental power that it was not capable of balancing.

It seems probable that the interests on both sides of the negotiating table will recognize that Britain needs to be kept as close as possible to the processes of EU foreign policy coordination. But whatever the legal position after the exit documents are signed off the UK will continue to have vital interests in the international politics of Europe, and to be connected in multiple ways to its neighbouring states. The tragedy is – unless Brexit can be reversed – that both British and European foreign policies will end up distinctly worse after their divorce. The two sides are now locked into a prisoners' dilemma in which the only issue is how to minimize the level of damage. On the upside, perhaps it is only through such turmoil that fundamental rethinking can take place about what Britain needs foreign policy for in the first place. Is it aiming to be an independent great power again? Can it be? Should it be? Do its citizens care?

Further Reading

Brexit has produced a mass of material both published and on-line, although the number of books on the subject is as yet limited. In order to understand the changing context of British foreign policy it is best to start with some general works that can provide the historical and European background. An excellent overview of British Foreign Policy since 1945 is that by Sanders and Houghton (2017). It is well complemented by Gaskarth (2013), which brings insights from constructivism to bear on a range of contemporary issues. The grand historical sweep on view in Simms (2016) shows how the European Union is only the latest in a long line of British entanglements with Europe.

Detailed accounts of Britain's up and down relationship with the European Union can be found variously in Geddes (2013) and Smith (2017). Young (1998) is something of a classic. A shrewd and informed history of the European project itself can be found in Gilbert (2012), while the tortuous story of European foreign policy cooperation is traced in Hill and Smith (2000). Tocci (2017) is a fascinating account of the EU's latest attempt to give itself an international strategy. Two insightful and well-written accounts by practitioners deeply involved in British European policy are Wall (2008) and Hannay (2013).

In terms of how Britain managed to stumble into a referendum on membership, and into a decision to leave, MacShane (2016) is a readable and well-informed account from someone who observed at close quarters many of the political players in both main parties. Evans and Menon (2017) is also essential for placing the vote in the context of the changing British political environment. Emerson (2015) is a succinct and expert account of the issues at stake, as analysed through the 'balance of competences' review that the British government launched in 2012 as 'an audit of what the EU does and how it affects the UK'. The reasoned findings of that review (and of Emerson's book) seem to have had little effect on the campaign of 2016. Thompson (2017) is an incisive analysis of how structural problems in political economy created the conditions for a split from the EU. As for the vote itself, the most authoritative publication yet is that by Clarke, Goodwin and Whiteley, though no doubt many more are in the pipeline. Oliver (2018) manages to cover the before, the during and the after both concisely and in detail.

On the new diplomatic era opened by the Brexit vote Armstrong (2017) provides a forensic account of the issues at stake in the negotiations from a politically-aware specialist in European law. Martill and Staiger (2018) have collected together a comprehensive set of essays dealing with the issues, the actors, the institutions and the implications of this crisis. Owen and Ludlow (2017), two authors who voted differently in the referendum, attempt to show that Britain can move forward constructively from here on a range of issues to provide a valuable 'independent voice' in the world. Interestingly, they do not refer to the Commonwealth, let alone the Anglosphere, which some Brexiters have looked hopefully towards. Kenny and Pearce (2018) argue that while neither are a feasible alternative to the EU it is only by understanding what they represent that we can explain why Britain came to the point of wishing to leave the European Union. Niblett (2015) and Whitman (2016) have outlined the theoretical choices that lie before the UK as it attempts to square its various circles.

As for some of the particular issues dealt with in this book, Gamble (2003) is still worth reading as a perceptive account of Britain's attempts to balance its European and transatlantic identities. It was also prescient in its focus on the English question, which has been so important in mobilising anti-EU sentiment. Dumbrell (2006) is the best history of what he carefully calls 'an' ever-diminishing 'special relationship', though it now needs updating. For Franco–British relations see Tombs and Tombs (2006), which looks at the *longue durée*, and Bell (1997), which covers the post-war period. Goodhart (2013, 2017) is indispensable for anyone wishing to understand the part that European immigration has played in the rise of populist attitudes towards Europe. Hill (2013) traces the ways in which foreign policy has interacted with multicultural society in Britain and other European countries, and how the European Union has only watched from the sidelines.

Much useful material is to be found on the websites of key think tanks. First among equals is *The UK in a Changing Europe,* funded by the Economic and Social Research Council and run by Professor Anand Menon, who has brought together a powerful team of academic experts able to provide accessible material for the British public. Chatham House, aka the Royal Institute of International Affairs, is as always an authoritative independent voice on matters of European and global affairs. The Centre for European Research, while never disguising its sympathies, is still Britain's best and most enduring source for specialist expertise on the EU and its external relations. Outside the UK, the Centre for European Policy Studies and the European Policy Centre, both in Brussels, provide a regular stream of valuable briefs and commentaries. Needless to say, keeping up with events also requires reading the serious press, even in the age of social media. The British government's websites seem to be designed to be unhelpful, although persistence usually means that one can get through to helpful experts in places like the National Audit Office or the Office for National Statistics.

References for
Further Reading

Armstrong, Kenneth A. (2017), *Brexit Time: How, Why and When* (Cambridge: Cambridge University Press).

Bell, P. M. H. (1997), *France and Britain, 1940–1994: The Long Separation* (London: Longman).

Clarke, Harold D., Goodwin, Matthew and Whiteley, Paul (2017), *Brexit: Why Britain Voted to Leave the European Union* (Cambridge: Cambridge University Press).

Dumbrell, John (2006), *A Special Relationship: Anglo-American Relations from the Cold War to Iraq* (Houndmills: Palgrave Macmillan).

Emerson, Michael, ed. (2015), *Britain's Future in Europe: Reform, Renegotiation, Repatriation or Secession?* (Lanham, MD: Rowman & Littlefield for the European Centre for Policy Studies).

Evans, Geoffrey and Menon, Anand (2017), *Brexit and British Politics* (Cambridge: Polity).

Gamble, Andrew (2003), *Between Europe and America: The Future of British Politics* (Houndmills: Palgrave Macmillan).

Gaskarth, Jamie (2013), *British Foreign Policy* (Cambridge: Polity).

Geddes, Andrew (2013), *Britain and the European Union* (London: Palgrave Macmillan).

Gilbert, Mark (2012), *A History of European Integration* (Lanham, MD: Rowman & Littlefield).

Goodhart, David (2013) *The British Dream: Successes and Failures of Post-war Immigration* (London: Atlantic Books).

Goodhart, David (2017), *The Road to Somewhere: The Populist Revolt and the Future of Politics* (London: Hurst).

Hannay, David (2013), *Britain's Quest for a World Role: A Diplomatic Memoir from Europe to the UN* (London: I. B. Tauris).

Hill, Christopher and Smith, Karen E., eds. (2000), *European Foreign Policy: Key Documents* (London: Routledge, in association with the Secretariat of the European Parliament).

Hill, Christopher (2013), *The National Interest in Question: Foreign Policy in Multicultural Societies* (Oxford: Oxford University Press).

Kenny, Michael and Pearce, Nick (2018), *Shadows of Empire: The Anglosphere in British Politics* (Cambridge: Polity).

MacShane, Denis (2016), *Brexit: How Britain left Europe*, 2nd edn (London: I. B. Tauris).

Martill, Benjamin and Staiger, Uta, eds. (2018), *Brexit and Beyond: Rethinking the Futures of Europe* (London: UCL Press).

Niblett, Robin (2015), *Britain, Europe and the World: Rethinking the UK's Circles of Influence* (London: Chatham House).

Oliver, Tim (2018), *Understanding Brexit: A Concise Introduction* (Abingdon: Policy Press).

Owen, David and Ludlow, David (2017) *British Foreign Policy after Brexit; An Independent Voice* (London: Biteback Publishing).

Sanders, David and Houghton, David Patrick (2017), *Losing an Empire, Finding a Role: British Foreign Policy since 1945*, 2nd edn (London: Palgrave Macmillan).

Simms, Brendan (2016), *Britain's Europe: A Thousand Years of Conflict and Cooperation* (London: Allen Lane).

Smith, Julie (2017), *Britain's Journeys into and out of the European Union: Destinations Unknown* (London: Routledge).

Thompson, Helen (2017), 'Inevitability and contingency: the political economy of Brexit', *British Journal of Politics and International Relations*, 19:3.

Tocci, Nathalie (2017), *Framing the EU Global Strategy: A Stronger Europe in a Fragile World* (London: Palgrave).

Tombs, Isabelle and Tombs, Robert (2006), *That Sweet Enemy: The French and the British from the Sun King to the Present* (London: Heinemann).

Wall, Stephen (2008), *A Stranger in Europe: Britain and the EU from Thatcher to Blair* (Oxford: Oxford University Press).

Whitman, Richard (2016), 'Foreign and security policy post-Brexit: future models of EU–UK cooperation', *National Institute Economic Review* 238: 43–50.

Young, Hugo (1998), *This Blessed Plot: Britain and Europe from Churchill to Blair* (London: Macmillan).

Notes

1 Brexit and UK Foreign Policy

1 Andrew Shonfield (1973), *Europe – Journey to an Unknown Destination* (London: Allen Lane).
2 Anand Menon et al. (2017), *Red, Yellow and Blue Brexit: The Manifestos Uncovered* (Swindon, Economic and Social Research Council: 'The UK in a Changing Europe' project).
3 Michael Emerson, ed. (2016), *Britain's Future in Europe: The Known Plan A to Remain and the Unknown Plan B to Leave* (London: Rowman & Littlefield for the Centre of European Policy Studies), pp. 150–1.
4 Jamie Gaskarth (2013), *British Foreign Policy* (Cambridge: Polity).
5 Brendan Simms (2016), *Britain's Europe: A Thousand Years of Conflict and Cooperation* (London: Allen Lane).
6 Julie Smith (2017), *Britain's Journeys into and out of the European Union: Destinations Unknown* (London: Routledge).
7 Malcolm Chalmers (2018), 'Brexit and European Security', RUSI Briefing Paper (London: RUSI); Kenneth A. Armstrong (2017), *Brexit Time: How, Why and When* (Cambridge: Cambridge University Press).
8 Benjamin Martill and Uta Staiger, eds. (2018), *Brexit and Beyond: rethinking the Futures of Europe* (London: UCL Press). On foreign policy see in particular the chapters by

Amelia Hadfield, 'Britain against the world? Foreign and Security Policy in the "age of Brexit"', and by the present author, 'Turning back the clock: the illusion of a global political role for Britain'.

9 Mark Powell (2017), 'Anti-Europeanism in contemporary American discourses: the media 2001–2011', PhD thesis, University of Cambridge.

10 Harold Macmillan is supposed to have replied 'events, dear boy, events' when asked what he most feared in politics, while James Callaghan was careful to monitor personally remote places like the Falkland Islands, which he feared could produce an unexpected crisis. Peter Hennessy (2000), *The Prime Minister* (London: Penguin), pp. 389–91.

11 The phrase occurs in the lyrics of John Lennon's song 'Beautiful Boy' (1980) although it may first have appeared in the *Readers Digest* in 1957, attributed to Allen Saunders. https://en.wikipedia.org/wiki/Beautiful_Boy_(Darling_Boy)

12 Robin Niblett (2015), 'Britain, Europe and the World: Rethinking the UK's Circles of Influence' (London: Chatham House Research Paper), https://www.chathamhouse.org/sites/files/chathamhouse/20151019BritainEuropeWorldNiblettFinal.pdf

13 See the insider accounts of two British iconoclasts of rather different casts: Carne Ross (2017), *Independent Diplomat: Dispatches from an Unaccountable Elite* (London: Hurst); Tom Fletcher (2016), *The Naked Diplomat: Understanding Power and Politics in the Digital Age* (London: Harper Collins).

14 Maurizio Carbone (2017) in Christopher Hill, Michael Smith and Sophie Vanhoonacker, eds. *International Relations and the European Union*, 3rd edn, p. 305.

15 *Guardian*, 27 January 2017. Of 890,000 British passport-holders living elsewhere in the EU about 189,000 are aged over 65, according to the Office of National Statistics.

16 See the account by a British citizen selected by Palestinian terrorists for execution on the basis of his passport: Michael, J. Thexton (2006), *What Happened to the Hippy Man? Hijack Survivor* (Richmond: Lanista).

17 https://ec.europa.eu/home-affairs/what-we-do/policies/borders-and-visas/visa-policy#stats

18 David Sanders and David Patrick Houghton (2017), *Losing an Empire, Finding a Role: British Foreign Policy since 1945*, 2nd edn (London: Palgrave Macmillan).

19 Fred Northedge (1974), *Descent from Power: British Foreign Policy 1945–73* (Hemel Hempstead: Allen & Unwin).

20 Denis MacShane (2016), *Brexit: How Britain left Europe,* 2nd edn (London: I. B. Tauris), pp. 108–25.

21 In May 2018 an incident occurred that was revealing of the identity dilemmas thrown up by modern international relations. The German Premiership footballers Mesut Özil, Ilkay Gündoğan and Cenk Tosun met President Erdoğan of Turkey during his visit to London, presenting him with signed shirts. On being criticized by human rights campaigners the three responded that they had only been showing courtesy to 'their president', which unleashed a further wave of criticism on the grounds that their actual president was Hans-Walter Steinmeier of the Federal Republic of Germany. 'Özil and Gündoğan's Erdoğan picture causes anger in Germany', *Guardian*, 16 May 2018. In their next international match they were booed by some German fans.

2 Falling Back on Europe

1 Pithily summarized in cultural terms by Denis MacShane (2016) in his *Brexit: How Britain left Europe*, pp. xxii–xxiv. MacShane regretfully concludes that Britain is not (any longer) European.

2 This is and always has been a matter of perception. One hundred and twenty years ago Joseph Chamberlain called for an alliance with Germany because 'We find our system of justice, we find our literature, we find the very base and foundation on which our language is established, the same in the two countries'. Speech in Leicester 30 November 1899, in James Joll (1967) ed., *Britain and Europe: Pitt to Churchill, 1793–1940* (Oxford: The Clarendon Press).

3 Michael Howard (1972), *The Continental Commitment* (London: Temple Smith), pp. 9–52; Max Beloff (1969), *Britain's Liberal Empire, 1897–1921* (London: Methuen), p. 90.

4 Christopher Hill (2013), *The National Interest in Question: Foreign Policy in Multicultural Societies* (Oxford: Oxford University Press).

5 Brendan Simms (2007), *Three Victories and a Defeat: The Rise and Fall of the First British Empire, 1714–1783* (London: Allen Lane), p. 672.

6 Brendan Simms (2016), *Britain's Europe: A Thousand Years of Conflict and Cooperation* (London: Allen Lane), pp. 130–42.

7 Templewood, Viscount (Sir Samuel Hoare) (1954), *Nine Troubled Years* (London: Collins), p. 129.

8 Zara Steiner (2005), *The Lights that Failed: European International History 1919–1933* (Oxford: Oxford University Press), pp. 610, 617–18.

9 Mark Gilbert (2012), *A History of European Integration* (Lanham, MD: Rowman & Littlefield), pp. 9–59.

10 It is worth noting that even in the dark days of late 1940 discussion had taken place in Cabinet about how war aims might need to include thinking about the future reorganization of Europe, whether on federal or confederal lines – in anticipation of Churchill's famous Zurich speech of 1946. See Christopher Hill (1991), *Cabinet Decisions on Foreign Policy: the British Experience October 1938 – June 1941* (Cambridge: Cambridge University Press), pp. 193, 195–6, 206, 210, 216.

11 See Susan Strange's still thought-provoking article (1971), 'Sterling and British policy: A political view', *International Affairs*, 47:2, 302–15.

12 Julie Smith (2017), *The UK's Journeys into and out of the EU: Destinations Unknown* (Abingdon: Routledge), pp. 7–24.

13 Richard Neustadt (1970), *Alliance Politics* (New York: Columbia University Press). President Kennedy agreed favourable financial terms (though ones constraining Britain's actual use of the system) partly out of a desire not to cause Prime Minister Macmillan political difficulties.

14 Harold Wilson (1971), *The Labour Government 1964–1970* Harmondsworth: Penguin Books), pp. 442–69, 619–24.

15 Simon Nuttall (1992), *European Political Co-operation* (Oxford: The Clarendon Press), p. 54.

16 Bernard Porter (1975), *The Lion's Share: a Short History of British Imperialism*, pp. 353–4. Cited in Paul Kennedy (1984), *Strategy and Diplomacy 1870–1945* (London: Fontana), p. 201.

17 David Edgerton (1996), 'The "white heat" revisited. The British government and technology in the 1960s', *Twentieth Century British History*, 7:1, 53–82. It should not be forgotten that Wilson was also the first economist to occupy 10 Downing Street.

18 *House of Lords Debates* 16 July 1969 vol. 304 cc282–5. This summarizes the government's immediate response to the Report.

19 Report of the Review Committee on Overseas Representation (Cmnd 4107, 1969) (Duncan Committee Report), available in the National Archives.

20 The Berrill Report is formally entitled 'Review of Overseas Representation'. It was conducted by the Central Policy Review Staff, a para-governmental ginger group based in the Cabinet Office and composed of young talent under the chairmanship of Sir Kenneth Berrill – an academic economist before he served in the Treasury. Henderson's private dispatch to the Foreign Secretary was soon leaked and appeared in full in *The Economist*, 2 June 1979. The quotation here is from p. 12 of the original document, sent to the Foreign Secretary on 31 March 1979, to be found online in the Thatcher Archive of Churchill College Cambridge. http://www.margaretthatcher.org/document/110961

21 Christopher Hill (1988), 'The historical background: past and present in British foreign policy', in Michael Smith, Steve Smith and Brian White, eds. (1988), *British Foreign Policy: Tradition, Change and Transformation* (London: Unwin Hyman), p. 26.

22 The actual figures were 67.23% who said 'yes' and 32.77 who said 'no', to the question 'Do you think the United Kingdom should stay in the European Community (the Common Market)?'

23 Robert Saunders (2018), *Yes to Europe! The 1975 Referendum and Seventies Britain* (Cambridge: Cambridge University Press), p. 9.

24 Monnet wanted Britain inside the EEC, and indeed believed in its 'three circles role' – British leaders did not return the empathy. François Duchêne (1994), *Jean Monnet: The First Statesman of Interdependence* (New York: W. W. Norton), p. 380.

25 Robert Jervis (2017), *How Statesmen Think: The Psychology of International Politics* (Princeton: Princeton University Press).

26 Alan Milward (1992), *The European Rescue of the Nation-State* (Abingdon: Routledge).

27 Anthony Eden (1960), *Memoirs: Full Circle* (London: Cassell), pp. 282–7, 291–4, 337.

28 Christopher Lord (1993), *British entry to the European Community under the Heath Government of 1970–4* (Aldershot: Dartmouth), p. 87. For more Labour volte-faces, see Mac-Shane (2016), pp. 42–3.

29 *House of Common Debates*, 9 February 1972.

30 Roy Jenkins, ed. (1983), *Britain and the EEC* (London: Macmillan), p. 4.

31 This is Christopher Lord's paraphrase, in Lord (1993), p. 130, citing a Witness Symposium on Conservative Party Policy-Making, 1965–1970, recorded in *Contemporary Record*, April 1990, pp. 34–7.

32 Christopher Hill, ed. (1996), *The Actors in Europe's Foreign Policy* (London: Routledge).

33 Stephen Wall (2008), *A Stranger in Europe: Britain and the EU from Thatcher to Blair* (Oxford: Oxford University Press), pp. 108–38.

34 Michael Emerson, ed. (2015) *Britain's Future in Europe: Reform, renegotiation, repatriation or secession?* (Lanham, MD: Rowman & Littlefield for the European Centre for Policy Studies), p. 122.

35 See Blair's speech in Warsaw, arguing for rapid expansion and accompanying reform: 'A superpower but not a superstate', *Guardian*, 7 October 2000.

36 'False beginnings' was the journalist Peter Jenkins' phrase from 1988, cited in Stephen George (1990), *An Awkward Partner: Britain in the European Community* (Oxford: Oxford University Press), p. 190. The 'stratégie minimaliste' was noted with frustration by Françoise de La Serre (1987) in her *La Grande Bretagne et la Communauté européenne* (Paris: Presses Universitaire de France), p. 112.

37 Denis MacShane (2016), *Brexit: How Britain left Europe,* provides an excellent account of the slow-burning rise of antagonism to the EU within British politics.

38 Christopher Tugendhat (1986), *Making Sense of Europe* (Harmondsworth: Viking), p. 119. Tugendhat was both British and a European Commissioner, from 1977 to 1985. He had been a Conservative MP, on its pro-European wing.

39 Charles Moore (2014), *Margaret Thatcher: the Authorized Biography: Volume I* (London: Penguin), p. 490, citing a meeting between the PM and Commission President Roy Jenkins on 26 November 1979, in the National Archives, PREM 19/55.

40 Christopher Tugendhat (1986), pp. 119–27.

41 Lawrence Freedman (1986), 'The case of Westland and the bias to Europe', *International Affairs* 63/2.

42 For a prescient though tendentious whistleblower's account of ERM diplomacy see Bernard Connolly (1995), *The Rotten Heart of Europe: the Dirty War for Europe's Money* (London: Faber & Faber). Connolly was a Commission economist dismissed for writing this frontal assault on his masters – and on many others. His reputation has survived the setback.

43 Norman Lamont (1995), *Sovereign Britain* (London: Duckworth). As a young man Lamont had been pro-EEC. See *The Independent*, 3 October 1992. It is interesting that he and Yanis Varoufakis, the one-time Greek Finance Minister and opponent of the monetary orthodoxy imposed by the European Central Bank (ECB), have become friends. Yanis Varoufakis (2017), *And the Weak Suffer What They Must? Europe, Austerity and the Threat to Global Stability* (London: Vintage), pp. xii, 125–9.

44 In fact, Labour was not unsympathetic to these concerns, and tried to limit the effect of the Social Chapter to health and safety issues, insisting that employment policy remained a national prerogative (as with the French 35-hour week, which Labour had no intention of following). Stephen Wall (2008), *A Stranger in Europe: Britain and the EU from Thatcher to Blair* (Oxford: Oxford University Press), pp. 164–6.

45 Gradually rebadged as 'Freedom, Security and Justice' after the Treaty of Amsterdam in 1999.

46 House of Lords Select Committee on the European Union: Home Affairs, Health and Security Sub-Committee (F). 'Inquiry on the EU's global approach to migration and mobility', 18 July 2012, p. 8.

47 Nicholas Watt and Patrick Wintour, 'How immigration came to haunt Labour: the inside story', *Guardian*, 'Long Read', 24 March 2015.

48 Harold D. Clarke, Matthew Goodwin and Paul Whiteley (2017), *Brexit: Why Britain Voted to Leave the European Union* Cambridge: Cambridge University Press) especially pp. 173–4, 222–7.

49 David Owen and David Ludlow (2017), *British Foreign Policy after Brexit: An Independent Voice* (London: Biteback Publishing)

50 Menno Spiering (2015), *A Cultural History of British Euros-cepticism* (Basingstoke: Palgrave Macmillan).
51 Although the UK is the biggest purchaser of French champagne. I am grateful to Mark Gilbert for his insight about the impact of 1846.

3   Does Britain Need European Foreign Policy?

1 Foreign policy was barely mentioned in the referendum campaign, and no reference to it occurs in the index of the authoritative work by Clarke, Goodwin and Whiteley, *Brexit: Why Britain Voted to Leave the European Union*. That book does, however, contain a figure (p. 156) summarizing the results of an opinion monitoring survey of perceptions of the costs and benefits of leaving the EU. This showed that 64% of people thought Brexit would make no difference to the conduct of foreign affairs, 21% thought the UK would have less international influence and 15% thought it would have more.
2 *Designing Europe's Future: Security and Defence*, Special Eurobarometer 461, April 2017, p. 9.
3 See Wong, Reuben and Hill, eds. (2011), *National and European Foreign Policies: Towards Europeanisation?* (London: Routledge).
4 Steven Blockmans and Sophia Russack (2015), *The Commissioners' Group on External Action – Key Political Facilitator* (Brussels: Centre for European Policy Studies), Special Report 125.
5 Speaking for the Coalition government in the House of Lords in 2013 Lord Wallace of Saltaire noted the 'generally extremely favourable comments from British ambassadors about the utility of EU delegations on the spot, particularly in countries some distance from the EU, and the way in which EU embassies – often only a few EU embassies – and the resident EU delegation have learnt to work together'. House of Lords Debates, 3 June 2013, Column GC146, Report on the External Action Service.
6 European Union (2003, December), *A Secure Europe in a Better World: Europe's Security Strategy*, https://www.consilium.europa.eu/uedocs/cmsUpload/78367.pdf; see also Asle Toje (2005), 'The 2003 European Union security strategy:

a critical appraisal', *European Foreign Affairs Review,* 10:1, 117–33.

7 At that time, before the Treaty of Lisbon, the High Representative only acted for the CFSP, and had less status, although Javier Solana brought personal weight to the post as an ex-Secretary-General of NATO.

8 European Union (2016), *Shared Vision, Common Action: A Stronger Europe. A Global Strategy for the European Union's Foreign and Security Policy* http://europa.eu/globalstrategy/sites/globalstrategy/files/regions/files/eugs_review_web_0.pdf. See also Nathalie Tocci (2017) *Framing the EU Global Strategy; A Stronger Europe in a Fragile World* (London: Palgrave). Dr Tocci drafted the document on behalf of HR Federica Mogherini.

9 Circular letter from Mrs Lynda Chalker, 6 January 1989 entitled 'European Political Cooperation'.

10 According to the Foreign and Commonwealth Office: see *Working in European Union Common Security and Defence Policy Missions: Deployee Guide* (London: FCO Stabilization Unit, October 2014).

11 Rosemary Hollis (2013), 'Europe in the Middle East', in Louise Fawcett, ed., *International Relations of the Middle East,* 3rd edn (Oxford: Oxford University Press), pp. 356–8.

12 The three 'pillars' set up by the Treaty of Maastricht were I: Community business (ie the only one with supranational content); II: Common Foreign and Security Policy; III: Justice and Home Affairs.

13 European Commission, Press Release, 13 April 2016: 'EU Official Development Assistance reaches highest-ever share of Gross National Income'.

14 Maurizio Carbone (2017), 'The European Union and International Development' in Christopher Hill, Michael Smith and Sophie Vanhoonacker, eds. *International Relations and the European Union,* 3rd edn (Oxford: Oxford University Press), p. 305.

15 See for instance Paul Johnson (1992) *The Offshore Islanders: A History of the English People* (London: Weidenfeld & Nicholson). Johnson write of England (sic) being 'pushed unwillingly into a Continental system from which it has been their historic mission to escape', a system that 'is in all essentials the historic concept of German expansionism...enshrining

the prospect that Europe must coalesce against the outer darkness of the world beyond' (p. 405).

16 Mario Draghi (2017), 'The Monnet Method: its relevance for Europe then and now', 4 May 2017. https://www.ecb.europa.eu/press/key/date/2017/html/ecb.sp170504.en.html

17 Stanley R. Sloan (2016), 'Was de Gaulle right on Britain's role in Europe?', Atlantic Council Blog, 9 August 2016. http://www.atlanticcouncil.org/blogs/new-atlanticist/was-de-gaulle-right-on-britain-s-role-in-europe

18 The claim 'This is the hour of Europe – not the hour of the Americans' was made in 1991 by Jacques Poos, then Luxemburg's foreign minister and responsible for the EC's rotating presidency when negotiating the issue of Slovenia's independence. See Josip Glaurdić (2011), *The Hour of Europe: Western Europe and the Breakup of Yugoslavia* (New Haven: Yale University Press), pp.1, 306–7.

19 Roger Morgan (1996), 'German foreign policy and domestic politics' in Bertel Heurlin, ed., *Germany in Europe in the Nineties* (Houndmills: Macmillan), pp. 158–61.

20 See in particular the indictment in Brendan Simms (2002), *Unfinest Hour: Britain and the Destruction of Bosnia* (London: Penguin Books).

21 Statement at the UN Security Council by the UK Presidency on Kosovo, 31 March 1998, reproduced in Hill, Christopher and Smith, Karen, eds. (2000), *European Foreign Policy: Key Documents* (London: Routledge in association with the Secretariat of the European Parliament), pp. 387–8.

22 So long as the abstentions do not amount to more than one third of the weighted votes.

23 Robert Kagan (2003), *Of Paradise and Power* (New York: Alfred Knopf), p. 23.

24 Catherine Gegout (2017), *Why Europe Intervenes in Africa* (London: Hurst), pp. 217–21).

25 Damien Helly (2009), 'EU NAVFOR Somalia: the EU Military Operation Atalanta', in Giovanni Grevi, Damien Helly, and Daniel Keohane, eds. *European Security and Defence Policy: The First Ten Years (1999–2009)* (Paris: European Union Institute of Security Studies), pp. 391–402. A more recent view is that even more could have been done with better

resources. See Monica Chinchilla (2017), 'Operation Atalanta: success or failure?', *Areté Online* https://www.areteassociation .com/single-post/2017/01/07/Operation-Atalanta-Success-or-Failure 2 March 2017.

26 Paul Williams (2012), 'Britain, the EU and Africa', in Adekeye Adebajo and Kaye Whiteman, eds. *The EU and Africa: From EurAfrique to Afro-Europa* (London: Hurst), p. 351. See also note 7 above.

27 Marissa Quie and Hameed Hakimi (2017), 'EU pays to stop migrants', *The World Today* 73:6, pp. 26–8.

28 European Commission Humanitarian Office Factsheet (2017, May) 'EU Response to the Ebola Outbreak' http://ec.europa.eu/ echo/files/aid/countries/factsheets/thematic/wa_ebola_en.pdf

29 Gianluca Quaglio et al. 'Ebola: lessons learned and future challenges for Europe', *The Lancet Infectious Diseases*, 16:2, 259–63.

30 For the chronology of this and what follows I rely on *Timeline of Nuclear Diplomacy with Iran*, Factsheet of the Arms Control Association, Washington DC, updated to August 2017 https://www.armscontrol.org/factsheet/Timeline-of-Nuclear-Diplomacy-With-Iran

31 'Statement by France, Germany, the United Kingdom and United States: Iran's space launch vehicle inconsistent with UNSCR 2231', 29 July 2017. https://www.gov.uk/government/ news/statement-by-france-germany-the-united-kingdom-and-united-states-irans-space-launch-vehicle-inconsistent-with-unscr-2231. 'Europe calls on Trump to keep Iran deal alive', *Financial Times*, 11 January 2018.

32 'UN Security Council wrangles over ceasefire', *Guardian*, 24 February 2018.

33 François Heisbourg (2016), 'Brexit and European security', *Survival: Global Politics and Strategy*, 58:3, p. 19.

34 Rosa Beckmann and Ronja Kempin (2017), 'EU defence policy needs strategy', *SWP Comment34* (Berlin: Stiftung Wissenschaft und Politik), pp. 1–4.

35 *Foreign Policy, Defence and Development: A Future Partnership Paper* (London: HM Government, Department for Exiting the European Union, 12 September 2017) https://www.gov. uk/government/publications/foreign-policy-defence-and-development-a-future-partnership-paper

4   Britain's à La Carte Menu

1 Christopher Hill (1983), 'Britain: A convenient schizophrenia' in Christopher Hill, ed. *National Foreign Policies and
   European Political Cooperation* (London: Allen & Unwin
   for the Royal Institute of International Affairs).
2 David Marsh (2009), *The Euro: The Politics of the New
   Global Currency* (New Haven: Yale University Press).
3 Kenneth Dyson, ed. (2008), *The Euro at Ten: Europeanization, Power and Convergence* (Oxford: Oxford University
   Press), p. 354.
4 A cappuccino, which had cost 1,500 lire, moved up to one
   euro, despite the conversion rate of one euro to 1936 lire.
   'Italy in a froth over euro cheats', BBC News 18 January
   2004, http://news.bbc.co.uk/2/hi/business/3407987.stm
5 Susan Strange (1998), *Mad Money* (Manchester: Manchester
   University Press). Reissued in 2015 (with an Introduction by
   Benjamin Cohen) given its prescience about the instability of
   the international financial system.
6 Andrew Rawnsley (2010), *The End of the Party: The Rise and
   Fall of New Labour* (London: Penguin Books), pp. 189–97.
7 Helen Thompson (2017), 'Inevitability and contingency: the
   political economy of Brexit', *British Journal of Politics and
   International Relations*, 19:3, 437–8; Helen Drake (2011),
   Contemporary France (London: Palgrave Macmillan).
8 France was the only state that could have halted, or at least
   slowed, the enlargement bandwagon. For the reasons why
   it did not see Helene Sjursen and Børge Romsloe (2006),
   'Protecting the idea of Europe' in Helene Sjursen, ed. (2006),
   Questioning EU Enlargement: Europe in Search of Identity
   (Abingdon: Routledge), pp. 142–64.
9 On the years building up to the 2004 enlargement see Karen
   E. Smith (2017), 'Enlargement, the Neighbourhood Policy
   and European' in Christopher Hill, Michael Smith and Sophie
   Vanhoonacker, eds., 3rd edn, *International Relations and the
   European Union*, pp. 330–40. On New Labour, see Simon
   Bulmer (2008), *New Labour and the European Union,
   1997–2007: A Constructive Partner?* Working Paper FG 1
   2008/05 (Berlin: Stiftung Wissenschaft und Politik). Also Simon
   Bulmer, 'New Labour, New European policy? Blair, Brown

and utilitarian supranationalism', *Parliamentary Affairs*, 61:4 (2008), 597–620.

10 Jan Zielonka (2002), ed. *Europe Unbound: Enlarging and Reshaping the Boundaries of the European Union* (Abingdon: Routledge).

11 Philp Leech and Jamie Gaskarth (2015), 'British foreign policy and the Arab Spring', *Diplomacy and Statecraft*, 26:1, 139–60.

12 IAI online c 28 October 2017. My translation.

13 'Pacificistic', in contrast to 'pacifist', means the tendency to give the benefit of the doubt to attempts to preserve peace. It does not have the historical baggage of 'appeasing', which strictly speaking means the same. On the trend of German and Italian attitudes see Philip Everts and Pierangelo Isernia, eds. (2001), *Public Opinion and the International Use of Force* (London: Routledge), e.g. pp. 262–3, and the same editors' 2015 volume *Transatlantic Relations and the Use of Force* (Houndmills: Palgrave Macmillan), pp. 170–7.

14 According to the Foreign and Commonwealth Office: see *Working in European Union Common Security and Defence Policy Missions: Deployee Guide* (London: FCO Stabilization Unit, Oct. 2014). See also 'UK–EU defence and security cooperation', (London: Institute for Government, 2017), https://www.instituteforgovernment.org.uk/explainers/uk%E2%80%93eu-defence-and-security-cooperation. For its part France has been a strong supporter of the missions though it is now cutting back given financial constraints and the seriousness of its commitments in Mali, Syria and on the home front. See Lisa Watanabe (2015), 'Keeping France in the CSDP', *Policy Perspectives* 3/3 (Zurich: Centre for Security Studies).

15 The operational centre was in fact established on 8 June 2017, with the UK no longer willing to carry out its immediately post-referendum threat of obstruction. See *Britain's fear of European army muddles EU defence plan* Reuters, 27 September 2016.

16 Megan Dee and Karen Smith (2017), 'UK diplomacy at the UN after Brexit: Challenges and opportunities'. *British Journal of Politics and International Relations* 19: 3, 527–42.

17 For more on Franco–British cooperation see Chapter 6.

18 Galileo has become both a substantive and symbolic obstacle in the UK–EU negotiation. Chancellor of the Exchequer Philip

Hammond responded to the prospect of being excluded from the programme by asserting that Britain could go it alone. 'Hammond: UK will build satellite rival if barred from Galileo', *Guardian*, 26 May 2018.

19 Stuart Butler, 'Our 60-year relationship with Euratom offers hard lessons for Brexit negotiators', *Guardian*, 2 August 2017; also Andrew Ward, 'Euratom Matters to the UK', *Financial Times*, 6 July 2017.

20 Data from the European Nuclear Society, November 2016. https://www.euronuclear.org/info/encyclopedia/n/nuclear-power-plant-europe.htm

21 Owen and Ludlow, in their *British Foreign Policy after Brexit*, p. 52, dispute this on the grounds that NATO deals with important foreign policy issues and that diplomats participate in its processes. But NATO does not have a common foreign policy, economic resources or systematic cooperation through missions in third countries – as even the Nordic states do.

22 The High Representative's first year report on the global strategy was enthusiastic about progress on defence, without mentioning the UK: *From Shared Vision to common Action: Implementing the EU Global Strategy Year 1* (Brussels: European Union, 2017). https://europa.eu/globalstrategy/sites/globalstrategy/files/full_brochure_year_1.pdf

23 *Foreign Policy, Defence and Development: A Future Partnership Paper*, paras. 12–22. (London: Department for Exiting the European Union, 12 September 2017). https://www.gov.uk/government/uploads/system/uploads/attachment_data/file/643924/Foreign_policy_defence_and_development_paper.pdf

24 Ibid., para. 63.

25 Office of National Statistics, 21 July 2017. https://www.ons.gov.uk/peoplepopulationandcommunity/populationandmigration/populationestimates/articles/overviewoftheukpopulation/july2017. Matthew Goodwin and Caitlin Milazzo (2017), 'Taking back control? Investigating the role of immigration in the 2016 vote for Brexit'. *British Journal of Politics and International Studies*, 19:3, 450–64.

26 Some projections see a further rise of 20 million over the next 40 years, which would represent a one-third increase in the size of the British population, which was around 40 million at the end of the First World War and is 66 million

today. See David Goodhart (2013) *The British Dream: Successes and Failures of Post-war Immigration* (London: Atlantic Books), p. 22

27 Migration Watch (2015), *Population Density Brief* MW356 March 2015.

28 That is, from 359 people per square kilometre to 401. Office for National Statistics, *Population Density Tables,* 25 June 2015. https://www.ons.gov.uk/peoplepopulationandcommunity/ populationandmigration/populationestimates/datasets/ populationdensitytables. Compare Germany at 229 and France at 121 (2012 Migration Watch 2015). In mid 2016 the estimated density for England was 424 people per square km. https://www.ons.gov.uk/peoplepopulationandcommunity/ populationandmigration/populationestimates/datasets/ populationestimatesforukenglandandwalesscotlandandnor thernireland

29 Erica Consterdine (2016), 'The huge political cost of Blair's decision to allow Eastern European migrants unfettered access to Britain', *The Conversation* 16 November 2016, https:// theconversation.com/the-huge-political-cost-of-blairs-decision-to-allow-eastern-european-migrants-unfettered-access-to-britain-66077

30 Carlos Vargas-Silva and Yvonni Markaki (2017), *Briefing: EU Migration to and from the UK*, 5th edn, 30 August 2017. Oxford University, The Migration Observatory. The most authoritative analysis so far of the 2016 Referendum vote is properly cautious about singling out one key factor, but clearly identifies concerns about immigration as having 'major role'. See Harold D. Clarke, Matthew Goodwin and Paul Whiteley (2017), *Brexit: Why Britain Voted to Leave the European Union*, p. 222 and pp. 146–74. See also Goodwin and Milazzo (2017), note 25 above.

31 'Hate crimes soared by 41% after Brexit vote, official figures reveal', *The Independent*, 13 October 2016.

32 Kenneth Coutts and Robert Rowthorn (2013), *Update of Prospects for the UK Balance of Payments*, Centre for Business Research Working Paper, 452, University of Cambridge December 2017, p. 1.

33 *International Trade in Services, UK: 2015*, Figure 3: UK international trade in services (excluding travel, transport and banking), exports by continent, 2011 to

2015 (London: Office for National Statistics, https://www.ons.gov.uk/businessindustryandtrade/internationaltrade/bulletins/internationaltradeinservices/2015. Also 'How Brexit will affect sectors of the British economy', *Financial Times* Briefing, 23 June 2017.

34 *Security, Law Enforcement and Criminal Justice: A Future Partnership Paper* (London: Department for Exiting the European Union, and the Home Office, 18 September 2017); Christopher Hill (1986), 'The political dilemmas for Western governments', in Lawrence Freedman et al. *Terrorism and International Order* (London: Routledge and Kegan Paul for the Royal Institute of International Affairs).

5 Regional or Global?

1 Margaret Thatcher (1993), *The Downing Street Years* (London: Harper Collins), pp. 816–28. Thatcher makes frequent reference to her success in the Falklands as having given her an understanding of what needed to be done in such a crisis.

2 John Kampfner (2004), *Blair's Wars* (London: The Free Press).

3 My italics. Christopher Hill and Karen E. Smith, eds. (2000), *European Foreign Policy: Key Documents* (London: Routledge), p. 156. The current Consolidated Treaty of the European Union, as amended by the Treaty of Lisbon in the renumbered Article 34, updates this to include the High Representative in the process of consultation but is otherwise unchanged.

4 On Panama and Libya, jointly with France and the USA. *Security Council Veto List* (New York, the UN: Dag Hammarskjold Library – http://research.un.org/en/docs/sc/quick

5 In April 2018 the UNSC went into emergency session at Russia's request, as a riposte to the solidarity shown to Britain over the poisoning of Sergei Skripal in Salisbury. This was the first time Britain had been the focus of a Security Council discussion since 1982.

6 The General Assembly supported a Mauritian Resolution (by 94 votes to 15) to ask the International Court of Justice for an opinion on the status of the Chagos Islands, including Diego Garcia, which Britain leased to the US in 1971, leading to the expulsion of its inhabitants. Only four EU

Member States voted with Britain. See 'Britain defeated in UN vote on Chagos Islands', *Financial Times*, 23 June 2017.

7 Megan Dee and Karen Smith (2017), 'UK diplomacy at the UN after Brexit: challenges and opportunities', *British Journal of Politics and International Relations*, 19:3, 527.

8 See 'IAEA Director General at the Edoardo Amaldi Conference: Nuclear Science has a Key Role to Play for Development', International Atomic Energy Agency, 9 October 2017. https://www.iaea.org/newscenter/news/iaea-director-general-at-the-edoardo-amaldi-conference-nuclear-science-has-a-key-role-to-play-for-development

9 Voting in these organizations is relative to the size of the subscription paid, which means that the richer countries, and particularly the US, dominate. The EU has increasingly sought to coordinate its positions over the years, with limited success. The future evolution of the Eurozone will have a determining effect on the position of both the EU and the UK in the international financial institutions. See Fraser Cameron (2012), *An Introduction to European Foreign Policy*, 2nd edn (London: Routledge), pp. 22–3, 120.

10 Jan Wouters and Sven van Kerckhoven (2017), 'The international monetary fund' Kund-Erik Jørgensen and Katie Verlin Laatikainen, eds. *The Routledge Handbook of the European Union and International Institutions* (Abingdon: Routledge), pp. 221–3

11 See Maurizio Carbone, 'The European Union and international development', in Christopher Hill, Michael Smith and Sophie Vanhoonacker, eds. (2017), *International Relations and the European Union* 3rd edn (Oxford: Oxford University Press), pp. 292–315.

12 As towards the end of Thatcher's premiership, when she was combative in both EU and Commonwealth summits. See Stephen Wall (2008), *A Stranger in Europe: Britain and the EU from Thatcher to Blair* (Oxford: Oxford University Press), p. 85. The relative lack of sharp tensions in recent years may betoken either an increasing closeness among members, or simply the lack of any significant common business.

13 See William Wallace, 'Introduction: Foreign Secretaries and foreign policy', p. 11, and Lord Howe of Aberavon, 'Politics and personality in the Thatcher years', pp. 76–7, both

in Graham Zeigner, ed. (2007), *British Diplomacy: Foreign Secretaries Reflect – the LSE Lectures*. (London Politico's).

14 Winston S. Churchill (1956–8), *A History of the English-Speaking Peoples* (London: Cassell).

15 See Daniel Hannan (2013), *Inventing Freedom: How the English-Speaking Peoples Made the Modern World* (New York: Harper Collins), and for commentary Charles Moore (2013), 'A reveille call to the slumbering Anglosphere', *The Daily Telegraph*, 24 November 2013. For attempts to rehabilitate the British empire see Niall Ferguson (2004), *Empire: How Britain Made the Modern World* (London: Penguin Books) and Andrew Roberts (2006), *A History of the English-Speaking Peoples since 1900* (London: Weidenfeld & Nicolson). Roberts sees the British and American empires as historically of a piece, and associated with pursuing a long 'civilizing mission' (p. 6) – a phrase anathema to post-colonial critics of empire. In the 1990s another historian, Robert Conquest, had been influential in turning Margaret Thatcher away from Europe and towards the Anglosphere. See Michael Kenny and Nick Pearce (2018), *Shadows of Empire: the Anglosphere in British Politics* (Cambridge: Polity); also the article by Kenny and Pearce (2015), 'The rise of the Anglosphere: how the right dreamed up a new Conservative world order', *New Statesman* 10 February 2015. The first scholarly treatment of the emergence of the idea of the Anglosphere, showing how it played into both Conservative hostility to the EU and growing English nationalism, was that by Ben Wellings and Helen Baxendale (2015): 'Euroscepticism and the Anglosphere: traditions and dilemmas in contemporary English nationalism', *Journal of Common Market Studies*, Special Issue on 'Interpreting British European Policy', 53:1,123–39.

16 Duncan Bell (2017), 'The Anglosphere: new enthusiasm for an old dream', *Prospect Magazine*, February 2017, p. 42.

17 Gareth Evans (2016), 'The Anglosphere illusion', *The Korea Herald* 21 February 2016. http://www.koreaherald.com/view.php?ud=20160221000311

18 Gareth Evans (2017), *Incorrigible Optimist: A Political Memoir* (Carlton, Victoria: University of Melbourne Press), p. 182.

19 Evans (2017), p. 183.

20 As Kenny and Pearce say 'while the net is sometimes cast wider to encompass Commonwealth countries and former

British colonies, such as India, Singapore and Hong Kong, the emotional and political heart of the project resides in these 'five eyes' nations'. Michael Kenny and Nick Pearce (2016), 'After Brexit: the Eurosceptic dream of an Anglosphere', *Juncture* 22/4, Spring 2016.

21 Cited in Kenny and Pearce (2018), *Shadows of Empire: the Anglosphere in British Politics*, p. 147.

22 The paper was written by the FCO's Directorate for Strategy and Innovation, the renamed Policy Planning Staff, at the time headed by Simon Fraser, subsequently Permanent Under-Secretary between 2010–2015 (Personal copy).

23 As did Theresa May when she came into office. See Sir Simon Fraser (2017), 'In search of a role: rethinking British foreign policy', speech at Chatham House 7 November. https://www.chathamhouse.org/sites/files/chathamhouse/images/events/2017-11-07-Fraser.pdf accesses 21 March 2018.

24 The UK's dependence on imported energy has been rising in recent years and is now just under 40%. In 2015 one third of the UK's fuel imports was crude oil, of which 6% came from Russia. Petroleum products made up 27% of fuel imports, of which 16% came from Russia. Russian natural gas is also important to the UK indirectly as continental Europe is ever more dependent on imports from Gazprom. Office for National Statistics, https://visual.ons.gov.uk/uk-energy-how-much-what-type-and-where-from/

25 https://www.gov.uk/government/publications/exporting-to-indonesia/exporting-to-indonesia

26 Thomas Lembong, quoted in 'Where should Britain strike its first post-Brexit trade deals? *The Economist*, 4 February 2017.

27 'Annual UK trade exports and imports by country 1999–2015', https://www.ons.gov.uk/economy/nationalaccounts/balanceofpayments/adhocs/006034annualuktradeexportsandimportsbycountry1999to2015

28 'The UK and Latin America', speech by Sir Alan Duncan, Minister of State for the Americas, 10 November 2016. https://www.gov.uk/government/speeches/the-uk-and-latin-america-latin-american-investment-forum-speech

29 'The strategic imperatives of a transformed global order demand that the United Kingdom aim to be the best networked state in the world'. House of Lords Select Committee on Soft Power and the UK's Influence, Report for 2013–2014:

Persuasion and power in the modern world, H/L 150 28 March 2014, para. 147.

30 William Hague, 'Britain's foreign policy in a networked world', Speech at the FCO, 1 July 2010. https://www.gov.uk/government/speeches/britain-s-foreign-policy-in-a-networked-world–2

31 Jamie Gaskarth (2013), *British Foreign Policy* (Cambridge: Polity), pp. 67–8.

32 According to the Lowy Global Diplomacy Index for 2017, compiled by Alex Oliver. https://globaldiplomacyindex.lowyinstitute.org/#

33 'French diplomatic service is the world's best, UK says', BBC News 8 November 2012, http://www.bbc.co.uk/news/uk-politics-20218377

34 See Christopher Hill and William Wallace (1979), 'Diplomatic trends in the European Community', *International Affairs*, 55/1, p. 58. Although the basis of the calculations is slightly different from those of Lowy above, the ratios are the same, with France in 1978 having 129 overseas missions, the UK 123 and Germany 120.

35 'Diplomatic excellence briefing document', FCO, October 2013. https://www.gov.uk/government/uploads/system/uploads/attachment_data/file/253590/Dip_Ex_MFA_briefing_Oct_13_finalv1_2.pdf

36 *Conflict, Security and Stability Fund, Annual Report 2016–2017* (London: HM Government, July 2017) https://www.gov.uk/government/uploads/system/uploads/attachment_data/file/630077/conflict-stability-security-fund-annual-report-2016–2017.pdf

37 It is intrinsically difficult to follow levels of spending on the Diplomatic Service, given the removal of the BBC World Service in 2014 to the department of Culture, and other base-line changes. The publicly available data is only decipherable by trained accountants, and does not measure up to standards of democratic transparency. I am thus grateful to the officials in the National Audit Office who helped me to make some sense of them.

38 *Guardian*, 1 February 2018.

39 These and other defence statistics relate to 2016 and are taken from data in *The Military Balance, 2017* (London: International Institute for Strategic Studies, 2017), ch. 2 'Comparative defence statistics'.

40 *The Military Balance, 2017*, pp. 82–9.
41 *The Equipment Plan, 2017–2027* (HM Government: National Audit Office 31 January 2018), Summary, para. 15. https://www.nao.org.uk/wp-content/uploads/2018/01/The-Equipment-Plan-2017-to-2027-Summary.pdf
42 Theo Farrell (2017), *Unwinnable: Britain's War in Afghanistan, 2001–2014* (London; Bodley Head).
43 Wikipedia (13 March 2018), 'History of the Royal Navy: trends in ship strength'.
44 *The Military Balance, 1989–1990*, (London: Brasseys for the International Institute of Strategic Studies), pp. 78–9; *The Military Balance, 2016–2017* (London: Routledge for the International Institute of Strategic Studies), p. 170.
45 For an excellent analysis of the difficulties, pointing to the need to think in new ways, see Malcom Chalmers *Decision Time: The National Security Capability Review 2017–2018 and Defence*, Whitehall report 1–18 (London: Royal United Services Institute, February 2018).
46 House of Commons Defence Committee (2018) *Rash or Rational? North Korea and the Threat it Poses*, 4th Report 2017–2019 HC327 (HM Government), 5 April 2018.
47 https://www.gov.uk/government/speeches/pm-speech-at-munich-security-conference-17-february-2018
48 Joseph Nye (2004), *Soft Power: The Means to Success in World Politics* (New York: Public Affairs). Christopher Hill and Sarah Beadle (2014), *The Art of Attraction: Soft Power and the UK's Role in the World* (London, British Academy).
49 The British Academy (2013), *Lost for Worlds: the Need for Languages in UK Diplomacy and Security* Report of a Steering Group, November 2013
50 *The British Council: Corporate Plan 2017–2020*, www.britishcouncil.org , Foreword by Chief Executive Sir Ciarán Devane.
51 Jamie Gaskarth (2013), *British Foreign Policy* (Cambridge: Polity), pp. 115–18.
52 In the 2015 *National Security Strategy and Strategic Defence and Security Review, 2015: A Secure and prosperous United Kingdom* (London: HM Government, November 2015, Cmd 9161), p. 6, Prime Minister David Cameron observed that: 'Our substantial aid budget means that Britain not only meets our obligations to the poorest in the world, but can

now respond rapidly and decisively to emerging crises overseas that impinge on our security at home – and with this
speed and agility of response comes greater influence in the
world.'

53 A European Parliament scenario-building exercise for ODA
after Brexit saw three possible kinds of British attitudes:
nationalist, realist and cosmopolitan, but under all of them
it saw the UK as inevitably repatriating much of the funds
it currently provides for the EU's Development Fund. *Possible Impacts of Brexit on EU Development and Humanitarian Policies* European Commission, Directorate General for
External Policies, EP/EXPO/B/DEVE/FWC/2013–08/Lot5/14,
April 2017.

54 These and other data are taken from *Statistics on International
Development 2017*, (HM Government, November 2017) https://
www.gov.uk/government/statistics/statistics-on-international-
development-2017

55 David Abulafia (2011), *The Great Sea: A Human History of
the Mediterranean* (London: Allen Lane).

6 A Tale of Two Special Relationships – Paris and Washington

1 P. M. H. Bell (1974), *A Certain Eventuality: Britain and the
Fall of France* (Farnborough: Saxon House).

2 In recent years theorists of International Relations have finally
started to take the issue of emotion in international politics
seriously – although foreign policy analysts have long done so.
Probably the first article in this 'emotional turn' was by Neta
C. Crawford (2000), 'The passions of world politics: propositions on emotion and emotional relationships' *International
Security*, 24:4, 116–56. See also Jonathan Mercer (2006)
'Human nature and the first image: emotion in international
politics', *Journal of International Relations and Development*, 9:3, 288–303; Roland Bleiker and Emma Hutchison
(2008), 'Fear no more: emotions and world politics', *Review
of International Studies* 34, 115–35.

3 Following Albert O. Hirschman (1970), *Exit, Voice and
Loyalty: Responses to Decline in Firms, Organizations and
States* (Cambridge, MA: Harvard University Press). Put simply,
exit means abandoning a situation, voice means engaging

with it, and loyalty means sticking with the status quo so as to allow a constructive engagement.

4 The notion of a 'coordination reflex' emerged among the practitioners of European Political Cooperation in the 1970s to describe the increasing instinct of the Member States to consult each other first when faced by some new international problem.

5 David Reynolds (1995), *Rich Relations: The American Occupation of Britain, 1942–1945* (London: Harper Collins).

6 This last phrase represents the angst *de nos jours*, given the rise of China, the surprising revival of Russian power, Donald Trump's hostility to multilateralism and the rise of 'illiberal democracy' in places like Poland, Turkey and the Philippines. See Stephen Walt (2016), 'The collapse of the liberal world order', *Foreign Policy*, June 2016, and *International Affairs*, special issue, 94/1, January 2018.

7 Mark Gilbert, *A History of European Integration*, pp. 26–32.

8 Alex Spelling (2009) Edward Heath and Anglo–American relations 1970–1974: A Reappraisal, *Diplomacy and Statecraft*, 20:4, 638–58.

9 Stephen Wall (2008), *A Stranger in Europe: Britain and the EU from Thatcher to Blair* (Oxford: Oxford University Press), p. 89.

10 Alice Pannier (2013) 'Understanding the workings of interstate cooperation in defence: An exploration into Franco–British cooperation after the signing of the Lancaster House Treaty', *European Security*, 22:4, 540–58; Alice Pannier (2017), 'The Anglo-French defence partnership after the 'Brexit' vote: new incentives and new dilemmas', *Global Affairs*, 2: 5, 481–90; Jean-Pierre Maulny, 'The French/UK defence relationship', *Tribune* (Paris: Institut de relations internationals et stratégiques) 22 June 2016. http://www.iris-france.org/78591-the-frenchuk-defence-relationship/

11 See especially P. M. H. Bell (1996), *France and Britain, 1900–1940: Entente and Estrangement* (London: Longman); P. M. H. Bell (1997), *France and Britain, 1940–1994: the Long Separation* (London: Longman); Isabelle and Robert Tombs (2006), *That Sweet Enemy: the French and the British from the Sun King to the Present* (London: Heinemann); Henrik Larsen (1997), *Foreign Policy and Discourse Analysis: France, Britain and Europe* (London: Routledge).

12 For some of the mutual demonology see Sudhir Hazreesingh
    (2016), *How the French Think* (London: Penguin), e.g. pp. 9,
    24–6, 159. In 1972 President Pompidou anxiously explained to
    Edward Heath that a referendum on the accession of Britain,
    Denmark and Ireland was a constitutional necessity in France.
    Heath drily recounted how 'I was able to assure him that I
    was not worried about it. As he said, it is a matter of dif-
    ferences in customs between our two countries, like the fact
    that we eat mustard only with beef and they eat it with lamb
    as well'. Edward Heath to Richard Nixon, 22 March 1972,
    National Archives FCO82/204-110814, reproduced in Ilaria
    Poggiolini (2004), *Alle Origini dell'Europa Allargata: La Gran
    Bretagna e l'adesione alla CEE (1972–1973)* (Milan: Edizioni
    Unicopli), Documents section.
13 For an example of the collaborative 'competence' shown at
    the UNSC by Britain and France see Rebecca Adler-Nilssen
    and Vincent Pouliot (2014), 'Power in practice: negotiating
    the international intervention in Libya', *European Journal
    of International Relations*, 20:4, 889–911, especially pp.
    898–902.
14 Gérard Errera, the experienced ex-French Ambassador to
    London, observed that France and the UK are 'the only ones
    in Europe' to have the political will and military capabilities
    to provide foreign policy leadership for Europe. 'Syria shows
    why Europe needs to flex more muscle', *Financial Times*, 24
    September 2013.
15 I discuss these issues at greater length in Christopher Hill
    (2016), 'Powers of a kind: the anomalous positions of France
    and the United Kingdom in world politics', *International
    Affairs*, 92:2, 11–14.
16 A point made by David Allen (2011) in his 'Die EU-Politik
    der britischen Koalitionsregierung: Distanz vor Pragmatismus',
    Integration, 34:3, 197–213.
17 For a sceptical view of this development, sealed at the EU
    Council in June 2017, see Jolyon Howorth (2017), 'EU defence
    cooperation after Brexit: what role for the UK in the future
    EU defence arrangements?' *European View* 16, 191–200.
18 See HM Government, *Security, Law Enforcement and Crimi-
    nal Justice: A Future Partnership Paper* 18 September 2017.
    https://www.gov.uk/government/uploads/system/uploads/

attachment_data/file/645416/Security_law_enforcement_and_
criminal_justice_-_a_future_partnership_paper.pdf
19 Pierre Briançon (2016), 'Brexit or not, France and Britain deepen military alliance', *Politico* online 7 May 2016. https://www.politico.eu/article/brexit-or-not-france-and-britain-deepen-military-alliance-lancaster-treaties-defense-david-cameron-nicolas-sarkozy/
20 HM Government, *Security, Law Enforcement and Criminal Justice*, p. 2.
21 See British American Security Information Council (2014), *Trident Commission Concluding Report*, pp. 9, 33–8. http://www.basicint.org/sites/default/files/trident_commission_finalreport.pdf
22 John Baylis (1984) *Anglo-American Defence Relations 1939–1984: The Special relationship* 2nd edn (London: Macmillan), pp. 153–7.
23 Michael Harvey (2011), 'Perspectives on the UK's Place in the World' (London: Chatham House Programme Paper).
24 Robin Niblett (2015), *Britain, Europe and the World: Rethinking the UK's Circles of Influence* (London: Chatham House) p. 30.
25 Barack Obama has expressed regret since the referendum result over having acceded to David Cameron's request to speak publicly in favour of the Remain option, and in particular over his remark that Brexit would put Britain at the back of the queue for a new trade deal. This was clearly counter-productive.
26 Wyn Rees (2017), 'America, Brexit and the security of Europe', *British Journal of Politics and International Relations*, 19:3, 562.
27 Graham K. Wilson (2017) 'Brexit, Trump and the special relationship' *British Journal of Politics and International Relations*, 19:3, 555.
28 *The Report of the Iraq Inquiry: Executive Summary* (The Chilcot Report, 2016) (London: HMSO), para. 365.

7 Nothing Good Out of Europe?

1 This intentionally ambiguous phrase is a reworking of Margaret Thatcher's famous remark that 'in my lifetime all our problems

have come from mainland Europe and all the solutions have come from the English-speaking world' – an observation soon criticized by Tony Blair in these terms: 'How can anyone seriously argue nothing good has come from Europe in the last half century?' *The Telegraph*, 19 March 2002.

2 Parts of this chapter are an updated version of a paper written for the Greek Public Policy Forum in Chania, Crete, 7–8 October 2016.

3 A case in point was the personal letter sent jointly by President Macron of France and Chancellor Merkel of Germany to President Putin of Russia to stop blocking a UNSC resolution on humanitarian relief in East Ghouta, Syria. Prime Minister May was notable by her absence. *Guardian*, 24 February 2018.

4 Private information.

5 Sir Simon Fraser (2017), 'In search of a role: rethinking British foreign policy', speech at Chatham House 7 November. https://www.chathamhouse.org/event/search-role-rethinking-british-foreign-policy

6 Up to 5% of UK electricity comes from France via interconnectors. See Deartment of Energy, Business and Industrial Strategy, *Digest of United Kingdom Energy Statistics 2017*, pp. 113–14. https://assets.publishing.service.gov.uk/government/uploads/system/uploads/attachment_data/file/643414/DUKES_2017.pdf

7 In December 2017. Permanent Structured Cooperation was originally envisaged as a way for states with serious defence capacity to push ahead with projects. It is now so inclusive (apart from Britain, Denmark and Malta) as to be indistinguishable from the CSDP and thus subject to the same drags upon it.

8 For some creative ideas see Salvador Llaudes and Ignacio Molina, 'Gibraltar, UK and Spain: how Brexit could be an opportunity', *The UK and a Changing Europe* website, http://ukandeu.ac.uk/gibraltar-uk-and-spain-how-brexit-could-be-an-opportunity/ 21 March 2018.

9 Personal information.

10 *Foreign Policy, Defence and Development: A Future Partnership Paper* (London: HM Government September 2017) para. 68 – italic type in the original.

11 Ibid., paras. 71–2.

12 Fraser Cameron (2017), 'After Brexit: Prospects for UK–EU cooperation on foreign and security policy', EPC Policy Brief, 30 October 2017 (Brussels: European Policy Centre).

13 Sir Peter Ricketts, 'What will Brexit mean for the UK as a foreign policy power?', ESRC project *UK in a Changing Europe*, 12 September 2016, http://ukandeu.ac.uk/what-will-brexit-mean-for-the-uk-as-a-foreign-policy-power/

14 The Duncan Report, named after its chairman Sir Val Duncan, was the *Report of the Review Committee on Overseas Representation, 1968–1969*. HM Government, Cmd 4107. See for analysis William Wallace, *The Foreign Policy Process in Britain* (London: Royal Institute of International Affairs), pp. 215–43.

15 As outlined by Ian Bond (2018, March), *Plugging in the British: EU Foreign Policy* (London: Centre for European Reform).

16 The phrase was Lord Franks, ex- Ambassador to the United States, in his Reith Lectures of 1954. Cited in Philip Darby (1973), *British Defence Policy East of Suez, 1947–1968* (Oxford University Press for the Royal Institute of International Affairs), p. 22.

17 An idea given much air time by the May government, but articulated more effectively by a past Labour Foreign Secretary and his collaborator. See David Owen and David Ludlow (2017), *British Foreign Policy after Brexit: An Independent Voice* (London: Biteback Publishing), e.g. p. 48.

18 Martin Kettle (2018), 'After Salisbury, surely it's clear our real friends are in Europe', *Guardian*, 22 March 2018. See also Anand Menon (2018), 'It is time to set out Britain's place on the world stage', *The Telegraph* 26 February 2018, and 'Globaloney', in *The Economist*, 15 March 2018.

19 *Global Britain*, House of Commons Foreign Affairs Committee, HC 780, 12 March 2018 (London: HM Government).

20 The view of Lord Hannay, as cited by the House of Commons Report *Global Britain*, para. 21.

21 In her Speech in Florence the Prime Minister called for a new Treaty between the UK and the EU on foreign policy cooperation. Theresa May (2017) 'A new era of cooperation between the UK and the EU', 22 September 2017 https://www.gov.uk/government/speeches/pms-florence-speech-a-new-era-of-cooperation-and-partnership-between-the-uk-and-the-eu

22 Richard Whitman (2016) 'Foreign and security policy post-Brexit: future models of EU-UK cooperation'. *National Institute Economic Review* 238: 43–50.
23 Jan Zielonka has led the way in pointing to the crisis of the EU and of the philosophy underpinning it. See his *Is the EU Doomed?* (Cambridge: Polity, 2014), and *Counter-Revolution: Liberal Europe in Retreat* (Oxford: Oxford University Press, 2018).

Index

Acheson, Dean 16, 133
ACP group 106
acquis communautaire 39, 53
acquis politique 53
Afghanistan 45, 56, 57, 59,
    67, 90, 91, 100, 119,
    120, 125, 127, 168
Africa, sub-Saharan 66–9, 94,
    100, 106, 109, 125, 127,
    142, 152, 169
Albright, Madeleine 89, 134
Amano, Yukiya 104–5
Amin, Idi 107
Amsterdam, Treaty of 39–40,
    65
Anglosphere 21, 101, 107–9,
    110, 126, 169, 173
armed services 43, 49, 56,
    62, 88, 89, 115, 116,
    118–20, 127, 147, 159
  British Army 25, 120, 128,
    142
  European army 61, 87–8,
    90

Royal Air Force 65, 100,
    118–19
Royal Navy 26, 118, 120
Armstrong, Kenneth 5
ASEAN 107
Ashton, Lady Catherine 70
Australia 10, 25, 108, 111,
    131, 172
Austria 26, 37, 84

Baldwin, Stanley 26
Balkans 21, 22, 63–6, 67, 84,
    88–9, 100, 120, 158,
    160, 163
BBC (British Broadcasting
    Corporation) 121,
    122–3
Belarus 85
Belgium 3, 6, 91
Bell, Duncan 108
Benn, Tony 36
Berrill Report 31–2
bilateralism 110, 118, 161–2,
    163

black Wednesday, 1992 43, 44
Blair, Tony 40–1, 46, 47, 55, 58–9, 66, 79–80, 83, 87, 89, 94, 99, 100, 114, 134, 168, 210n1
Brazil 70, 111, 113–14, 117, 124, 173
Brexit scenarios 175–6
BRICS (Brazil, Russia, India, China, South Africa) 106
British Council 121, 122
Brown, Gordon 79–80, 83
Bulgaria 46
bureaucratic politics 60, 75
Bush, George W. 59, 69, 136–7

Cabinet Office 11
Callaghan, James 7, 42
Cameron, David 16, 47, 110, 135, 170, 205n52, 209n25
Canada 10, 25, 108, 111, 172
CANZUK 108, 109
Carrington, Lord 39, 58
Chagos Islands (Diego Garcia) 104, 147
Chalker, Baroness Lynda 56
Chamberlain, Joseph 187n2
Charles, Prince of Wales 107
Chilcot Report 153
China 70, 91, 103, 110, 111, 112–13, 117, 118, 124, 126, 127, 128, 129, 142, 158, 170–1
Chirac, Jacques 134
Churchill, Sir Winston 8, 32, 34, 108, 111, 132
City of London 79

Clarke, Charles 46
Clarke, Kenneth 48
climate change 13, 18, 123, 137, 148, 174
Coalition government 2010–15 45, 59
Cold War 28, 33, 159, 172
end of 39, 40, 44, 58, 79, 120, 134
Commission see European Commission
Common Agricultural Policy 13, 42, 48, 83
Common Commercial Policy 13, 49, 97
Common Foreign and Security Policy (CFSP) 9, 16, 19, 21, 38, 39, 40, 53, 56–63, 65, 72, 83, 88, 92, 115, 153, 155, 156, 157, 161, 162, 165, 167, 174
see also European foreign policy cooperation
Common Security and Defence Policy (CSDP) 3, 56, 63, 67, 162, 165
see also European defence cooperation
Commonwealth 8, 10, 17, 21, 30, 34, 37, 62, 67, 69, 75, 78, 86, 101, 104, 105–7, 126, 150, 172, 174
Conference on Security and Cooperation in Europe 88
conflict prevention 68, 92
Conflict, Stability and Security Fund (CSSF) 116

Conservative Party 4, 16, 32,
     37, 40, 43, 45, 47, 59,
     63, 75, 79, 82, 96, 108,
     110, 165
Consterdine, Erica 199n29
contact groups 65, 73, 174
Cook, Robin 39
Cooper, Sir Robert 55
Coordinated Annual review
     on Defence (CARD) 73
Corbyn, Jeremy 47
COREU 103
Cotonou agreement 106
Council of Europe 130
Council of Ministers 39, 74
Coutts, Kenneth 95
Crawford, Neta C. 206n2
cyber war 151
Cyprus 65, 84, 86, 100, 114,
     147

Da'esh (ISIS) 91
de Gaulle, General Charles
     17, 29, 30, 35, 63, 74,
     132, 133
decolonization 30, 37, 62, 99
defence budget 118, 119
Delors, Jacques 44
Denmark 15, 61, 163
Department of the
     Environment, Food and
     Rural Affairs (Defra) 13
Department for Exiting the
     European Union
     (DEXIT) 7
Department for International
     Development (DfID) 12,
     13, 61, 68, 116, 123,
     156, 158
Department of Trade 7, 13,
     113, 116

diasporas within the UK
     169
Diego Garcia see Chagos
     Islands
Diplomatic Service 55,
     115–16, 118, 166
Douglas-Home, Sir Alec
     (Lord Home) 32
Duchêne, François 34
Duncan Report 31, 168
Duncan, Sir Val 31

East of Suez
  UK's military role 30, 78,
     99
Ebola virus 68
ECOWAS 107
Eden, Sir Anthony (Lord
     Avon) 32, 35
Egypt 29, 113, 129
Elizabeth II, Queen 105, 107
embassies 116–18
Emerson, Michael 4
emotion 206n2
  see also sentiment
energy
  UK sources of 91, 162,
     203n24
England 26, 93
enlargement of the European
     Union 10, 20–1, 40, 41,
     52, 59, 66, 71, 81–7,
     160
Erdoğan, Recep Tayyip 110,
     114
Errera, Gérard 208n14
ethnocultural minorities 17,
     139
EU-3, leadership group 70,
     72
Euratom 91, 104–5

euro (EU currency) 20, 44,
    77–80, 81, 83, 146, 157
European army 61, 87–8, 90
European Arrest Warrant
    (EAW) 96, 143–4
European Central Bank 62
European Commission 17,
    35, 36, 54, 61, 71, 74,
    94, 124, 151, 152, 158,
    160, 167
European Commission
    Humanitarian Office
    (ECHO) 68–9
European Council 7, 40, 41,
    44, 50, 54, 74, 83, 171
European Court of Justice
    (ECJ) 49
European defence cooperation
    40, 82, 87, 134, 135,
    143, 150–1
  battlegroups 45, 61
  Permanent Structured
    Cooperation (PESCO)
    73, 143, 162
  St Malo declaration 22, 40,
    87, 89, 134, 136, 162
European Development Fund
    (EDF) 12, 157
European Economic Area
    (EEA) 3, 98
European External Action
    Service (EEAS) 3, 8,
    39, 54–5, 83, 116, 165,
    166
European foreign policy
    cooperation 30, 38, 39,
    49, 53, 134, 157–8, 177
  see also Common Foreign
    and Security Policy
European foreign policy (EFP)
    51–2, 55–6, 65, 74–6, 92

European Free Trade
    Association (EFTA) 3, 98
European integration 1, 25,
    27–8, 35–6, 37, 39, 41,
    45, 47, 49, 53, 62, 75–6,
    77, 81–3, 133, 138, 146,
    163
European Monetary Union
    (EMU) 44
European Parliament 46–7,
    61
European Political
    Cooperation (EPC) 11,
    30, 38–9, 52–3, 56–63,
    88
European Security and
    Defence Policy (ESDP)
    40–1, 45, 59, 67–8, 87,
    89–90, 162
European Space Agency 130
European Union
  enlargement of 10, 20–1,
    40, 41, 52, 59, 66, 71,
    81–7, 160
  free movement of people
    14, 16, 46, 49, 83, 86,
    92–7
  freedom security and justice
    area 161
  as global power 127
  Global Strategy 55–6, 92,
    109
  High Representative (HR)
    40, 52, 54, 60, 70, 71,
    83, 103
  Justice and Home Affairs
    46
  as normative power 51
  Political and Security
    Committee 165, 175
  problems 7

rotating presidencies 39
Strategy of 2003 55, 109
Single Market 14, 20, 36,
    47, 53, 57, 81, 93–4, 97,
    164
Social Chapter 44–5
Social Charter 39
Europeanization 19, 53, 73,
    77, 108, 159, 167
Euroscepticism 36, 41–2, 48,
    80, 83, 86, 93, 95, 108,
    110, 115, 138
Eurosceptics 39, 44, 45,
    48, 57, 59, 61, 79, 80,
    177
Eurozone 7, 20, 78, 80, 105,
    146, 166–7
Evans, Gareth 108, 109
Exchange Rate Mechanism
    (ERM) 36, 43, 78
expatriates 14

Falkland Islands 18, 58,
    99, 100, 103, 119, 134,
    148
Farage, Nigel 48
Finland 84
fisheries policy 160
fishing industry 42
'Five Eyes' intelligence
    grouping 109, 174
Five Power Defence
    Arrangements 108
food security 13
Foreign Affairs Council 54,
    175
Foreign and Commonwealth
    Office (FCO) 3, 7,
    10–12, 13, 30, 31, 75,
    116, 118, 119, 122, 123,
    158, 159, 176

foreign policy
    nature and concept of 2,
        51, 87, 88, 174
France 3, 6, 10, 12, 15, 17,
    21–2, 25, 26, 27, 28, 34,
    40, 41, 45, 46, 59, 62–3,
    64, 65, 66, 67, 68, 69,
    70, 71, 72–3, 77, 82, 83,
    87, 89, 90, 91, 92, 93,
    94, 98, 99, 102, 103,
    104, 105, 106, 116, 117,
    118–19, 128–46, 155,
    156, 161–3, 169
Franco-British relations 29,
    135–6, 137–46
Francophonie 107

G7 130, 167, 174
G20 113, 116, 117, 174
Galileo programme 91,
    159
Gaskarth, Jamie 4–5
GCHQ (Government
    Communications
    Headquarters) 147
Gegout, Catherine 66
geography
    foreign policy and 73,
        125–7
Germany 6, 10, 12, 22, 26,
    27, 28, 34, 39, 41, 45,
    46, 50, 58, 59, 64, 65,
    66, 70, 71, 72–3, 77, 78,
    80, 82, 83, 90, 94, 103,
    105, 107, 116, 117, 118,
    124, 128, 132, 134, 140,
    141, 143, 146, 150, 152,
    156, 162, 163
Ghaddafi, Muammar 135
Gibraltar 163, 164–5
Giscard d'Estaing, Valéry 42

global Britain, concept of 4, 8–9, 21, 26, 101–2, 110–11, 114–15, 118, 120, 121, 123, 125–6, 127, 168, 173–4
globalization 34, 77, 79, 100, 110
Gorbachev, Mikhail 58
Greece 27, 38, 65, 84, 94, 113
Grenada 58, 107, 148

Hague, William (Lord) 114–15, 116, 165
Healey, Denis 36
Heath, (Sir) Edward 32, 35, 36, 42, 48, 133, 208n12
Heisbourg, François 73
Helsinki Accords 1975 57
Henderson, Sir Nicholas 31–2
Heseltine, Lord Michael 43
Hollande, François 135
Home Office 143, 158
Hong Kong 15, 170
Howe, Sir Geoffrey (Lord Howe of Aberavon) 39, 43
Hungary 38
Hurd, Douglas (Lord) 100
Hussein, Saddam 45, 100, 168

identity
   British senses of 9, 16–17, 19, 150
   issue of 4, 8, 16–18, 23, 27, 51, 133, 164, 169
immigration 20, 46, 47–8, 86, 92–7, 157

India 10, 25, 32, 94, 106, 107, 109, 110, 117, 122, 124, 169, 172
Indonesia 111, 113
intelligence services 12, 147
International Atomic Energy Agency (IAEA) 69, 70, 104–5
International Court of Justice 104
international financial institutions (IFIs) 105, 146, 166, 167
International Monetary Fund (IMF) 79, 105, 167
interventions 25, 63, 65, 68, 85
Iran 63, 69–72, 81, 92, 103, 111, 112, 137, 158
Iraq War 2003 41, 45–6, 55, 59, 63, 80, 83, 90, 91, 100, 102, 119–20, 127, 131, 134, 136–7, 138, 148, 168
Ireland 38, 40, 41, 113, 114, 151
   border with Northern Ireland 163–4
ISIS (Da'esh) 91
Islam in British society 86
isolationism 8, 100
Israel 58, 69, 72, 92, 129, 131
Italy 10, 34, 50, 68, 71, 77, 80, 85, 87, 94, 96, 103, 117, 128, 150, 156, 163, 169

Japan 37, 105, 111, 112, 117, 124, 128, 132, 173

Jenkins, Roy (Baron Jenkins
  of Hillhead) 37, 48
Johnson, Boris 48, 97, 109

Kagan, Robert 65
Kenya 66, 67, 125
Keynes, John Maynard 74
Kissinger, Henry 133–4
Korea see North Korea;
  South Korea
Kosovo 65, 66, 100, 134,
  136

Labour Party 4, 29, 32, 34,
  35, 36, 37, 40, 42, 43,
  45, 46, 47, 58–9, 63,
  79–80, 82–3
  New Labour 41, 59, 79,
  80, 82–3, 110
Lamont, Norman, Lord
  Lamont of Lerwick 44
Lancaster House treaties 22,
  91, 135, 142, 162
Lavrov, Sergey 111
Lawson, Nigel (Lord Lawson
  of Blaby) 36, 43, 48
Le Pen, Marine 138
Le Touquet, Treaty of 140,
  145
Leave campaign/Leavers 4,
  95, 153, 168–9
Lembong, Thomas 203n26
Liberal Democrats 4, 82
Liberal Party 35
Libya 22, 63, 66, 67, 68,
  85, 90, 91, 100, 102,
  118, 135, 136, 137, 141,
  163
Lisbon, Treaty of 40, 45, 54,
  83
Litvinenko, Alexander 148

Lomé Convention 106
Luxemburg 61

Maastricht, Treaty of 39,
  44–5, 53, 75, 88, 102
Macedonia, Former Yugoslav
  Republic of 86
Macmillan, Harold (Earl of
  Stockton) 7, 32, 34
Macron, Emmanuel 135, 162
Maghreb 66, 86, 145, 152
Major, Sir John 40, 43, 44,
  79, 88, 100
Mali 66, 68, 92, 118, 142
Malta 84, 93
Marshall, General George 74
Martill, Benjamin 5
May, Theresa 2, 8, 11, 85,
  96, 121, 135, 158, 162,
  165, 171, 172, 175
media 5, 49, 61
MERCOSUR 107
Mexico 111, 113, 114, 173
migration 7, 15, 20, 46–8,
  68, 86, 92–7, 126, 140,
  145, 157, 161, 162
Miliband, David 39, 114
Milward, Alan 35
Ministry of Defence (MoD)
  12, 119, 143, 159
Minsk process 73
Mogherini, Federica 54
Moldova 85, 86
monetary policy 43–4,
  76–81
monetary sovereignty 76–81
Monnet, Jean 34, 48
Mozambique 106
Mugabe, Robert 67
multiculturalism 25, 48, 94,
  139, 169

multilateralism 4, 34, 68,
    110, 173–4

National Security Council 11,
    12, 118
NATO 6, 16, 19, 21, 22, 27,
    29, 34, 35, 41, 49, 52,
    56, 63, 65, 66, 67, 82,
    83, 84, 87, 88, 89, 91,
    99, 101, 114, 118, 130,
    131, 134, 135, 136, 143,
    147–8, 150, 156, 159,
    162, 167, 174
neo-colonialism 106, 124
Netherlands, the 6, 15, 25,
    91, 93, 94, 98, 123, 163
New Zealand 5, 17, 25, 62,
    108, 111, 131, 172
Niblett, Robin 149–50
Nigeria 10, 111, 113, 125,
    169
Normandy contact group 73
North Korea (Democratic
    People's Republic of
    Korea) 71, 120, 127
Northern Ireland
    border with Ireland 163–4
Norway 6, 160

Obama, Barack 143, 148,
    209n25
Oppenheimer, Robert 74
Organization for Economic
    Cooperation and
    Development (OECD)
    116, 117, 130, 174, 177
Organization for Security and
    Cooperation in Europe
    (OSCE) 130
Overseas Countries and
    Territories (OCT) 15

Overseas Development
    Assistance (ODA) 61,
    123–5, 156
Owen, Lord David 48

Pakistan 107, 111, 113,
    124–5, 169
Parliament 11, 12, 28, 33,
    119, 123
passport controls 3
passports 14
Philippines 111, 113
Plowden Report 31
Poland 10, 27, 38, 131, 163,
    169
Polaris system 29
Pompidou, Georges 208n12
population 46, 106, 111,
    112, 113, 138, 169, 170
population density 93, 94
populism 49, 93
Portugal 6, 24, 84, 98
Pound Sterling 29, 30, 31,
    43, 44, 78, 79, 146, 167
proliferation of nuclear
    weapons 69, 71, 152,
    163
Prüm 144
public opinion 18, 33, 47,
    53–4, 62, 64, 88, 92, 95,
    127, 129, 170
Putin, Vladimir 73, 91, 111,
    172

Reagan, Ronald 58
Rees, Wyn 153
referendum
    1975 16, 32, 36, 42
    2016 1, 4, 6, 9, 13, 44, 45,
        46, 47, 48, 52, 93, 115,
        118, 138, 143, 167

refugees 7, 13, 47–8, 94
Regeni, Giulio 85
Remain campaign/Remainers 47, 168–9
residence rights 14
resources 115–25, 126–7
Ricketts, Peter, Lord Ricketts of Shortlands 166
Roberts, Sir Frank 31
Romania/Roumania 27, 46, 65, 110, 169
Rome, Treaty of 28, 38, 75
Rouhani, Hassan 70
Rowthorn, Robert 95
Rushdie, Salman 72
Russia 7, 18, 20, 26, 57, 65, 70, 73, 84, 85, 87, 91, 103, 111, 117, 118, 119, 125, 127, 128, 131, 142, 147, 158, 164, 170, 171–2
    invasion of Crimea 7
    Skripal poisonings 2018 52, 85, 167, 171, 172
Rwanda 64, 100, 106

Sadat, Anwar 129
St Malo declaration 1989 22, 40, 87, 89, 134, 136, 162
sanctions
    use as foreign policy tool 52, 67, 70, 71, 72, 85, 158, 160, 167, 174
Sarkozy, Nicolas 135
Saudi Arabia 72, 111, 112, 118, 171
Schengen Information System (SIS) 15, 96, 144
Schengen system 14, 15, 40, 46, 94, 96, 145, 157

Schmidt, Helmut 42
security, issue of 5, 15, 20, 22, 27, 40, 52, 56, 67, 82, 87–92, 96, 120–1, 133, 134, 136, 143–4, 145, 147, 150, 151, 152, 157, 158, 161–2, 172, 174, 175
sentiment 79–80, 129, 132, 146, 153
    see also emotion
Serbia 64, 65, 86, 134
service industries 95–6, 121
Shonfield, Andrew 2, 31
Simms, Brendan 5, 25–6
Single European Market (SEM) 2, 39
Skripal poisonings 2018 52, 85, 167, 171, 172
Skybolt missile 29
Slovakia 65
Smith, Julie (Baroness Smith of Newnham) 5
Social Chapter 44–5
Social Charter 39
soft power 116, 121–3, 176
Solana, Javier 55
South Africa 10, 25, 30, 106, 124, 173
South Korea (Republic of Korea) 120, 173
sovereignty 9, 17, 28, 35, 36, 37, 44, 48, 64–5, 88, 90, 97, 107, 112, 155, 171, 174
Spain 10, 14, 25, 59, 65, 68, 84, 93, 94, 116, 117, 163, 164–5, 169

special relationship, concept
     of 9, 22, 29, 62, 82,
     110, 128–54, 156, 163,
     170
Steiger, Uta 5
Sterling *see* Pound Sterling
strategic partnerships 10, 21,
     101, 109–15, 126
Suez crisis 17, 22, 29, 30, 45,
     133, 136
Sweden 61, 84
Switzerland 160
Syria 7, 47–8, 56, 71, 73, 94,
     100, 114, 118, 125, 135,
     149

terrorism 17, 46, 59, 68, 69,
     86, 88, 109, 126, 139,
     160–1, 164
   counter-terrorism 15, 52,
     56, 92, 96–7, 113, 118,
     125, 144, 161
Thatcher, Margaret (Lady
     Thatcher of Kesteven)
     23, 36, 39, 42–4, 58, 78,
     79, 100, 209n1
three circles concept 8, 35,
     105, 149
trade 9, 13, 17, 20, 51, 64,
     69, 71, 73, 95, 110–14,
     123, 124, 147, 160, 166,
     172
Treasury 11–12, 75, 79, 80,
     101, 118, 122
Treaty of Amsterdam 39–40,
     65
Treaty of Le Touquet 140,
     145
Treaty of Lisbon 40, 45, 54,
     83
Treaty of Maastricht 39,
     44–5, 53, 75, 88, 102

Treaty of Rome 28, 38, 75
Trevi group on airport
     security 96
Trident nuclear weapons
     system 90, 119
Trump, Donald 72, 129, 135,
     137, 143, 148, 151, 176
Tugendhat, Christopher (Lord
     Tugendhat) 42
Tunisia 69
Turkey 6, 21, 37, 59, 70, 86,
     100, 111, 113, 114, 117,
     125, 160

Uganda 66, 67, 107, 125
UKIP (United Kingdom
     Independence Party) 17,
     46–7, 86, 94
Ukraine 21, 73, 85, 86, 160,
     163
United Nations 9, 13, 34, 56,
     64, 90, 101, 102–5, 123
   General Assembly 104,
     107, 160
   Security Council (UNSC)
     21–2, 34, 58, 62, 70, 83,
     97, 101, 102, 103, 104,
     115, 126, 132–3, 139,
     141–2, 147, 152, 155,
     161, 163
   specialized agencies 107,
     126, 166
United States 5, 7, 9–10, 12,
     16, 17, 22, 25, 27, 29,
     34, 35, 37, 40, 45, 52,
     55, 57, 63, 64, 65, 69,
     70, 71, 72, 87, 89, 92,
     97, 99, 100, 103, 104,
     105, 107, 108, 109, 112,
     114, 117, 118, 120,
     128–54, 156, 158, 163,
     168, 170, 171

University of London 122

variable geometry Europe,
    concept of 76, 161
Venice Declarations 1980 58
Vietnam War 29, 45, 78, 100,
    133, 136, 149
visas 15

Wallace, William (Lord
    Wallace of Saltaire)
    192n5
Warsaw Pact 27, 107
    ex-members of 40, 41, 64,
    82
Western European Union
    (WEU) 88

Westland affair 43
Whitelaw, William (Viscount
    Whitelaw) 37
Whitman, Richard 175
Williams, Shirley (Lady
    Williams of
    Crosby) 48
Wilson, Harold (Lord Wilson
    of Rievaulx) 29, 31, 32,
    42, 149
World Bank 105, 167

Xi Jin-Ping 170

Yugoslavia 58, 63–4, 88,
    134
    republics of 58, 84, 86

CPSIA information can be obtained
at www.ICGtesting.com
Printed in the USA
FSHW020252190920
73455FS